Imprisoned Minds

Lost Boys, Trapped Men, and Solutions from Within the Prison

ERIK S. MALONEY AND KEVIN A. WRIGHT
Foreword by Shadd Maruna

Rutgers University Press

New Brunswick, Camden, and Newark, New Jersey
London and Oxford

Rutgers University Press is a department of Rutgers, The State University of New Jersey, one of the leading public research universities in the nation. By publishing worldwide, it furthers the University's mission of dedication to excellence in teaching, scholarship, research, and clinical care.

Library of Congress Cataloging-in-Publication Data

Names: Maloney, Erik S., author. | Wright, Kevin Andrew, 1982– author.
Title: Imprisoned minds : lost boys, trapped men, and solutions from within the prison / Erik S. Maloney, Kevin A. Wright ; foreword by Shadd Maruna.
Description: New Brunswick, New Jersey : Rutgers University Press, [2025] | Series: Critical issues in crime and society | Includes bibliographical references and index.
Identifiers: LCCN 2024016203 | ISBN 9781978837263 (paperback) | ISBN 9781978837270 (hardcover) | ISBN 9781978837287 (epub) | ISBN 9781978837294 (pdf)
Subjects: LCSH: Prisoners—United States—Case studies. | Criminals—Rehabilitation— United States—Case studies. | Imprisonment—United States.
Classification: LCC HV9471 .M326 2025 | DDC 365/.6092273—dc23/eng/20240717
LC record available at https://lccn.loc.gov/2024016203

A British Cataloging-in-Publication record for this book is available from the British Library.

♾ The paper used in this publication meets the requirements of the American National Standard for Information Sciences—Permanence of Paper for Printed Library Materials, ANSI Z39.48-1992.

rutgersuniversitypress.org

This book is dedicated to our moms.
   Jacqueline (Penni) Jones
   May 6, 1951–June 2, 2021
Thank you, Mom, for loving, supporting, and encouraging me.
You knew I could write this book before I did. I only wish you
could be here to see it become a reality. I love and miss you dearly.

And to
   Kelly Wright
   June 10, 1942–January 5, 2021
Miss you terribly, Mom.

Contents

Foreword

There are few people who can see the future. Most of us can barely see what is happening right in front of us. The critical criminologist Stan Cohen was one of those exceptional few who could see both—anticipating what was coming largely because he was such a keen student of the world. In his more than slightly surreal essay, "The Last Seminar," Cohen (1988) imagines a nightmare scenario for a university in which the human "subjects" of academic theories start appearing on campus. A professor teaching a class on mental illness is faced with two students having real-life mental breakdowns in the classroom. A professor of South American politics is confronted by a revolutionary straight from combat in South America. As for the criminology professor, he is having a great deal of trouble explaining his theories of punishment to a particularly cynical student named Jeff, who of course turns out to be a released prisoner himself: "You don't know anything about it, do you? It's all a game to you. . . . Prison. You think because you've spoken to a few cons you understand it all. Well, you don't, you just don't."[1]

The essay—which I should point out appears in a book titled *Against Criminology*—brutally challenges the value of academic knowledge. (There is a painful scene when, fleeing from campus, never to return, the criminologist momentarily pauses to decide which of his hundreds of books he wants to take with him—punchline: not many.) In doing so, the essay also makes a case for the ability of lived experience to disrupt our taken-for-granted understanding of expertise. As such, the essay has become a staple in writings by so-called convict criminologists—formerly incarcerated academics who draw on both lived experience and academic scholarship when teaching about prisons and other criminological topics.

The essay is clearly meant to be humorous and much of the writing is over the top, but the basics of the fantasy are indeed coming true in more ordinary ways. That is, although universities are still a long way from being "decolonized" (in the new parlance), we are no longer fully comfortable with traditional models of the learned (white, Western, middle class) expert descending into the jungle or the slum and reporting back what the natives there are up to. For most of us, there is a real discomfort in this very traditional, imperialistic model of the so-called academic expert.

Further, just as Cohen anticipated, this change has been at least partially motivated by the changing nature of university students. Yes, student enrollment still skews white, middle class, and suburban, but campuses have become far more diverse in recent decades, in all sorts of ways. Long gone are the ivory tower days when politics professors could pontificate about developing countries to all-white classrooms of naïve students as they did in Cohen's story. Likewise, any professor discussing mental health with students in the 2020s is fully aware that a huge proportion of those in attendance will have been diagnosed with a mental health issue, many will be taking psychiatric medication for depression or anxiety, and all will know family members, friends, or others who have experienced acute mental health episodes.

Most of all, the sight of a student who had been to prison in the back of one's seminar on prison studies would no longer cause as much as a batted eye. Indeed, in my first semester of teaching at the university level at the University at Albany, State University of New York, way back in 1998, I had two such students in my class. Far from leading me to abandon criminology, these students became the inspiration for nearly every decision I have made throughout my career. Like many of my colleagues, I decided to abandon what I call "behind their backs" criminology—the kind of criminology where we talk about "them"—these "offenders" and what is wrong with them. Instead, from that first-ever seminar, from the moment the two students identified themselves as formerly incarcerated, I realized that "they" were "us." At first, every word said in the seminar had to be chosen carefully so as not to accidentally offend, but then it simply became second nature for all of us to talk about those in prison and those working in prisons as fully human and no different than any of us (except for the extraordinary circumstances they found themselves in). Everyone who left that seminar emerged as a better criminologist (myself very much included), not as a diminished one.

As such, I have been chasing that experience in all of my educational work ever since. Like the authors of this book, I have helped to facilitate dozens of prison–university partnerships over the decades (in my case under the UK model of "Learning Together" rather than the U.S. "Inside Out" model, but the idea is the same). In these classes, students from a university sit side by side with prison-based learners inside a correctional facility, learning about criminology from the inside, together, peer to peer, where the best sort of learning is done. To his credit, Cohen had also done this sort of teaching inside prisons, and it was surely this experience that triggered his realization of the disruptive power of lived experience.

I part with Cohen only on his ultimate conclusion—made clear in the title of his book—that the criminological enterprise should be abandoned, that what we do cannot withstand the interrogation of those experts who actually have lived the experience of crime and punishment. I think criminology definitely can redeem itself, but unquestionably we need to change our ways. In short, my vision of a postimperial criminology is precisely the one that is put forward in this book. For one, this incredible work blurs the distance and the distinction between researcher (expert) and the researched (subject), integrating lived experience and academic theory. The fundamental tools of criminology are still very much here on display (especially our secret weapon—the narrative interview). Gone, however, is the usual translation process through which these raw and visceral truths are chopped and dissected into "data" for the academic to manipulate. Instead, we are presented with life stories in powerful detail, complete with the unique subjectivity that Maloney and Wright call the "imprisoned mind."

Importantly, the book has two authors, and the contributions of both of these voices (Maloney and Wright) are clear throughout, even when the other one has "the floor," yet so are the voices of these other research collaborators. In the end, the book reads as if it was written collectively by the subjects (the "data") themselves, unfiltered by the obfuscation of academic jargon. The most important thing I can say about this work (and the highest praise I can give it) is that one will put down this book, like the students in that first seminar I "taught" in New York, a much better criminologist than before they opened it up. They may even be able to see the future of criminology.

—Shadd Maruna

Shadd Maruna is a professor in the School of Social Sciences, Education and Social Work at Queen's University Belfast. His book *Making Good: How Ex-Convicts Reform and Rebuild Their Lives* was named the Outstanding Contribution to Criminology by the American Society of Criminology (ASC) in 2001.

Prologue

I sat in a maximum custody jail cell, two weeks after my initial arrest, and read a newspaper article that was about me. It was full of inaccuracies and untruths, but something else bothered me that I was unable to grasp. I read it repeatedly, and each time became more perplexing than the last. I continued to read the first sentence until it finally stood out to me. It read, "A twenty-one-year-old man was arrested. . . ." It would be troubling for most people to read about their own arrest, and it was for me too; however, there was one word used to describe me that was difficult for me to read.

The word *man*.

I didn't understand why being called a "man" troubled me so much. Certainly, I considered myself to be a man prior to my arrest. I had a job, a fiancée, and a newborn daughter. My fiancée's pregnancy had been deemed high risk by her doctor, so she was unable to work. This made me the sole and primary breadwinner. We had our own place, and I paid the rent (mostly) on time. By then, I'd owned and operated my own business for eight months before it failed. Of course I considered myself a man! I would've been offended had anybody said differently. So why did it trouble me? I couldn't figure it out, and I put it out of my mind. Nearly two years later it occurred to me that I'd been deceiving myself for the better part of my life. I'd convinced myself I was several things that in reality I wasn't. One of those things was a man. I later understood that similar acts of self-deception were but one aspect of a mindset that I call "the imprisoned mind."

I first noticed the imprisoned mind in my father when I was a child. Both of my parents were incarcerated for separate crimes in the late 1970s. They met in a co-ed prison where I was conceived and born. My mother was released early for good behavior shortly after my birth and never returned to prison. My father, however, was a habitual recidivist who eventually died in prison of natural causes. I only met him a handful of times throughout my childhood. He spent those times attempting to impress me with stories of his past criminal acts and how "respected" he was in prison. That was confusing for me because all that I cared about was whether he was going to stay out of prison and be my father. Up until that point, the few interactions we did have consisted of him promising me the world, only to never deliver on those promises. I was devastated by his lies, as any child would be. I later understood that he never intended to lie or let me down. He truly believed that he could and would deliver on those promises each time. It was his misfortune that sent him back to prison and that absolved him of any responsibility for breaking his promises. He convinced himself that he never lied to me and couldn't understand my disappointment. Self-delusion epitomizes the imprisoned mind.

I thought my father was crazy back then. My opinion of him would evolve over time as I encountered and became more familiar with the imprisoned mind. I vowed to never be like my father. And that I would never adopt his mentality or lifestyle. It took a cell door to one day slam behind me to realize that life's circumstances were such that I'd become him without even realizing it. I learned firsthand that the imprisoned mind causes us to deceive ourselves by rationalizing our illogical behavior. It causes us to convince ourselves that we have life figured out, and anyone who doubts or questions us is intellectually inferior. Unlike most men with the imprisoned mind, my incarceration lifted the fog of deception, allowing me to view reality once again. My newfound clarity brought about the realization that not only had I lost sight of my vows, but my life's course had been drastically impacted because of it. My cell became tangible evidence that my life had taken an unexpected turn. Visiting my daughter through glass brought back memories of doing the same with my own father. That memory shocked my conscience. I realized that the ripple effect of my decisions impacted more than just myself. The fact that something so obvious had never occurred to me was troubling. The unpleasantness of my newfound reality demanded that I attempt to understand what the mindset was and figure out why I'd unknowingly adopted it. To determine this, I began to look back upon my life in hopes of detecting where it all went wrong. What I discovered was life-altering, but I never imagined where it would lead me.

When I was twenty months old, my sisters, cousins, and I were taken hostage in our home by two crazed drug addicts who'd previously stabbed our neighbor in a drug deal gone wrong. Family members of the neighbor, who'd been stabbed, pursued his attackers, who then ran to our house, kicked in the front door, and took us hostage. We were eventually rescued by the police, but not before one attacker was killed in front of us. A few months later, I suffered a traumatic injury after being pushed off of a roof and breaking my leg. Both incidents are my earliest memories and continue to affect me today.

I thought about the hardships of growing up biracial during the 1980s. I recalled how emotionally overwhelming it was to experience racism from both races whose Black and white blood coursed through my veins. I remember feeling inadequate as neither of my parents' families seemed to want anything to do with me. At six years old, I developed separation anxiety and abandonment issues after two of my three sisters ran away from home. At eleven years old, I experienced depression after my third sister left home, leaving me alone. I then convinced myself that smoking marijuana would make me happy. The effect that it had on me allowed me to break from the anxiety and depression that afflicted me. I didn't know it at the time, but that's when I believe my imprisoned mind started.

I experienced a series of violent events at thirteen years old that caused me to quit caring whether I lived or died. As a result, marijuana and alcohol became staples in my life that I believed provided a sense of gratification in a time of chaos and stress. I embraced gang life to have a sense of security and family. A gun in my waistband gave me confidence in such a violent world, and selling drugs allowed me to feel financially secure. My thought process hardened with each adverse experience I encountered, and it took coming to prison to add flexibility back into it.

So here I am. Twenty-four years later, a forty-five-year-old man once arrested as a twenty-one-year-old boy. I sit in a medium-security prison, serving a life sentence, surrounded by people with imprisoned minds. Their stories are not unlike mine. I am more convinced than ever that the unaddressed traumas of our youth contributed to our wayward path to adulthood. I tell our stories so that others can be freed from their imprisoned minds. I tell our stories so that today's youth never develop this mindset. And I tell our stories so you can better understand why men can be trapped in a cycle of incarceration.

Imprisoned Minds

Introduction

The Imprisoned Mind

Everyone has a story. The stories of men with an imprisoned mind may seem more incomprehensible than others. When you have a comprehensive understanding of the mindset, however, you begin to better understand the actions of the men who are trapped with it.

I once came across an episode of the television show *Cops*. I watched as the police pulled a man from a wrecked vehicle and handcuffed him. The surrounding pandemonium suggested that I'd missed a car chase, and, as was the premise of the show, the "good guys" had nabbed the "bad guy." The exasperated officer, clearly familiar with the suspect, placed his prisoner in the back seat of his squad car and huffed, "How many times have you ran from the police?"

With a smirk on his face and in a casual tone, the prisoner answered, "Twenty-six times."

I can only imagine the average viewer's reaction to hearing that: "Damn! Twenty-six times? That man's crazy!" or, "What the hell's wrong with that dude? He must enjoy getting arrested!"

These viewer responses seem rational given the circumstances, but I've yet to hear anyone accurately explain why people, such as this man, continue to believe they can get away with breaking the law after having been caught so many times. Clearly, this man wasn't so crazy that he didn't know he'd broken the law—he wouldn't have run from the police otherwise. And I've yet to find one prisoner who actually enjoys being arrested, so that must not be the problem. It was obvious to me there was something wrong with this man, and those like him, but what?

* * *

1

Tracing the development of the imprisoned mind begins with childhood. Stories of unimaginable childhood abuses and neglect are prevalent throughout "the hood" and prisons. Growing up, I remember listening to "homies" openly talk about their adverse childhood experiences. A homey once told me about watching his mom kill his dad. It was chilling to hear him describe seeing the bullet pierce his father's chest as if it was a scene from a movie and not his actual life. Another spoke of his backside being beaten by his stepdad in such gory detail that I was reminded of hearing similar stories of slaves being whipped by their master. I remember feeling uneasy each time I listened to one of these stories. I mean, what's a kid supposed to say to someone who's being so open about such horrific personal experiences? All I'd say was, "Damn! That's messed up," or, "Man! That ain't right." I thought it was a coincidence when I began hearing many of the same stories in prison. Sure, each story is different, but they're all still painfully similar. It was clear to me that each individual continued to be plagued by their past experiences as if they had only recently happened. Yet each man had no clue how their past continued to affect their present.

It didn't take long for me to notice how emotionally detached everyone seemed to be while recalling their vividly horrific experiences. Some told their stories as if they were no big deal, casually joking about them. One person laughed about being beaten, at the age of seven, by his mother's boyfriend. He had a gun put to his head because he'd urinated while asleep on his mom's couch. "Shit," the man chuckled as he recalled the story, "it made me stronger, and best believe I didn't piss myself again after that!" Of everyone who has told me a story of childhood traumas, only one person ever choked up while recalling his traumatic experience. Even then, he continued to tell his story with such numbness that I began to wonder if there was a relationship between childhood trauma and incarceration. By that point, I'd become aware of my own emotional detachment and subsequent imprisoned mindset due to childhood trauma, but I wondered just how common this link was in prison. I set out to find the answer.

The *development* of the imprisoned mind starts with emotionally sensitive children who've experienced trauma that is left untreated. The child then begins to experience mental and emotional distress. Without knowledge of healthy coping mechanisms, they eventually turn to drugs and alcohol and begin making other risky decisions. These behaviors don't heal the trauma; they only serve to temporarily numb or distract from the agony of the mental and emotional distress. The individual becomes so focused on achieving this temporary relief that their willingness to engage in criminal endeavors becomes habitual. With each illegal act, the mindset evolves into a rigid criminal mentality, one that arrests all future development.

I recognized prominent and recurring themes in the lives of everyone I believed showed signs of having an imprisoned mind. Like me, everyone readily admitted to being an emotionally sensitive child prior to their initial traumatic experience. My own mother and sisters would describe me as a crybaby. I wondered if this predisposition factored into the intensity of the symptoms of having post-traumatic stress disorder. Additionally, the individual with an imprisoned mind often experienced the absence of one or both parents during childhood. This absence, I found, caused some to seek out a semblance of a family or brotherhood, such as joining a gang or the military, to fill the void left by their own fractured family. Being a part of something we feel is bigger than ourselves gives us a sense of belonging to the "family" we feel we never had.

The *progression* of the imprisoned mind is highlighted by denial and deflection. The individual who possesses an imprisoned mind is generally unaware that anything is wrong with them. It's as if we develop a form of tunnel vision and become hyper-focused on satisfying our desires and needs. The problem with this mentality is its self-deceiving nature: the imprisoned mind causes us to believe that things we simply want are so important that we are required to have them. Our inability to differentiate between our wants and our needs leads to a sense of urgency and a lack of patience when it comes to acquiring what we feel we must have. We then develop an egoistic attitude. Our imprisoned mind leads us to believe that everything is about us and produces behavior that seems rude or inconsiderate. We lie and manipulate to get what we want. We believe that we have honor and integrity, but in reality they're foreign concepts to us. If there are rules that hinder our ability to do as we feel, then we will attempt to find ways around those rules or just ignore them. It doesn't occur to us that our actions affect anyone outside of ourselves. When faced with the consequences of our actions, we deny culpability, we feign ignorance, and we deflect responsibility. Saying "everybody does it" is a typical excuse, and one that is indicative of the irrationality of the imprisoned mind, yet it's suitable enough for us to justify committing unethical or illegal acts. Once we're caught and suffer the consequences of our actions, the imprisoned mind causes us to see ourselves as victims, virtually blind to our own accountability.

The *permanence* of the imprisoned mind is dependent upon the further traumas we're exposed to while involved in the criminal underworld. Witnessing violence firsthand as a child causes us to be more likely to engage in violent behavior as adults. The imprisoned mind's self-deceptive nature convinces us that our learned violent behavior is the only way to respond to perceived threats. We then end up in precarious situations that expose us to more trauma, thus intensifying the mindset. Those who are repeatedly exposed to violence can develop an antisocial attitude that is often misunderstood as sociopathic. In our minds, the violence we engage in tends to be more reactive than senseless. We detest having to engage in it, and we typically only do so when we believe it's necessary to protect our well-being, our way of life, or the well-being of those we care about. This attitude seems to result from overexposure to hypervigilance and lasts as long as we feel threatened in an apparently hostile environment. Once we're removed from our hostile environments, this attitude can begin to dissipate and is eventually replaced with shame and a desire to better ourselves.

I've been interested in human behavior since I can remember. Figuring out why people do the things that they do consumed much of my childhood curiosity. And it continues to this day. I began my informal studies in psychology during middle school. These studies only intensified during my incarceration. I've formally taken classes and informally read whatever books I could get my hands on to better understand myself and others. Through my studies, I discovered sociology, and I began research in criminology after taking an Inside-Out Prison Exchange Program class in 2016. I've taken human subjects and qualitative interviewing training through Arizona State University, and I've personally interviewed over 200 prisoners for two groundbreaking Participatory Action Research projects.[1] Together, my studies, my training, and over two decades of experience with prisoners and incarceration make me uniquely qualified to write this book.

But I struggled with how to best advance the imprisoned mind idea. I wasn't even sure who, if anyone, would be interested in an argument from someone who is incarcerated and lacks an academic degree. That is, until a wise man told me, "It's not about the degree. It's the experience living that life and with being incarcerated, having the access to prisoners who can support the idea that's unique." I decided the only way to lend credibility to my claim would be to tell the stories of the men who I'm referring to as having the imprisoned mind: prisoners. I set out to find those on the unit who had the mindset and were willing to share their life story with me and the world. I was surprised and pleased to discover that many prisoners were eager to have their stories told. I sat with each man and took notes by hand, as recording devices are prohibited, while they recounted their life stories to me. I interviewed in our cells. I interviewed in the middle of the prison yard. I interviewed in the Arizona heat. Each meeting had to be broken down into several sessions as time permitted. We had to work around lockdowns and count times. I processed the information acquired from each discussion and wrote each subject's story in the first person. Each individual's story is compiled as a chapter, detailing how instances of trauma can contribute to a singular, common outcome: prison.

The chapters that follow are real-life accounts based upon the lives of six men who were emotionally damaged during the most vulnerable time in their life. Each chapter provides detailed descriptions of the harm, pain, and anguish some boys have experienced, and then later caused. I believe all six men have an imprisoned mind, but each of their stories better represent different stages of the mindset. In the first part of the book, Kidd's and Sergeant's stories epitomize the childhood trauma and neglect that contribute to the development of the imprisoned mind. In the next part, Oso's and Dee's stories show how denial and deflection contribute to the progression of the imprisoned mind. In the last part, Oakland's and Unique's stories demonstrate how the mindset can be fortified through continued victimization and trauma. These stories are not told to excuse our behavior or to justify our incarceration. Rather, the following brief life histories are meant to highlight the origin of the irrationalities that drastically influence the criminal mind, and to educate those who believe they have criminality all figured out. At times, what's told here isn't pretty. But sometimes the most meaningful lessons are born from ugliness.

Dr. Kevin Wright joins me in the final part of the book on outside and inside solutions. Kevin and I have worked together on this book for over seven years. He has provided feedback and assistance on all aspects of the book, from helping me to refine the idea of the imprisoned mind to leading our efforts to secure a publisher to copyediting all drafts of the book. Here he contributes a chapter that leverages his outside knowledge as a correctional scholar to complement my inside knowledge as someone who has lived through an imprisoned mind. Where "imprisoned minds" could suggest an individual pathology, Kevin's chapter makes clear that our life circumstances—especially our adverse experiences as young boys—limit our opportunities for healthy physical and mental development. He writes about the value of combining his outside knowledge with my inside lived experience to suggest solutions to enhance the lives of people who are living and working in the correctional system. I conclude the book with a chapter that identifies what needs to happen outside of the correctional system to prevent the development, disrupt the progression, and reverse the permanence of the imprisoned mind. In simplest terms, we need to support both the lost boys and the trapped men—especially when they are experiencing and working through the trauma that can derail their opportunity to find purpose and meaning as humans.

I never thought I'd end up in prison. Nobody with an imprisoned mind ever does. We're perpetually caught up in a moment that is our life. For me, that moment was proving that I was "a man" and making money. Others' form of self-deceit differs, but the results are all the same. Days, weeks, months, and years go by without us even realizing that all aspects of our personal development have ceased. Once you have the imprisoned mind, I believe that there are only two destinies: death or incarceration. Unfortunately, we're unable to comprehend that we're blinded by our own compulsions, slaves to our impulses, while deceived into limiting our own options in life. When our perceived options are limited (and none of them seem good), then it stands to reason why we make the wrong decisions. We become trapped by an irrational mindset. While I'm unable to tell the stories of the men whose mindset led them to their demise, I can tell the stories of the men who are incarcerated.

Part 1

Development

Kidd

I was never allowed to have closure,
and because of that, it still doesn't
feel real to me.

I was born in Tucson, Arizona, in 1993. I'm the second youngest child of five kids. I have one older brother, two older half-sisters, and one younger half-sister. Two of my siblings have the same father, and the other three—including myself—have different fathers, so my mom had four different "baby daddies." All of my mom's kids are biracial. My mom was white, so my siblings are both Filipino and white or Mexican and white. I'm her only child who's half Black and half white.

We moved to Mesa, Arizona, when I was two years old. My earliest memory is of my first day of kindergarten when I started at Harris Elementary. I remember going out to play during recess. I didn't know anyone at the school and just wanted to be a kid and play. I spotted some kids playing soccer and wanted to play with them, so I went onto the field and asked if I could play. I remember a Mexican kid telling me I couldn't play with them because I was Black. I didn't understand, but I knew I didn't like it. So we fought. After fighting with the kid, we became best friends. One day I went to his house to play video games and his dad came into his room and began beating him for playing video games with me because I was Black. That wasn't my first experience with racism, though.

My own mom used to discriminate against me. She used to tell me, "Quit acting like a n——boy!" It wasn't until I learned to read, at the age of four and a half years old, that I realized what the word "n——" meant. Even then, I didn't fully understand. I knew it was a bad thing said to Black people by "ignorant" racist people. It really hurt me to be called that by my mom, and it made me feel as if she hated me because I was Black. I began noticing how she looked at me differently than my siblings. She also talked to me and treated me differently. There were times when she fed my siblings, yet withheld food from me. She once tried to drown me, and she'd even locked me in a closet for long periods of time and spanked me for the smallest things. My siblings received no such treatment. Each time my grandparents (my mom's parents) would come to visit, she'd find a reason to punish me before they arrived. Once I was withheld food for three days. The hunger became so bad that I had to go to the store and steal candy to eat. I was about five years old then.

Even my grandparents were racist. They treated me differently than my siblings too. My grandfather accepted that I was his grandson, but it seemed to me like all he wanted to do was "customize" me by changing me into one of the "good n——s." This made me feel bad for being Black. I never felt like I fit in with my own family. I felt alienated. I used to wonder why my mom even gave birth to me if she didn't want me. The best excuse I could come up with was maybe she became pregnant by a Black guy because of a one-night stand— of course, I was a little older when I came to that conclusion. I knew Mom drank and did drugs. I began using this to excuse her behavior toward me. I'd tell myself, "She's only acting like that because she's drunk or high." I never knew how true (or how far from the truth) that was. I'll never know for certain what the answer really was.

One morning, when I was nine years old, I awoke to find my mom had cooked a big breakfast for all of us kids. It was unlike her to cook breakfast. She made pancakes, eggs, and bacon that day. She even had a box of my favorite cereal just for me—Cookie Crisp. My siblings and I normally took the bus to school, but this morning she drove us. We were shocked, but I thought nothing of her behavior at the time as being out of character. I was just excited I was being treated normally. She even let me sit in the front seat. That's something I'd never been able to do. It felt great riding in the front seat of my mom's Mustang too. I remember feeling like I was the man! I was shocked when she said to me while driving, "You know that I love you a lot?" I couldn't believe what I was hearing, but I liked it. She went on to tell me that I had to be there for my brother and sisters. She told me, "They're not gonna survive like you will." She told me I was strong and independent. It was weird hearing her say these things, but I dismissed it. I was just happy to live in the moment. I remember leaving the car feeling as if everything, from that moment on, was about to get better.

I was upbeat and jovial at school that day. We had what was known as a "fun run"—kind of like a mini-carnival. There were a lot of games like slip-n-slide, basketball tournaments, and all sorts of fun stuff to do. It turned out to be one of the best days at school I'd ever had.

My friend Kelsie and I rode the bus home from school together. Kelsie lived a few houses down from me, so when we arrived at my house he and I parted ways. I went to the front door and knocked, thinking it was locked, as usual. I'd never been trusted enough to be given a key, so I waited for my mom to open the door. There was no answer after what must have been five or ten seconds, but it felt like forever. I tried to turn the door handle and, to my surprise, it turned. I pushed the door open and yelled, "Mom, I'm here!" I closed the door behind me and walked into the living room. There I found my mom's body lying in a pool of blood. She had a gun in her hand and a hole in her head.

I don't know how long I stood there looking at her before I panicked. I remember realizing I needed to get help, so I ran to the neighbor's house. My mother had committed suicide. My best day had become my worst day—I felt betrayed and left behind. To make matters worse, Child Protective Services (CPS) separated me from my siblings. My oldest brother and sisters were sent to live with their uncle. My younger sister was sent to a foster home, and I was sent to a group home.

It was very difficult for me to be separated from the only family I had left. I was nine years old, and I quickly missed my family. I desperately wanted to be with my brother and sisters, so I began running away from my group home to be with them. My group home was in Tempe, Arizona, so one evening I decided I was going to live with my siblings. I began walking from Tempe to Mesa at five P.M. and arrived at my siblings' uncle's house at approximately three A.M. In my mind, I thought I'd be welcomed and celebrated for being there. But my siblings' uncle called the police. He told me he had to because if he didn't, he'd get in trouble. I didn't want to get anyone in trouble. When the police arrived, they called my group home and told them to come and pick me up. I felt restricted from my family, like I was being punished. I blamed the police and CPS for my mom's death. I didn't know my dad, and I couldn't be with my brother and sister. I was alone, with no home and no sense of belonging.

I can't even count how many group homes I've been in. I was treated like shit in most of them, like I was a burden or a nuisance.

I really hated the second one that I stayed at. The staff would talk to me crazy all the time. One day, I ended up getting into an argument with a staff member. They said I disrespected him. The staff member responded by hitting me so hard that I bit off part of my tongue. I threw a tantrum after seeing all the blood coming from my mouth—it reminded me of finding my mom's body. I don't remember much about the tantrum except for them saying I threatened to kill myself. I only said that hoping it'd force them to remove me from the group home and send me to a better one. I wanted to be someplace I felt I belonged; instead, I was taken to Arizona State Hospital—a mental health facility.

I was thrown into a cell and placed on suicide watch. I still remember the sound of the first time the door slammed shut behind me and locked. I flipped out! Before, I could always run away, but in the cell I was stuck. I couldn't go home. I couldn't see my brother and sisters. I was locked up. I cried so much that I stopped producing tears. It was there they convinced me something was wrong with me. Although I was only there for a couple of weeks, the experience left me feeling as if I was more of an outcast.

To be fair, not every group home was bad. I stayed in two that treated me well. I always behaved in the ones that treated me well. I didn't want to give them a reason to ship me off to a group home that was worse. I also found that if I behaved, I could earn a home pass that allowed me to see my brother and sisters.

On my tenth birthday, I was moved to Kenwood group home. It was there I met Miss Bobby. Miss Bobby was the manager of the group home. She was an older Black lady. She brought me in and welcomed me. She even recognized it was my birthday and cooked me hot dogs and macaroni. She took me shopping for clothes and had my hair cut. On our way back, she took me to ride go-carts. It was the first time anyone took an interest in me and recognized it was my birthday. I felt special. It was a whole new experience for me. I remember thinking the lady was an angel.

I'd never had anything special done for my birthday prior to that day. I'd been to other kids' birthday parties, but I'd convinced myself I wasn't special enough to have my own. It was obvious to me I wasn't loved enough to enjoy the recognition of the day I was born. Because of Miss Bobby, my tenth birthday has always been a special memory to me. It was the first time I really viewed a woman as a mother figure.

I spent about three months with Miss Bobby. The entire time I was on my best behavior. I didn't want Miss Bobby to be disappointed or angry with me, I was happy there. Unfortunately, all good things come to an end. Miss Bobby received a promotion and was transferred to another group home.

Around the same time, I was assigned to a new CPS caseworker. The guy who replaced Miss Bobby turned out to be alright. His name was Mario. He was a younger Black guy. The first time we met, he quickly eased my concerns about the type of person he was. He handed me his phone and let me listen to rap music on it. Under his care, I wasn't abused or made to feel like I was a burden, but I wasn't at home either.

When I was eleven, my caseworker established contact with my dad. I was able to meet him for the first time and get acquainted. Like any young boy who never knew his father, I always dreamed about meeting him. I remember being nervous and excited while waiting for him to arrive. When I saw him for the first time, it was unreal. I immediately noticed I looked like him. It kind of scared me, too. I knew he was my dad, but I didn't know if he'd love me or treat me like my mom did.

We were accompanied by my caseworker for our first meeting. We went to the mall and ate at a place called the Rainforest Cafe. After that, we went to a place called Dave & Busters and played games—Dave & Busters is like a sports bar and arcade combined. I had a great time that day, but it was awkward because I didn't know how to express myself. It made getting acquainted quite difficult. I did ask my dad how he felt about meeting me. He explained that he'd known I existed since I was two years old, but my mother had told him I wasn't his child. He seemed excited to have a son, but we never talked about what I'd been through.

After meeting my dad, I had an incentive to stay out of trouble—staying out of trouble meant I could get a home pass and be with him. The next time we met, I was taken to meet his whole family. I met his mom, my grandma, her sister, my great aunt, and a few cousins. It was the first time I had a family that looked like me. I even met my dad's daughter, my older half-sister. They made me feel so welcomed. I finally felt like I belonged to a family again.

Soon after my dad was awarded custody of me, I was allowed to go home with him. Having a father was unreal to me, after not having one the first eleven years of my life. I'd been in so many group homes that I began to believe I'd never have a home—that I'd always be unwanted and unloved.

My dad was a successful businessman. He owned three businesses and lived in a three-bedroom, two-bath house in a small community situated on the outskirts of Tucson called Vale, Arizona. He had a fiancée and a daughter who was a few years older than me. I was excited to have a new big sister, and she seemed excited to have a little brother—as excited as a teenage girl could be given the situation. My dad's fiancée seemed pretty cool. She welcomed me into their home, and I was given my own room. Prior to that day, I'd always shared a room with my older brother. Having my own space felt great. My dad bought me posters so I could put my personal touch on the room. It was nice, too. I had a bunk bed, a computer, and an entertainment center. I felt like my life was finally perfect.

It didn't take long for reality to set in. I thought my dad and I would be able to make up for lost time and be together all the time. I had a list of all sorts of father-and-son things we could do. However, my dad worked a lot and I barely saw him. I didn't understand why he was never home. To make matters worse, it turns out the neighborhood we lived in was predominantly white. I began to feel like an outsider again.

Much like my new neighborhood, my new middle school was predominately white. There were a handful of Mexican kids, but I was the only Black kid.

I met a kid named Jesus, and he seemed pretty cool. He was my age, so we hung out at school a few times. One day, he asked if I wanted to go to his house and play video games. Of course, I had nothing else to do, so I accepted. As we played video games in his living room, a light-skinned Black kid walked into the room. I pretended as if I didn't see him and just kept playing the video game. I was excited to see another Black kid, but I did my best not to let on. I was curious who he was, so I kept glancing over at him. He looked to be a few years older than me, and he carried himself with a certain swagger that I immediately admired. Once the video game had ended, Jesus introduced me to his big brother. His name was Rico. When his brother introduced us, Rico flicked his head upward, saying "What's up," and with a smile asked, "What'cha doin' hangin' with this lame?" referring to his brother. I knew I liked him from the moment I met him, and we instantly became friends.

Rico was half Black and half Mexican and, much like me, he was the only mixed-race child of his mother. He and I connected because we were the only two Black kids in the neighborhood. The fact we had similar backgrounds, given our family dynamics, only strengthened our bond. Rico was only two years older than me, but at thirteen he was already an imposing figure. He stood about six feet two inches tall and dressed in that New York "gangsta" style T-shirt, baggy jeans, and signature Timberland boots. He didn't go to the same school as me because he was kicked out prior to my arrival. I was impressed. He was tough, cool, and for an eleven-year-old boy who'd never really had a Black friend, he was THAT DUDE!

My dad was at work all the time. Because of that, I always hung with Rico when we weren't in school. I became popular with the girls at my school, but that seemed to only make the boys dislike me even more than they already had. I started getting into fights and began getting suspended from school. It was cool, though, because each time I was suspended Rico and I would end up skipping school and partying. He smoked weed and drank alcohol, so naturally I smoked weed and drank. And even though I hadn't smoked or drunk before meeting Rico, I acted as though I had. When I was with Rico, I felt like I fit in.

My dad purchased my clothes from either Ross or Walmart. For an adolescent, that gear wasn't cool. I had to keep up with my popular image, and the gear I wore wasn't helping. I decided I needed to get better gear. To do that, I needed money. At first I started raking people's yards for money. That, however, wasn't cutting it. Rico suggested we sell weed to make money, which I thought was a good idea. I also thought it'd further my "rep." We started selling small amounts of weed, and I was able to start buying better clothes. My "rep" began to grow thanks to the gear. I figured out the larger amounts of weed you buy, the cheaper it was. I wanted to make more money, so it was only logical to buy larger quantities. I suggested to Rico that we save our money and buy a pound of weed. He agreed, and that's exactly what we did. After doing that, we started making pretty good money.

I felt like the man when I hung with Rico. Selling weed and wearing fresh gear made the girls love me more. The boys hated me, but they couldn't beat me up, so I didn't worry about them. I had an established "rep," so everybody began to know who I was.

Rico and I started buying larger amounts of weed after a few years, and our clientele grew. At fifteen, Rico had enough money to buy himself a car. We also bought dirt bikes so we could go out in the desert and ride with other kids. My dad would ask me about my new possessions, and I just lied to him. I'd tell him they belonged to someone else, which he seemed to believe, or maybe he just didn't want to know the truth. Perhaps he did know and was cool with not having to spend money on me. I don't know. I was providing for myself, so I was cool with him not pressing me too hard.

By my sixteenth birthday, I saved up enough money to buy myself a car, a Honda Civic. I also found out my dad's businesses weren't doing very well. I was surprised to find out he smoked weed too. When I found out, my dad seemed cooler to me, but finding out his businesses weren't doing so well made me feel like I was a burden on him. By then I'd been providing for myself for some time. I sold weed, so I convinced myself I had to step up my game in order to take care of myself. By this time, my dad's daughter had been doing drugs and had gotten pregnant. My dad was helping her with money, so I felt like I was doing him a favor by not having to spend money on me.

I began selling different types of drugs in order to make more money. I grew to six feet tall and had the build to go with it. Together, Rico and I were imposing figures. This only seemed to bring more hatred from the white and Mexican guys. We were getting into fights all of the time—mainly when someone would call us the N-word. And we won every one of our fights. Our opponents always outnumbered us, so at some point they just started to jump us. One night after getting jumped, these guys tried to rob us of our money, so Rico and I decided to buy guns. *That was the game changer.* We now had protection. Having a gun proved to be a deterrent, but thankfully we never had to use them.

A few months before my seventeenth birthday, my dad told me he was breaking up with his fiancée, and they were losing their house. This news was devastating to me. While I hated the neighborhood, I had a good thing going on. I had a family, a friend, and I was making money. I finally felt like I fit in somewhere, and now I was losing my sense of security. My dad told me I had to move to Tucson and live with his mom. He ended up renting a one-bedroom townhouse, and, once again, I felt abandoned.

It was all good, though, I thought. *I could be going to someplace worse*, I told myself. In the five years of knowing my grandma, I'd come to love and appreciate her. She'd made me feel special since day one. Each time my dad went to the city, I enjoyed going to visit her. While I felt abandoned by my dad, I knew living with my grandma would be a safe place for me—at least it wasn't a group home.

My grandma was pretty cool. She was born in England and had a British accent. I always got a kick out of hearing her speak. Until then, I'd never heard a Black lady speak with a British accent. Every time I saw her, she was the typical Black grandmother—you know, churchgoing, welcoming, and always offered to cook something to eat if I was hungry. At the age of seventy-six, she continued to work as a registered nurse. She'd always taken good care of people regardless if they were family or her patients. One thing that always stuck out to me was the fact she was a no-nonsense type of woman. My grandma did *not* play.

Knowing I was going to live with my grandma meant I had to be proper. I knew I'd have to go to church and go to school. I knew I'd have to do my homework before I even thought about going anywhere. It felt good to have someone who cared about me like that. I didn't hate the structure, but it did take some getting used to. The problem was I felt stuck in my ways, so it was difficult for me to get used to. It didn't help that I had trust issues. I couldn't shake the feeling that my grandma would die or leave me like everyone else. I became determined not to get used to the structure, or even to try and embrace it, because it was temporary. I did everything asked of me while I was in her house, but I continued to "do me" once I was outside of her house.

My grandma lived in a four-bedroom, two-bath house. She used to be a certified foster parent, so I guess she was accustomed to keeping a full house. When I moved in, my cousin had already been living there. He was twenty years old at the time and thugged out. He was a light-skinned Black man who stood about five foot nine inches and was very stocky. He had green eyes, wore his hair in cornrows, and had a cocky demeanor. One glance at his brand-name clothes, new shoes, silver chain, and expensive watch told me he sold drugs. I knew he belonged to a gang, and I knew he had "connections." I saw him as an opportunity to establish myself in this new city. By then, I treated selling drugs like it was my job, and I had work to do. I still had some money from selling drugs at my dad's house, so my cousin helped me to buy a half ounce of coke. I was excited because I was in a bigger city, and that meant more people. And more people meant more money.

My cousin was a Crip, so naturally I wore blue all the time. I began going to Palo Verde High School while living with my grandma. There were a lot of Bloods there, so I began getting into fights because I wore blue. Those fights led me to the principal's office often. The principal came to really dislike me because of my attitude—and for the fact that it appeared as if I caused all of the trouble. I wasn't about to snitch on anyone, so I always refused to cooperate with the principal. I just took the suspension rather than telling him what'd happened. For some reason, people never seemed to like me due to how I carried myself. That's always been something I could never quite understand. It wasn't as if I walked around like I was some kind of tough guy. I was just determined never to back down from anyone.

One day while I was in school, I had words with a guy who made a remark to me. I could have ignored his remark, but if I had it would have made me appear weak. I said some disrespectful things back to him, hoping he'd fight me. He didn't respond. I thought it was the end of it as we went our separate ways. After school, he was waiting for me with some of his friends. They ended up jumping me and beating me up pretty good. The minute I stepped foot on campus the next morning, security grabbed me and took me to the principal. Apparently, the school received a report that I was going to bring a gun and use it on someone. They searched me, my locker, and my book bag but found nothing. The situation, however, was the perfect excuse to kick me out of school, given my history of suspensions and my attitude with the principal.

Grandma wasn't too pleased with me. She immediately enrolled me in a school for troubled kids called Southern Arizona Community Academy (SACA), and I decided I'd really try to keep up with school in order to make my grandma happy. The problem with SACA was nobody there tried to understand me, what I'd been through, or what I was going through. To their credit, when I brought this to their attention, they tried to help me. They sent me to a place called La Frontera after school each day.

La Frontera turned out to be pretty cool. In addition to counseling, they offered nontraditional classes such as photography and cooking. I recognized that I needed counseling, so I didn't protest. I met a counselor there I immediately respected. His name was Rob. Rob was a long-haired white guy who looked like a hippie. However, he gave off a vibe that said, "I've been there and done that." He took an interest in me, and I began to really look up to him. I could talk to him, and, more importantly, he'd listen. He encouraged me to take a photography class and a cooking class. I was doing well, too. I had a lot going on, and I really enjoyed it. Rob used to always tell me, "When life gives you lemons, you paint that shit gold!" I didn't quite know what that meant, but I got a kick out of hearing him say it. It was always said after I was doing something good, so I took it as his way of telling me he was proud of me.

I went to school one day and Rob was waiting on me with a sad look on his face. I knew that look—bad news was coming. Rob informed me he was being transferred to another facility that was way across town. I was devastated. Once again, I felt like I was being abandoned. To his credit, he tried to call me every now and again to check up on me. He even came by once and took me hiking with him. Unfortunately, he became too busy and the phone calls stopped—I also stopped going to La Frontera.

Mano was a guy I knew who one day asked me to drive him to the park so he could fight someone. He was afraid if he didn't bring someone with him he'd get jumped, so I agreed to go. The kid he was after wasn't there. However, he saw another kid he didn't like and decided to rob him. He pulled out what turned out to be a BB gun and robbed the kid. I just went along with it. We then jumped into my car and left. The kid called the police and reported the incident. He gave a description of my car, and shortly after leaving the park we were pulled over and arrested. The BB gun was found in my car, and we were taken to juvenile hall. I was charged with theft by control. I spent two weeks in juvie before the charges were dropped and I was released.

I had no desire to go back to school once I was out of juvie. I figured school was where the majority of my problems came from. *Besides*, I thought, *school isn't puttin' money in my pocket*. It was my junior year, and I decided I was done. As expected, my grandma was not too happy with my decision. She tried to talk me out of it, but I wasn't hearing it. After a while my grandma reluctantly gave in.

I longed for a sense of belonging, and school was a constant reminder I didn't belong. I joined my cousin's gang, and I quickly found I didn't belong there either. One day, while I was selling weed in the park, I spotted her. She was sitting with a girl I knew named Daniella. I saw her before she saw me. I decided to go and meet her, but I acted as if I was going to talk with Daniella. I walked up to the table and said, "What's up" to Daniella, and I immediately noticed this girl was even more beautiful up close. After speaking to Daniella, I introduced myself to her, and she told me her name was Rachel. I was instantly in awe of her.

Rachel was Mexican, but she looked like a white girl. She had hazel eyes and long black hair. Her makeup was nicely done. She wore just the right amount, not too much. I couldn't help but stare at her. She caught me staring at her once and quickly grabbed her purse and pulled out a compact mirror. As she opened it and looked at herself, she asked me, "What, do I have something on my face?" While shaking my head "no," I had to smile because I liked her sense of humor.

Rachel went to Santa Rita High School. After we met, I wanted to be around her all the time. She gave me her phone number, and we talked every day. That was not good enough for me, so I tried to get switched to her school. When that didn't work out, I began going and seeing her when she was out of school. My life became dedicated to selling drugs and being with Rachel. I felt like nothing else mattered when I was with her.

Rachel disappeared several months after we met. One day when I tried to call, there was no answer. I went to her school and no Rachel. I went to her house, and her mother answered the door. Rachel's mom informed me she was sent to Sahuarita, Arizona, to live with family. Apparently, Rachel hadn't been concentrating on school, and they decided she needed a change of scenery. I didn't quite know where Sahuarita was—I just knew it wasn't close to Tucson. The conversation with Rachel's mom was weird and vague. I left there with more questions than answers, and I didn't understand why Rachel would just leave without letting me know. It was clear to me her mother wasn't telling me everything, but I didn't want to press her. I thought everything was going well between us, and the turn of events left me puzzled. I decided it was her way of breaking up with me.

Not having answers made it difficult to move on from Rachel. What she did hurt me and triggered my abandonment issues.

I received a phone call from Rachel's mom around seven months later. She told me Rachel was back in town and wanted me to know her phone was turned on. I couldn't believe the nerve of the woman. I thought, *Who leaves someone without so much as a word only to turn up seven months later and expect that person to call them?* I considered not calling her, but I decided she owed me an explanation. So I called.

I expected Rachel to explain everything on the phone, but after answering the phone she only asked me if I wanted to go to dinner so we could talk. I was confused, but based on the seriousness of her voice, I agreed. When I arrived at her house to pick her up, the second she walked out of her house, it all made sense. She was pregnant.

My jaw dropped when I saw her pregnant belly. She looked like she was about to give birth right there. I was speechless. When she got into my car there was an awkward hello and then silence. My mind was racing as we drove to the restaurant. *This is my baby?* I wondered. *If so, how could she keep it from me?* These thoughts only made me angry. I could feel her glancing over at me as I drove. I could tell she was expecting a reaction, but I never gave her one. I didn't even look at her. I couldn't look at her.

When we arrived at the restaurant, I was just happy to be done with the awkward silence. I jumped out of the car and rushed to the passenger side to open the door for her, but she was already getting out. I closed the door behind her and walked with her in silence into the restaurant. I held the door for her and was pleased to be seated immediately. After we ordered and the waiter left, Rachel began to explain everything. I just sat there and listened.

Rachel told me about when she found out she was pregnant. She talked about how scared she was, and how she told her mom first. And it was her mom who insisted she go to Sahuarita and finish school. Apparently, her mom thought I'd be too much of a distraction for her to finish school. She told me she didn't want to go, but her mom had made her. She apologized for not calling, and

I continued to sit there and listen. I didn't doubt that I was the father since prior to her leaving we were together all of the time. As I sat there listening, I looked as if I was calm and composed, but the truth is I was freaking out! All I could think about was how a baby would ruin my life. I was aware my life was not great as it was, but I thought a baby would definitely not improve it. But I wasn't about to run from my responsibility, so we ended up getting back together.

I rented an apartment for me and Rachel, and I even had enough money to buy us a few pieces of furniture. Her mom and my grandma helped us out with some basic essentials. I tried to go out and find a real job, but it seemed like nobody would hire me. Let's face it, it's not like I had any work experience, so I continued to sell drugs in order to pay the bills.

Rachel went into labor in September of 2010. I called Rachel's mom from the hospital to let her know, and I began to experience anxiety as I told her what hospital we were in. I went back into Rachel's room after hanging up with her mom, and reality began to set in. I was about to be a father. The thought made me panic. *I'm not ready to be a father!* I thought. *I can barely take care of myself, let alone a child!* Before I knew it, I was in my car and driving away.

I found out later that Rachel gave birth to our daughter shortly after I left. I hadn't told my grandma about Rachel's pregnancy, so when I went into her house, I knew I had to finally tell her. She knew from the moment she laid eyes on me that something was wrong, so I told her about the pregnancy and labor. She responded by promptly taking me back to the hospital. Rachel was holding Trinity when we walked into the room. I held my daughter for the first time and instantly felt an overwhelming love for her, but the pressure of being responsible for her was even greater. Later, when Rachel asked me why I wasn't there for the birth, I lied. I told her I thought I'd had enough time to go and get my grandma. I've never told anyone about panicking that day, until now.

Holding my daughter for the first time motivated me to go out and get a job. I ended up getting hired at a Vans shoe store. I immediately felt out of place working a nine to five. Working for minimum wage didn't sit right with me, either. I had become used to making more money selling drugs. I felt like I knew my worth, and looking at my paycheck didn't reflect it. One day, a few of my homies came to me with a money-making opportunity. The prospect of making a significant amount of money was too great to turn down. The problem was, the opportunity required me to go out of town for three weeks. I agreed to do it and went. As expected, when I returned to work I didn't have a job to go back to; fortunately for me, the money I made enabled me to pay the bills, buy some things for Trinity, and buy some more drugs to sell. I wasn't concerned about losing my job because I made more money selling dope than I did working anyway. At least, that's what I told myself.

I wasn't at home much for the first year of my daughter's life. I treated selling drugs like it was my job, and I worked a lot of overtime. Trinity was my heart. I never knew I could love someone so much, and the love propelled me to "work" harder each day to take care of her.

I decided to stop off at a discount store to pick up a few things while I was on my way home from work. After getting what I needed, I presented the checkout lady with the items I needed to have rung up. The total amount my items came to was about five dollars, so I handed the lady a hundred-dollar bill. She gave me back change as if I'd handed her a ten-dollar bill. Before she could close the register, I stopped her saying, "Excuse me, but you gave me the wrong change. I handed you a hundred-dollar bill." She denied it. I informed her that I write my name on my hundred-dollar bills, and if she checked the bills in the register she'd find one with my name on it. I pulled out my driver's license so she could see my name and compare it to the name on the bill. Once again, she denied it.

While I was standing there with my ID in hand, another customer put his items on the counter for the lady to ring up. When she opened the register, I spotted the hundred-dollar bill and said, "See, there it is! It's on top of all the tens and my name's right there!" She gave the customer his change, closed the register, calmly looked me in the eyes, and said, "If you don't leave then I'm gonna call the police." I couldn't believe what I was hearing. I became infuriated as I realized the lady was deliberately trying to rob me. I pulled out my gun, and without pointing it at her, I said, "Oh, you think you're just gonna rob me?" The lady saw the gun and put her hands up. I was determined to get my ninety-five dollars' worth of stuff, so I just started grabbing things. I felt like they owed me. I left the store with my arms full and was quite proud of myself for not allowing the lady to rob me.

I was riding my bike approximately two weeks later, when out of nowhere a cop appeared behind me and turned on his lights and siren. It spooked me, so I tried to run. I ended up getting caught and taken to jail. They put me in an interrogation room, and two detectives came in and questioned me about the incident in the store. I was shocked when they brought that up. I thought I was in jail for running from the cops. Apparently, they'd been looking for me since the day it happened. It turns out showing the lady my ID was not a good idea. While she didn't catch my name at the time, the store's surveillance system did. When they showed me the video, I could clearly see my name on the ID—I was impressed by the clarity. I was charged with armed robbery and aggravated assault. I served eight months in jail before the prosecution gave me a plea bargain that I accepted. It was my first offense as an adult, because I'd recently turned eighteen, so I ended up getting nine months in prison and probation. By the time I was sentenced, I only had to serve a few days in prison before being released.

I went back to the apartment with Rachel and Trinity after I was released from prison. It was great being home and holding my daughter. I didn't want to leave them again. That is, until reality set in and I noticed all of the bills. I had no skills, no job, and no prospects of a job, so I went back to selling drugs to provide for my family.

I completed probation without any violations. But no sooner had I completed it than Trinity ended up getting really sick. She began coughing badly, and it seemed to last forever. At first, we thought she only had a cold, but we realized how serious it was when she began having breathing problems. We took her to the hospital, and the doctor gave us the bad news after he ran some tests. Trinity was diagnosed with a direct immune virus. Apparently, her body was unable to fight off infections. The doctor explained to us just how serious her condition was and told us she'd have to go to the doctors a few times a week. This news shook me to the core.

Rachel and I took Trinity to her appointments together, in the beginning. After a few weeks, Rachel insisted that she take Trinity by herself. I didn't have a problem with that. By then we understood her appointments were going to be an ongoing thing. Besides, not going freed me up to go out and make money.

I received a call from the doctor one day. He informed me that Trinity had missed a couple of doctor's appointments. This was news to me! When I confronted Rachel about it, she had no explanation. I couldn't understand why she wouldn't take our daughter to her appointments. I was also pissed that she couldn't seem to explain why. Rather than fighting with her, I just left. I packed some things and went to stay with my grandma. I wanted to take Trinity with me, but I decided against it. I worried that Rachel would call the police, or CPS, and tell them how I made my money. I couldn't risk having my daughter taken away from me and put into foster care. It was obvious I couldn't trust Rachel anymore, so I began taking Trinity to her appointments myself. Each time I'd pick her up, I gave Rachel money to pay the bills, but I hated having to leave Trinity with her. I just didn't feel like I had much of a choice, though.

Rachel and I ended up getting back together after having been broken up for a few months. I cared about her—she's the mother of my child. However, I only went back with her because of Trinity. Being apart from my daughter when I didn't have to be was just too much for me to handle. I loved my daughter to death and felt like I had no choice but to get back with her for Trinity's sake. She was sick and needed both of her parents.

Things went great for the first few weeks of being back with Rachel. Trinity was making it to her appointments, and her health seemed to be improving. Rachel and I were getting along great. We were a team and a family again.

One day, my grandma offered to have Trinity over to her house to spend the night. I thought it was a great idea. I was excited to spend some alone time with Rachel. Only she didn't seem to feel the same way.

When I returned from dropping Trinity off at my grandma's house, I walked into the apartment and discovered that Rachel had invited a few friends over. They had the music playing loudly and were drinking alcohol. I decided not to make a big deal out of it and grabbed a drink. A little later, a few of my friends showed up, and we began smoking weed. Before I knew it, we were having an all-out party. This went on all day and well into the night. Everyone was drunk and high. Spending alone time with Rachel became the furthest thing from my mind.

We were playing beer pong when I noticed a handful of guys had walked into my apartment. They were with my homeboy Devonte, so I didn't trip. I didn't know the guys with him very well, but I knew them well enough to know I didn't really like them. I decided to keep an eye on them.

At one point, Rachel's friend hooked her phone up to our stereo system—she wanted to play music that was stored on her phone. I watched as one of the guys who had just shown up acted as if he was changing the song that was playing. Instead, he unplugged the phone and plugged in my MP3 player. Once the music was playing, I didn't think anything of it. I didn't say anything because I quickly concluded that he just wanted to listen to another song. A little while later, I spotted the same guy take some weed off of the table and put it in his pocket. I became angry but decided against saying anything right then. I got out of my seat and went into my bedroom to grab my cigarettes.

When I opened the drawer to my side stand and grabbed my cigarettes, I noticed my daughter's gold wrist band was gone. I remembered it being there a few hours earlier. The fact that someone would steal her bracelet pissed me off. I immediately thought of the guy who took the weed. I went into my closet and grabbed my gun. I put the holster on my belt and pulled my shirt down to conceal it. I was drunk, high, and determined to get to the bottom of this. I grabbed my shotgun from behind my bedroom door and walked out of the room. I handed the shotgun to one of my homeboys and told him, "Lock the front door and don't let anyone leave." He tried to ask me why, but I had no time to explain. "Just do it!" I yelled. "You'll see what's going on!" I walked over to the stereo and turned off the music. Suddenly, I realized Rachel's friend's phone wasn't there. With the music suddenly off, everyone was looking at me asking, "Hey! What are you doing?" I shouted at Rachel's friend, "Did you grab your phone?" She replied, "No, it's there playing music." I immediately knew the guy stole it when she said that. It was time to confront the prime suspect.

My plan was to confront him about the missing phone, my daughter's bracelet, and the weed I saw him take. I figured he'd see my homeboy with the shotgun and realize how serious the situation was. I believed he'd get scared and give the stuff back with apologies. After he did, I was simply going to let him leave. However, my drunken plan didn't go as planned.

When I walked up to the guy and confronted him about the missing items, he had the nerve to deny taking anything. "Bro, I saw you take the weed off the table!" I told him. As soon as he started to deny it again, I hit him in the face and demanded that he empty his pockets. He quickly did as he was told. He produced the phone and the weed from his pockets, but no bracelet. I patted him down but found nothing. "Where's my daughter's f-cking bracelet!" I yelled at him. "I don't know nothing about a bracelet!" He pleaded, "I only took this stuff, man!" With that said, I shoved him so hard that he fell over the coffee table and onto the floor. Before I knew it, I was on top of him patting him down again. I pulled off his shoes and out fell my daughter's bracelet. Right then, this guy's homeboy hit my homey over the head, causing him to fall, giving his homeboys access to the door. They quickly opened the door and ran out. When the guy I caught stealing tried to run away, I attempted to hit him again but missed. This allowed him time to run out the door. No sooner had he cleared the door, three gunshots rang out. My front window shattered while everyone dove to the ground. I pulled out my gun and ran out of the apartment. Once outside, I spotted them getting into a car and opened fire as they sped off.

Once I was done shooting, I turned to find my homeboy Devonte yelling at me. These guys were friends of his that he'd brought, yet he was angry at me for hitting the guy and shooting at them? I couldn't believe he was angry at me and not them. I was confused. After all, it was his friends who tried to steal from me, and then shot up MY apartment. Next thing I knew, Devonte and I were fighting. Rachel stepped in the middle of the fight, and I accidentally hit her. When I stopped to focus on her injury, I heard Devonte yell that he was going to grab his AK-47 and come back. I knew he had an assault rifle and believed he'd use it. He lived in the same complex, and I became determined to not allow him to follow through with his threat. As he began walking up the steps toward his apartment, I started shooting at him. When I emptied my clip, I heard a woman's voice yell, "I'm calling the police!" I knew I had to leave before they showed up.

All I could think about was getting rid of my gun and shotgun before the cops showed up. After all, it was illegal for me to possess a firearm due to my past conviction. So I ran back into my apartment and grabbed the shotgun. I handed it to my homeboy and yelled, "Take this and leave before the cops come!" He said, "Okay" and quickly left the apartment with the few guys who remained. I ran toward the back of the apartments and hid my gun under the first bushes I saw. With both of my guns gone, I headed back inside to wait for the police.

I spotted the cops when I rounded the corner of the building. They had their guns out and were searching everywhere. "Let me see your hands!" one cop yelled when he saw me. "Put your hands up!" I heard another cop scream. I just ran. The next thing I knew, a dog was biting me on the arm and pulling me to the ground. The painful sensation of being attacked by a dog caused me to begin hitting it. I was then tackled by the police and handcuffed.

Initially, I was charged with a whole slew of crimes. While the police ended up catching the guys who shot up my apartment, they never found the gun used to do it. The one good thing those guys did was refuse to talk to the police. They never snitched. However, I wasn't as lucky as I thought. Somebody saw me stash my gun in the bushes and told the police where to find it. I was drunk, high, and full of adrenaline. That made me forget to take off the holster from my hip. I also forgot I had bullets in my pocket. I was caught red-handed. Because I had a prior conviction, I could expect to have my sentence determined to be aggravated if I went to trial and lost. I was looking at thirty years in prison. That thought scared the hell out of me.

One thing I learned from my past experience with the legal system was, if you can't afford a private attorney, you're screwed. I couldn't imagine doing thirty years for a crime when nobody was hurt. I ended up calling my grandma and explained to her what was happening. Thankfully, I had $7,500 stashed at her house, and she agreed to retrieve it for me and hire an attorney.

Seventy-five hundred dollars isn't a lot of money in the legal world, especially with the serious charges I had. After retaining an attorney, he explained that for the amount of money I had, he could only help me get a plea bargain. He told me I didn't have enough money to pay him to represent me if I went to trial. He also advised me not go to trial due to the "overwhelming amount of evidence against me." He told me, "The fact of the matter is you're going to prison. Maybe I can get you five years because nobody was hurt." All I could think about after hearing that was Trinity and how I'd let her down.

Because the guys who'd shot up my apartment refused to press charges, the only victim was the police dog. My attorney did his job and negotiated a plea bargain. All my charges were to be run concurrently. I pleaded guilty to illegally discharging a firearm, prohibited possession of a firearm, misconduct with a weapon, aggravated assault on a peace officer, and possession of a stolen firearm. I was given four and a half years in prison. The decision to sign was a hard one. All I could think about was how Trinity would almost be seven years old when I came home. After thinking about that, the answer was obvious.

The thought of going to prison after turning just twenty years old was sobering. I felt like my life was over. I became well aware that I'd let my daughter, Grandma, and Rachel down. I understood very quickly that Trinity would be without a father, my grandma would be without a grandson, and Rachel would be without a partner to help raise our child. I understood my actions were what got me to that point in my life, but I couldn't help but blame the guy who'd caused the whole thing.

* * *

I began doing time on a medium-security yard in Buckeye, Arizona. My first day in prison, I was immediately approached by some Black guys and escorted to the guy who was in charge of my race in prison. Arizona prisons were racially segregated, with each race having a "shot caller." The guy who ran the yard for my race informed me of the rules all Blacks are expected to follow. The rules are very simple: "If you get into debt you must pay it, keep all noise at a minimum inside of sleeping quarters from ten P.M. to ten A.M., and if someone disrespects you, then you must fight." These were some of the rules explained to me. I quickly understood what the punishment would be if I didn't follow them. I was on a lower-custody yard because of the amount of time I was given. As such, there wasn't a lot of violence. However, the atmosphere suggested there could be violence at any time. I didn't expect to get into debt, I had no problem with fighting, and, since I wasn't a loud person, I really didn't feel like I was going to have a problem.

I quickly settled into a routine, but after a month I was moved to another medium-custody unit in Tucson, Arizona. I was excited about the move because it put me closer to my family. The possibility of seeing my daughter excited me. Unfortunately, Rachel never brought her to see me. After about six months in prison, I was transferred to a minimum-custody facility.

The problem with a minimum yard is the prisoners on these yards are what is commonly known as "short timers"—because their sentences are short. These guys are a rowdy bunch because they're about to go home. I ended up getting into a few fights because these guys acted like children. One fight even landed me in "the hole," and I was transferred to another facility north of Tucson.

After a few months of good behavior, I was given a job working at Swift Trucking. I made good money working there, according to prison standards. Working there meant I had access to the streets. At first it wasn't a big deal to me, but it quickly became a problem. You see, access to the streets meant access to drugs. I loved smoking weed, and I ended up getting my hands on some weed. My first priority was to sell it inside of prison, but I also smoked some, too. Not long after smoking weed, I was forced to submit to a drug test. Of course, I tested positive for marijuana. The consequence for failing the drug test was a disciplinary violation. I lost my job, my visits, and my ability to purchase food from the commissary. At this time, I'd been in prison for two years so I didn't care about the consequences. All I cared about was going home to my daughter. I knew as long as I didn't do anything big to pick up more time, then a dirty urine sample wouldn't stop me from going home.

I was placed on the kitchen work detail after losing my job. Most prisoners dislike working in the kitchen, so I guess it was part of my punishment. In August of 2015, I was told to report to the yard office immediately—the yard office is a smaller administrative office and security control in the middle of the facility. When someone is called to the yard office, it usually means they're in trouble for something. Either that or you have to submit to a drug test. I concluded they must be calling me for another drug test, as I didn't do anything that would get me into trouble. I wasn't concerned with taking a drug test because I knew I was clean, so I walked in the yard office with confidence.

I was greeted by a correctional officer (CO) named Ms. Black. She was known on the yard for being one of the most disrespectful COs, so I immediately prepared myself for a confrontation. The second she saw me and looked at my ID, she asked, "How're you doing?" I knew something was up the second she began being nice to me. "I'm fine," I replied. There was an awkwardness in the room as I stood there looking at her. As I waited for her to tell me why I was there, she asked, "How're you feeling today?" Sensing my frustration, she quit the small talk and explained that the chaplain wanted to see me. In prison, when the chaplain wants to see you, it usually means a family member has passed away, and it's his job to inform you. I immediately became concerned and instantly thought of my grandma.

The chaplain and I went way back. He worked at the same church my grandma attended. I met him when I was eleven years old, when I first met my grandma and she took me to church with her. His name was Chaplain Helms. I never really liked him, so we never got along. However, I thought it was fitting for him to be the one to break the news to me about my grandma.

The look on his face as I approached him told me I was right to think someone had passed away. I braced myself to hear the news as I walked into his office. He offered me a seat and grabbed a chair for himself, positioning himself across from me. What came out of his mouth was something I never expected. He said, "In life there are lots of twists and turns, but sometimes God has a plan for you." Not wanting to hear the whole speech, I cut him off by asking, "What happened?" He paused and looked me in the eyes and said, "Your daughter passed away."

I heard what he'd said, but for some reason it didn't register. "Wait, what?" was all I could muster to ask. "Your daughter passed away today," he repeated. Hearing it for a second time made it real, and my heart stopped. I sat stunned as the chaplain explained that my aunt was on the phone and wanted to speak to me. It took every fiber of my being to grab the phone and say, "Hello?" I heard my aunt say, "Talk to your sister." I heard my sister's voice, but I don't recall exactly what she said. All I remember hearing her tell me was that Trinity's heart failed, how sorry she was, and how much she loved me. The last thing I remember is hanging up the phone thinking *this isn't real*.

I felt like my world had just abruptly ended. In tears and in shock, I walked back to my housing unit and laid on my bunk. I stared at the ceiling and tried to process everything that had just happened. I ended up falling asleep for maybe twenty minutes. When I opened my eyes, I decided to go outside and get some fresh air. A few guys noticed my sadness and asked what was wrong. At first, I said nothing. I simply didn't know if I could say it. Another guy asked me and I was able to tell him. He tried to say some kind words, but I stopped him and asked for some space. He understood and left. I was thankful for that.

The next day, I went back to the chaplain's office to make arrangements to attend my daughter's funeral. When a prisoner's immediate family member passes away, the prisoner may be approved to attend the funeral provided they're not an escape risk and can pay for the overtime of the COs who transport him. The chaplain allowed me to call my aunt, but it seemed like he'd already spoken to her about me not attending the funeral. She explained to me that she didn't have the money to pay for me to attend. I accepted that and hung up. I expected the chaplain to allow me to call other family members, but he refused to allow me to call anyone else. I was furious! *How could they keep me from my daughter's funeral?* I thought. It seemed as if there was some sort of conspiracy to keep me away. To this day, I don't have an answer as to why they didn't want me to attend. By not allowing me to attend Trinity's funeral, I was never allowed closure, and because of that, it still doesn't feel real to me. A part of me knows it's true, but another part of me feels like it's some sort of cruel joke.

I started smoking spice to cope with the pain—spice is a synthetic marijuana that has replaced weed in prison because it's harder to detect. I began getting into it with the COs and getting into trouble. I became aggravated and argued with the COs when I felt like they were being petty or messing with me, and I was transferred from a minimum-custody unit back to medium-custody because of the disciplinary violations I'd received. I was taken to Florence, Arizona, to a yard called East Unit.

Since coming to East Unit, I've tried to fly under the radar. Shortly after arriving here, I found out my older brother passed away while in another prison. I feel like the death of my daughter and brother has forced me to grow up. I know I don't want to be in here when another person I love passes away, so I'm focused on getting out of prison. My earliest release date is December of 2016. This last year has been the hardest of my incarceration and perhaps my life. I'm curious as to what my future will bring. Only time will tell.

Sergeant

> This kind of robbed us kids of our
> childhood.

When I think of my childhood, my initial thought would be to say it was shitty; however, after a second of reflection, I would correct myself and say, "It could have been better." I come from a broken Mexican family. I was born in El Paso, Texas, in July of 1984. El Paso is a medium-sized city located on the Texas and Mexico border. There weren't many employment opportunities back then, so I constantly reminded myself that I needed to leave as soon as I was old enough. That's exactly what I did.

I've only met my dad a handful of times, so I can't really say I know him. What little I knew about him as a kid was learned from others. Before I met him, I heard family members call him a "drug dealer" and "womanizer." I didn't really want to know him because of the bad things I'd heard about him. Plus, his absence in my life spoke volumes as to the type of person he was.

I must've been about eight or nine the first time I met him. We were living at my mom's parents' house when a lady showed up one day. My mom seemed to know who she was, but I didn't. I did meet her some months earlier, though it was never made clear to me who she was at the time. I thought it was strange when she showed up at my grandparents' house and spoke with my mom alone in the living room. Being a curious kid, I eavesdropped on them. "Don't you think he should meet him?" I heard her ask my mom. I wondered just who it was they were talking about. A few days later Mom put me in the car and drove me to a nice neighborhood. We stopped at a beautiful house and Mom walked me to the door and knocked. We were greeted by a bunch of people and, once inside, I was introduced to my dad's mother and two sisters. There were a lot of people there, and everyone focused on me. They all made me feel welcome, but my grandma and aunts kept asking me to do things like, "Mijo! Walk over there." When I did as asked they marveled, saying, "He even walks like him!" and, "He's a spitting image of him!" Two Mexican guys walked into the room while everyone was busy being fascinated by me. One guy was short, and the other one was tall. Both were well-dressed and good looking. "Mijo! Which one of them is your dad?" They asked me. The room fell silent. I remember feeling uncomfortable while looking up at both men with all eyes on me. I tried to figure out which one my dad was but I really had no clue. I just pointed to the shorter guy and was told I'd picked the wrong one. That's all I remember from the first encounter.

A few months later my dad came and picked me up for the weekend. I remember calling him by his first name because it felt weird to call him Dad. He took offense to it, though. "Don't call me that! Call me Dad," he said. I didn't understand how he expected me to do that when I didn't even know him, but I did as instructed. Don't get me wrong, I was happy to finally be around him. I actually thought he'd be a steady presence in my life. That was the first time I was really wrong about him.

He took me shopping that weekend. I remember feeling spoiled when he bought me all kinds of clothes and shoes that were all brand name. It was the first time I remember having brand new anything, let alone brand name. The last thing I remember was him dropping me off at Mom's house once we were done shopping and leaving. He dropped off a Christmas present for me a few months later. It was a Sega Genesis video game. Attached to it was a card that read: "To son, from dad." I slept with the card under my pillow.

I was twelve years old the next time I saw him. He had showed up a year later with his girlfriend and new son to pick me up. I hadn't heard anything about his new son, so having a brother came as a surprise to me. His son was sitting on his lap in the passenger seat, and my dad was holding him closely when he introduced him to me. It made me jealous, and I wished he'd been that way with me as I climbed into the back seat. I quickly noticed rock 'n' roll was playing on the radio. I desperately wanted to have something in common with him, so I asked, "Hey, Dad! Do you like rock?" He never took his eyes off his son when he responded, "Yeah." I didn't know what else to say, so I just sat in silence as we drove to his sister's house. He dropped me off and left, and I didn't see him for the rest of the weekend. I've listened to rock 'n' roll ever since.

I became angry with my dad after that visit. I refused to talk to him whenever he'd call. I refused to see or talk to his family either, because they were a reminder of his absence in my life. I saw him a couple of times after that but those experiences proved to be much like the previous ones.

I know very little about my mom's background. I guess you could say she and I didn't have much of a "traditional" mother and son relationship. There's never been very much communication between us. I know she was born in Juárez, Mexico, in September 1968. I don't remember who told me she was brought here illegally. While I don't know the details, I know she grew up with both of her parents and two sisters. And I know she was devastated to learn she'd been adopted as a teenager. It never occurred to me to ask about the details of that story, though.

Mom was fifteen years old when she met my dad. He was twenty-one and didn't stay around throughout her pregnancy. She dropped out of school when she gave birth to me. I don't know how she and my dad met. I just figured it had something to do with my mom's beauty. At forty-eight years old, she continues to be a very beautiful lady. She stands five feet seven inches. She's a thin, light-skinned Mexican woman with green eyes. I always noticed other guys checking her out, but for some reason she's very insecure. And with her insecurity came promiscuity. Two years after giving birth to me, she gave birth to my brother Michael. We still don't know who his father is.

Mom met a guy named José when I was about a year old. They were just "acquaintances" at first, but they began to get serious after Michael was born. I was eight years old when I finally met him. I remember being surprised that my mom would be with someone like him. He was a gang member and a drug user. He stood about five foot nine inches and weighed about 180 pounds. He was a heavily tattooed Mexican man and looked very dangerous. I found out some years later that he was a "shot caller" for his gang.

My first memory of Mom and José is of them fighting. I was eight years old, and I didn't like him after that. My grandparents didn't like him either. We lived with them at the time, and they made it clear to Mom that he wasn't welcome at their house. She had to go to his place to see him. I didn't want to be around him, so Mom would take Michael with her instead of me. I always worried about their safety when they went.

I've always been quiet and shy. As a kid, I always sat quietly in the back of the class. I was timid and quite sensitive. I never spoke up when Mom came home with black eyes and bruises. I just cried alone in the bathroom. I kept quiet when Michael came home with Mom visibly shaken from what he'd seen. I didn't object when we moved out of my grandparents' house and into an apartment with José. I didn't think my opinion mattered, so I said nothing.

Not long after moving in with José, I awoke one morning to the sound of Mom screaming, followed by furniture and glass breaking. I laid in my bed and listened to the fight. I was frightened, and when the sounds died down I thought, *Did he do it? Did he kill her?* I finally found the courage to get up and check. I made Michael stay in the room out of fear of what I'd find.

I walked out of the room and the living room was destroyed. Everything was turned over and there was broken glass everywhere. I heard my mom crying and whispering in the kitchen. When I walked in, she was on the floor in her bra and panties crying on the phone. She was bloodied and asking José to come back home.

Mom's relationship with José was a tumultuous one. They argued and fought regularly. It was always the same story. Mom would antagonize him for whatever reason, and they would begin arguing. José would then proceed to beat her up before eventually storming out of the house and declaring their relationship was over. But it was never over. Each time Mom would beg him to come back, only to repeat the cycle.

Mom gave birth to José's son, Joey, when I was nine years old. I knew then that she'd never leave him. We were stuck.

Mom always put José before her kids. She waited on him hand and foot while we were forced to take care of ourselves. José never put a hand on us, but it seemed as if each beating he gave Mom had a trickle-down effect on us. When he beat her, she'd find some reason to beat us. I learned very quickly what I could and couldn't do to avoid a beating. The fact that I didn't speak much became an asset for me. I was usually overlooked because I was quiet, and it allowed me to escape a lot of ass-whoopings.

We were continuously forced to move because of all the fights between Mom and José. This kind of robbed us kids of our childhood. We were never able to make friends because we didn't stick around long enough to form bonds with other kids. I became apprehensive of going outside to play with others out of fear of getting attached to them or the neighborhood. We lived in so many places it all became jumbled in my mind. It seemed as though I started a new school every few months or so, and each move came on the heels of a fight where the police were called.

I remember sitting in a cop car when I was ten years old. José had beat Mom up, and a neighbor called the cops on them. I recall seeing the look of horror on the cop's face when he saw me and my brothers huddled in the corner of our destroyed apartment crying. I can't remember if one or both of them went to jail that night. I do remember the officer taking me and my brothers to my grandparents' house and dropping us off. The most vivid memory I have today is of sitting in the back of the police car wondering if other people thought I was a criminal.

José broke my mom's arm when I was eleven. I was living with my grandparents at the time. Mom told us she fell down the stairs, but I knew better. I felt guilty for not being there when it happened. I know I couldn't have prevented it, but it feels as though I should have been there for my mom. I knew being around the violence was having a negative effect on me, though. I didn't know how much more I could take at that point.

My grandparents were good people. They lived in a three-bedroom, one-bath house in a nice middle-class neighborhood. I began going there when I was thirteen to escape the chaos at home. I also started to participate in whatever activity would keep me away from home. I liked going to school because it meant nine hours away from home. I played soccer, basketball, and street hockey after school to avoid going home. I rode my bike, so I began riding across town to my cousins' house to play with them. Anything to stay away from home as much as possible. I only returned once it was time for me to go to sleep.

I discovered the Reserve Officer Training Corps (ROTC) once high school began. I'd always been fascinated with the military as a kid, so I joined the first chance I got. I desperately wanted to be a part of something and to experience belonging to a normal family. ROTC offered that and more. I fell in love with it, too. It felt like a brotherhood, and that felt good. It felt right when I put the uniform on. I felt like I was somebody for the first time in my life.

I realized I was better off living with my grandparents while I was in high school. I became tired of the chaos at home and the stress it caused me. I felt guilty about leaving my brothers, but I knew I had to leave in order to make something of myself.

Living with my grandparents turned out to be a good decision. Joining ROTC made them proud. Grandma even loved to iron my uniforms. I always had the sharpest creases because of her. I participated in everything ROTC. I was in the color guard, the drill team, the sabre team, the rifle team, and the pride team. As the color guard, we presented the colors, or flags, during each football game. As the drill team, we marched in formation and put on a show by spinning our rifles in competition with other schools. We placed second in the city that year. As the rifle team, we shot Olympic-style rifles and qualified as marksmen. The sabre squad was the coolest. We dressed up in our Class "A" uniforms for prom. We carried a sabre on our hips and had a ceremony with our swords. The prom king and queen would walk beneath our swords to be crowned. I had a blast doing that. For pride team, we went around and performed at all kinds of schools and talked with kids about staying away from drugs. That was cool, too.

I kept busy during high school and even had friends. I opened up with my friends but continued to be shy with others. That didn't bode well for me with the ladies. I had a hard time approaching them, so I rarely had a girlfriend. One thing Mom did teach me about girls was how to be courteous and respectful. I once had a crush on a girl while in the sixth grade. When I told my mom about her, she took me to the store and showed me what to buy her. I bought her a teddy bear, chocolates, and balloons. Mom taught me to be a gentleman with girls and to NEVER put my hands on them. Unfortunately, I wasn't able to get a lot of practice in high school.

My biggest challenge came at the start of my junior year. The upper class-man who led our ROTC program graduated, and nobody was willing to step up and lead the program. It was unfortunate because it caused everyone to lose interest and move on from it. I was fifteen years old, shy, and unable to break out of my shell. I tried to step up and lead the program, but I failed to take charge and recruit. The feeling of failing myself and the program overwhelmed me. ROTC folded and I felt as if I was to blame. That's when I began drinking and partying. I started smoking weed, and, thankfully, that's as far as it went. I never experimented with hard drugs—which is why I believe I was able to go on and graduate.

I was determined to join the military once I graduated. My friend, Joe, wanted to join the navy. He had a car, so I went with him to the navy recruiter one day. I liked what he had to say. I never thought of myself as a navy guy, though. I went to an army recruiter afterward and felt as if I was being disloyal to the navy recruiter for going there. Joe and I later spoke and agreed to join the navy on the "buddy system." However, Joe backed out after I signed up. I went back to El Paso on leave a few years later and found him still living with his mom, smoking weed, and having no job. At the time, I remember being thankful because I was traveling and seeing the world. I had money and a cell phone while he wasn't doing anything with his life.

I was excited to finish basic training and begin my military career. I was stationed in San Diego aboard the USS *Stethem*, a guided-missile destroyer. I was trained as a damage controlman, or shipboard firefighter. I found out pretty quickly the navy was NOT what I'd expected it to be. It didn't feel like the military to me. I felt like I was just working on a ship. I began to feel as if I'd made a mistake by not joining the army or marines. I wanted to fight for my country. There were two wars going on, Iraq and Afghanistan, and I felt as though the navy wasn't contributing. I wanted to do my part, but I felt restless doing menial tasks like polishing brass on a ship.

I met a lot of good people in the navy, though. While the navy didn't quite feel like the "brotherhood" I'd hoped for, it did allow me to feel as if I was a part of something good. It helped me to break out of my shell and become one of the guys. I made a lot of friends, and we all partied together whenever we made port and left the ship.

When you're stationed in San Diego it's tradition to go to Tijuana (TJ), Mex-ico, and party. You only have to be seventeen years old to legally drink alcohol there, so it was ideal for a lot of underage navy crewmen to go and drink. It's not lost on us in the military that you can sign up to serve your country and put your life on the line at eighteen, but can't even buy a beer. My friends and I felt strongly about this, and it made us want to party even more. As Mexico is a foreign country, military personnel must receive written permis-sion from their commanding officer and be accompanied by other military personnel in order to go. The problem was, commanding officers rarely gave permission to go, so a lot of people falsify documents to go in case they were stopped by shore patrol.

Now, if you're not causing problems, the shore patrol rarely stops and asks for papers. We were unable to get permission and had to falsify our documents to go to TJ, but we went and partied hard! We had a great time, too. Only we were stopped by shore patrol on our way back, and they asked for our papers. They discovered our papers were fake and detained us. Our commanding officer was called and we were held until someone was sent to collect us. I didn't think what we were doing was that big of a deal—that is, until we were caught and sent to the captain's mast for disciplinary. I was given 45-45, which means forty-five days extra duty and forty-five days of ship restriction. I also had to forfeit a half month's pay for two months. It seemed to me they made a bigger deal out of it than need be, and that proved to be true when our punishments were handed out. At nineteen years old, the punishment was a slap on the wrist.

I began to receive a lot of write-ups and negative evaluations after my disciplinary. At the time, I felt as though I was being treated differently than the rest of the crew. It felt like I was being singled out for the smallest of things. While others got away with doing things, I didn't. I started to really resent the officers who were giving me a hard time.

My ship docked in Mazatlán, Mexico, in 2005. Each time a ship docks in another country, the captain gets on the loudspeaker and reminds the crew of the rules of conduct. He tells us what our country expects of us as guests in another people's country. One rule didn't sit right with me: we were forbidden from riding quads, scooters, and motorcycles. Being that I'm of Mexican descent, I took offense to them telling me I couldn't do something so trivial there. I wasn't the only one who felt that way, either. The day after arriving, my buddies and I went on liberty—left the ship for free time. The first place we went to was a restaurant and goofed around while eating and drinking. It was a Friday, and we weren't due back on the ship until midnight on Sunday. The restaurant was on the beach and we had plenty of time to kill. My buddy spotted a place that rented ATVs and suggested each of us rent one and go for a ride. It sounded like a great idea, so I encouraged everyone to go. Once each of us had our ATV, we decided to race. I was going fast and was winning the race when I suddenly hit a sand dune and the ATV flew into the air. I held on for dear life. When it came back down to the ground, the impact caused my face to hit the handle bars. I broke my nose and split my chin open. My buddies took me to a doctor, and I paid $500 for five stitches and some painkillers. We had to come up with a cover story: *We were at the pool drinking, and I slipped and hit my face on the ground.* I thought for sure we'd get away with it.

Nothing went as planned when we went back to the ship. Everyone noticed I had two black eyes and began asking questions. I stuck with the cover story, but my two buddies spilled the beans. I was demoted, docked a half month's pay for two months, and I was sent to correctional custody unit, or military jail, in Bangor, Washington, for thirty days for disobeying the captain's order and then lying about it. Of course, I felt like the captain overreacted.

I returned to the ship once I completed my thirty days correctional custody. It was kind of awkward, too. The ship was out to sea and I had to be flown in. I felt like everyone looked at me as if I was some sort of "bad apple" or something. I was also bitter because I'd spent time in jail because my "buddies" snitched on me. I felt betrayed. We were supposed to be a brotherhood and have each other's backs. So once back on the ship I just put my head down and did my job. I went back in my shell and waited for my time in the navy to come to an end.

I was honorably discharged from the navy in 2006. I went back to El Paso and found nothing had changed in the four years I'd been gone. It was like time had stood still. Mom and José continued to argue and fight. My brothers weren't doing anything with their lives, and I missed the structure of the military. I began to realize the mistakes I made in the navy, and how I took it for granted. I guess the monotony of civilian life quickly took a toll on me.

I'd only been home for a month when a friend invited me to her wedding. I didn't have anything else to do, so I went. I regretted my decision to go at first, but then I saw her. She was a beautiful, light-skinned Mexican woman with blondish-brown hair. She was short and petite. *Just my type!* I thought. I couldn't find the courage to talk to her, though. I noticed she kept looking at me during the ceremony. Afterward, I went outside to smoke a cigarette, and she followed me. She tried to act as if she was there to play with the kids and not because she'd followed me. I got a kick out of watching her act as if she didn't know I was looking at her. I finally worked up the nerve to talk to her. I found out her name was Jessica. She was eighteen and lived with her parents in Chapparal, New Mexico. We exchanged numbers and began talking on the phone. It didn't take long before I was making the one-hour drive to pick her up and bring her back to El Paso with me.

Jessica didn't turn out to be my type, though. I kept her around to fill a void in my life. I was out of work, out of the military, and she was a young girl who didn't see me as the loser I felt I'd become. She made me feel wanted, so I stayed with her. After a few months, she told me she was pregnant. I didn't want a kid and made that pretty clear at the time, but she decided to keep the baby anyway. She also decided to move to Phoenix, Arizona. I felt like a jerk for letting her go, but I told myself it was for the best.

I stayed with an old navy buddy after Jessica left. I was watching TV one night when they began talking about the wars in Iraq and Afghanistan. Seeing soldiers fight and die over there lit a fire in me that I'd never experienced before. The next day, I went to an army recruiter and signed up for active duty infantry. Maybe I had a death wish or something, but I wanted to die for my country. I imagined being buried in my uniform with honors. I knew I'd made the right decision when I walked out of the recruiter's office.

I departed for boot camp in March 2007. Having prior service meant I didn't have to go to Fort Benning, Georgia, with the regular recruits. All prior service recruits, including myself, were sent to New Mexico and put through a fast-paced, two-week-long boot camp refresher course. There'd been so many prior service recruits coming in that it made no sense to put us through an entire boot camp. After our refresher course was complete, we were sent to Fort Benning and placed with the regular boot camp. However, we weren't required to participate until the end of camp. In order to become infantry, everyone must earn their infantry status by being put through infantry training. It was at that phase that prior service had to participate, and it was there I learned just how out of shape I'd become as a civilian. I failed my six-mile and ten-mile ruck-sack marches, but I was able to pass the second time around to earn my "cross rifle" pin—infantry status symbol.

I received orders to my first duty station around June 2007. I was stationed in Oahu, Hawaii, at Schofield Barracks. I was assigned to 25th Infantry Division, 3rd Brigade, Unit 2-27, The Wolfhounds. However, 3rd Brigade had already been deployed to Iraq and was due to rotate home soon. 3rd Brigade was to be replaced by 2nd Brigade. I received word that some of 2nd Brigade's units were undermanned and were asking for volunteers, so I quickly agreed to fill in for them.

In December 2007, I was assigned to 2nd Brigade, Unit 1-21 and was finally deployed to Iraq. I was excited and prepared to go to war. A whole range of emotions came over me when we set out on our journey. I was excited, nervous, and a bit scared. I realized pretty quickly that everyone was overcome by emotions, but the great thing about the army is there's always someone to lighten the mood by making you laugh. We were well aware of the risks, yet we were still ready to go. I quickly fell in love with the army because of that. I'd found the brotherhood I was looking for, and it was much stronger than the navy.

It was an experience just getting to Iraq. We took a flight from Hawaii to Alaska. From Alaska we flew to Ireland. Finally, from there we flew to Kuwait. We arrived at night. While getting off the plane, I remember thinking, *Damn! It's cold as hell!* I'd prepared myself for the heat, so I was surprised it was cold at night.

We stayed in Kuwait for two weeks. During that time, we trained and watched videos of real in-the-field scenarios we were likely to encounter. We were trained on how to respond to each scenario in the videos. They really tried to prepare us for the field. It helped, too. Each time I went into the field, I went over a mental checklist of each scenario.

My job was to be a SAW gunner—SAW is a squad automatic weapon. It's a belt-fed machine gun that fires 5.56 caliber bullets. Each squad has a SAW gunner. His job is to put down suppressing fire during an attack—basically fire as many bullets toward the enemy during an attack. In addition to being a SAW gunner, I was trained as the equipment radio operator, ERO; eventually that became my primary assignment.

It was a short plane ride from Kuwait to Iraq. We flew into Camp Liberty, which is a huge military base. It was really a town full of military personnel and contractors. The first thing that stood out to me was the Burger King, Popeye's chicken, and Starbucks. Someone yelled, "Capitalism is alive and well, gentleman!" We were dropped off at our sleeping quarters, and we found our vehicles were already there. We were a Stryker unit. A Stryker is an armored personnel carrier. It has a driver, a gunner who operated either a .50 caliber machine gun or a Mark 19 grenade launcher, a vehicle commander, two rear gunners, and carried ten soldiers. We unloaded and took the rest of the day to prepare for the next day's mission.

Camp Liberty seemed like it was under attack on a daily basis. An alarm went off every other hour, signaling an attack or an incoming round. Nowhere on base was truly safe, as people had been shot and killed while eating in the chow hall. Incoming mortar rounds were a regular occurrence and had been known to kill soldiers while they performed PT—physical training.

After a few days in Camp Liberty, we finally headed to our AO—area of operations. We were to operate out of a small infantry base in Abu Ghraib known as FOB—forward observation base—Warrior. It was in an area known as "the triangle of death"—and happened to be the home of the insurgency.

Each platoon was tasked with an assignment for either three consecutive days or nights. There were three-day missions, three-night missions, three days QRF—quick reaction force—and three days "in house." We provided our own security, so "in house" was tasked with that. Being that I was the SAW gunner, my weapon was placed in one of the towers during "in house" in case of an attack.

The first time we prepared to go out on a mission was intense. Everyone was nervous. We loaded up in our Strykers and formed a column. We were ready to depart when all of a sudden we heard the thump of a Mark 19 firing followed by an explosion. I didn't know what to think. It turned out that someone's nerves had gotten the best of them, and that person had accidentally fired their Mark 19. Unfortunately for us, the incident caused our first mission to be cancelled so it could be investigated. A lot of guys acted disappointed, but I was genuinely disappointed.

We were tasked with "in house" at FOB Warrior. After being on watch for a few hours in the tower, I was replaced. I must've only been lying on my cot for ten minutes when an explosion rocked the base. I jumped up and ran outside. I was greeted by a black cloud of smoke, right in front of my tent. Turns out a suicide bomber drove in front of the base and blew himself up, trying to kill civilians. One person was killed and ten others were injured. I was unable to leave the base and provide security for the wounded to be evacuated, because my weapon was positioned in the tower. Instead, I helped to triage the wounded who were brought in for treatment.

That was the first time I witnessed such gruesome injuries. One civilian's foot was barely hanging onto his leg while the femur was sticking out of the other leg. I didn't know what to do. I just did as the doctor instructed and helped put the man on a stretcher and prepare him for medevac. My squad leader ordered me to get the civilian who was killed and place his body in a body bag.

Sometimes when I close my eyes I can still see the body.

His face was half gone and his legs had been blown off. That wasn't even the worst part. The worst part was the smell of burnt flesh. I almost threw up. We quickly placed the man in a body bag and turned the body over to Iraqi police. The smell of burnt flesh seemed to linger in my nostrils and later did cause me to throw up.

Each time we left the base on foot patrol was an adrenaline rush. My biggest concern was sniper fire. One of the videos in Kuwait that scared me the most was the one where a sniper shot a soldier. My second biggest concern was a suicide bomber. Both scenarios were almost impossible to foresee coming and defend against. That tends to make every soldier feel vulnerable. I experienced a lot of scenarios while in Iraq. I was fortunate to never experience a sniper or a suicide bomber.

We were sent on a long mission in February of 2008. We were tasked with supporting an engineering platoon who were going to clear mines and IEDs—improvised explosive devices. We linked up with them and left the base at 0400 hours. We provided security until 1700 hours before deciding to escort engineering back to base. We dropped them off and turned right back around and went on patrol. There was a route we hadn't been down for quite a while, so we decided to clear it. My squad had a three-Stryker convoy. Normally, my Stryker had always been the second vehicle; however, that day we took the lead position. As we drove down the street, we came upon an object in the road that looked to be covered by a carpet. We stopped, dismounted, and established a perimeter. We suspected it to be an IED. The object in the road was checked out and determined to be trash that was covered by a carpet. On the way back into the Stryker, a buddy of mine slipped and turned his ankle, so I grabbed him and helped him back into our vehicle. I sat him in my seat, so I took a seat in his. We must've only been underway for a minute or two when I heard a loud hissing sound followed by an explosion, chaos, and darkness.

The weight from our vehicle activated a pressure plate that had been attached to 500 pounds of explosives buried in the ground. There were nine of us in the

Stryker, four of whom were killed instantly. The other five, including myself, were severely injured. I remember waking up on grass, my jaw was hanging to the side of my face, and I was covered in oil and blood. Sergeant Erickson, from the second Stryker, was at my side telling me everything was going to be alright. I saw a helicopter take off and I tried to assess my injuries as I lay there. I couldn't move or talk. I didn't know how bad I was, but I knew I was messed up. I remember being placed into a helicopter, and a medic tried to stabilize me before I blacked out. I awoke in a hospital room to a nurse giving me oxygen while another one was cutting my clothes off. I blacked out believing I was in good hands.

My command sergeant major and battalion commander were pinning a Purple Heart on my bed, and telling me what a good job I did when I came to. I didn't understand how someone could do a "good job" being blown up. My jaw was wired shut, I had a compression fracture in my spine, and my ankle was broken. On top of that, I suffered a traumatic brain injury. I was later diagnosed with what they call "survivor's guilt." I tried to be strong, but there were times I'd cry thinking of my brother who'd been killed *while sitting in my seat.*

I was flown back to the States and given a choice as to which military hospital I preferred to be treated at. I chose Brook Army Medical in San Antonio, Texas. I stayed there for six months while I recovered. My jaw was wired shut, and my leg was in a boot for three months. I also had to wear a back brace for six months.

I met a girl named Tara while stationed in Hawaii, awaiting deployment. We only went out a few times before I was deployed, but we had a connection. She was originally from San Antonio, but her stepdad was in the army and stationed in Hawaii. She lived there with her parents when we met. Her stepdad had been deployed to Camp Liberty when I was wounded, and he told her about what happened to me. She was waiting for me the night I showed up in San Antonio and was at the hospital every day helping to take care of me. I began to feel as if I owed her, so I proposed to her once I was out of the hospital. I thought, *Why not? She's beautiful, and she cares for me. Maybe it's time to settle down.* We were married a few months later.

I was ready to go back to my unit after getting married. Tara and I flew back to Hawaii and I reported back to Schofield Barracks. It was August 2008. At the time, I didn't know I had issues. I thought I'd just be sent back immediately, but I learned I had to meet certain physical and mental requirements to be cleared to return to active duty. To determine that, I had to meet with a psychiatrist and show up for physical training each day. Once I was put through a series of tests, the results would then be given to a medical evaluation board. They'd determine if I was "fit for duty."

Tara and I moved into a really nice house on base. Once we were back in Hawaii, it seemed as if the honeymoon was over quickly. I didn't know it then, but I wasn't fit to be a husband. I began experiencing mental problems after I came back from Iraq. The things I'd seen and experienced had left me with PTSD. I was having a hard time. I couldn't sleep, so I began drinking while on medication in order to sleep. Tara and I began arguing a lot, too. In November 2008, my buddy and I went out for a few drinks and I ended up getting a DUI. With all of my turmoil, Tara and I were married and divorced within a year.

In January 2009, I received a phone call from my mom telling me José had suffered a brain aneurysm and was in a coma. I was trying to get back into shape at the time so I could go back to Iraq. However, my training wasn't going very well, so I decided to ask for a compassionate reassignment and be transferred back to Texas. It was granted and I was transferred to Fort Bliss. We found out later that José had suffered an aneurysm after using cocaine. I know people might wonder why I cared about the man after he beat my mom for years. Well, even though he wasn't the best example of a father figure, he was all that I'd had. I came to care about him and accepted him as my stepdad. He was in a coma for a month and a half. When he woke up, he was a totally different person. He had a childlike mentality and a speech impediment. He was never the same again.

I had a lot of idle time once José was released from the hospital. I began getting restless and became very aware of the void in my life since coming back from Iraq. My cousin, Chris, introduced me to riding motorcycles. I found going fast gave me an adrenaline rush, much like combat did, and that seemed to help ease my restlessness. Even though the rush wasn't quite the same, it was a temporary fix, so I became hooked. I took all my savings and bought my own "crotch rocket."

I was notified by the army medical review board that I was determined to be medically unfit to return to duty in May 2010. I was medically discharged from the army. To say that I was devastated would be an understatement. I didn't know what I was going to do. Not only did I feel as if I was letting my brothers in Iraq down by not returning, but I hadn't even thought about what I'd do after the army. I was lost and began drinking more to cope.

Mom discovered her newfound freedom after José was released from the hospital. She began leaving my ten-year-old brother, Angel, to take care of José. My little brother Joey began running the streets and hanging with a gang, and my brother Michael's mind was messed up from growing up around so much violence. My family was all screwed up, and I wanted to be the one who stabilized it. But I realized I had some mental wounds I needed to deal with before I could do that, so I started seeing a psychologist at the VA hospital.

It didn't take me long to realize the psychologist didn't know how to do his job. He seemed to think my problems were strictly combat-related, but I'd begun to think differently. However, since I didn't have a PhD, the psychologist didn't seem to agree with me. Our sessions became a sort of tug-of-war between us, so I decided to stop the treatment. I didn't need the kind of stress it was bringing me.

I met Gabby when I was twenty-five. My cousin invited me to her baby shower, and I saw her as soon as I walked in. She stood about five foot six inches and had short, curly dark hair. She was a beautiful, light-skinned Mexican woman, and I liked everything about her. She came up to me while I smoked a cigarette and began to explain how smoking was bad for me. We started talking and eventually exchanged numbers. We started dating, and I met her parents within a couple of weeks. She was twenty years old, but her parents were pretty strict with her. I made it a point to ingratiate myself to her father because I knew he'd judge me harshly because of all my tattoos.

It seemed as if Gabby's dad started to like me after about a month. I learned that he liked to build things, so I began spending time with him, helping with his projects. I volunteered to help him build a table one day, and I wrecked my motorcycle while on the way to his house. I was going about forty-five miles per hour when I made a left turn. All of a sudden, the front end of my bike lifted up. I opened up the throttle hoping to drive through it and was thrown off. My bike kept going and crashed into a fence. A bunch of people came running to my aid as I laid in the middle of the street. While one person called for an ambulance, I gave my phone to someone else and asked them to call Gabby. She was on the scene before the ambulance showed up. I had a broken wrist, broken collarbone, and I tore my left knee up pretty good. I was more devastated about wrecking my bike, though.

Gabby moved in with me at my grandma's house. She just wanted to take care of me after I was released from the hospital. Her parents were pretty conservative and had a problem with that, so they requested that I move in with them—I think to keep a closer eye on Gabby. Gabby had a two-year-old daughter, Jaylen, who I really took a liking to. Together, they made me feel as if I was a part of a family, and I was a "family man." I treated Jaylen like she was my own daughter, but Gabby's mom had a problem with that for some reason. It started causing problems in the house, which led to Gabby's parents beginning to make me feel like I was imposing upon them. This caused more tension in the house. I suppose I just wore out my welcome with Gabby's parents.

It all came to a head one night when Gabby informed me we were going to attend a cookout with her parents. I got upset because she didn't discuss it with me before agreeing to go. We argued about it, but I lost and ended up going.

Gabby's parents left prior to our argument, so Gabby's dad was already drunk by the time we arrived at the cookout. Jaylen hadn't taken her nap and began screaming and crying after only being there for about an hour. That caused Gabby's dad to snap. "Get her the hell out of here!" he yelled and startled Jaylen. I took exception to him yelling at Jaylen. He and I almost came to blows because of it, so I decided it was time to leave the cookout and their house. We went back to Gabby's parents' house and packed our things.

We found an apartment in Las Cruces, New Mexico. Our only income was my VA check, which amounted to $1,200 a month. We scraped together what furniture we could from friends and family after we moved in. No sooner than we moved in, something happened to me. I began having flashbacks and started sleepwalking in the middle of the night. It started to rain one night while we were asleep. Gabby told me she woke up to find me crawling on the floor in the living room. I guess I crawled to the window and got into shooting position. I don't remember doing that, but Gabby said it really scared her. I even started to have fits of anger and began losing my temper. I pushed and choked Gabby for no reason. I caught myself each time before it went further, but I couldn't explain why it was happening. The thing that bothered me the most was the fact that Jaylen had witnessed it. My behavior put a lot of strain on our relationship. We began breaking up and getting back together—just like my mom and José used to.

One day Gabby talked me into going to school to become a motorcycle mechanic. I did some research and found a school called Motorcycle Mechanic Institute, or MMI. It was located in Phoenix, Arizona. My VA benefits covered the tuition, so we decided to move to Arizona. In April 2011, we packed up a U-Haul and moved. We settled in a one-bedroom apartment and I started school that July.

I met a couple of guys from New York while attending school, Cavo and Swift. I started talking to them and we got along great. They belonged to an outlaw motorcycle club. They came to Arizona to go to school and scout the area to start a new chapter for their club. They talked up their club a lot. What really interested me was how they described it as a "brotherhood." I was intrigued, so I started hanging out with them. It didn't take long for me to realize their type of brotherhood wasn't for me. I continued to hang with them even though joining their club wasn't an option for me. Ever since coming back from Iraq, I felt as if I didn't fit into society. They were veterans like me, so I felt comfortable with them. Even though they hadn't been to war, we still had the military in common.

I found a job with Cavo and Swift. We became bouncers at a nightclub. They were built like bouncers, but I certainly wasn't. At five foot eight inches and 165 pounds—riddled with injuries—I wasn't a very effective bouncer, so I became a barback.

I was doing great in school. I'd go to my classes during the day and go to work at night. But I'd get lost mentally when I didn't have anything to keep me occupied. I'd hallucinate, thinking I was in Iraq. I became temperamental, and I'm ashamed to say Gabby bore the brunt of that. I went back to the VA and sought help for that and was prescribed Ambien. It didn't really help me, though.

Gabby finally had enough of me in January 2013. She took Jaylen and left me for good. They went back to El Paso and refused to speak to me again. My mood swings, outbursts, and hallucinations became too much for her when I blew up on her one night. I realized after she left that I was reliving my mom's relationship. I'd somehow turned into José. What's worse, I put Jaylen through what José had put me through.

I became depressed after Gabby left me. Work became boring, and I was lonely. I tried to keep busy to avoid becoming restless. One day, I received a phone call from my little brother Joey. He asked if he could come and live with me. He wanted to attend MMI. He'd graduated high school and didn't know what else to do. Plus, he wanted to get away from El Paso. I was excited that he'd finally created a plan for his life and was attempting to execute it. I was also happy to have someone around for me, so I agreed to let him come.

It felt good to have my little brother around. I quickly enrolled him in school the day he arrived. He had a learning disability, so I helped him go over what he'd learned in school each day. I didn't mind it. In fact, I quite enjoyed doing it because it kept me busy. It also made Joey really start to look up to me as his big brother. I liked that.

I received a phone call from a friend and former coworker one night. He used to be the head bouncer at the nightclub I worked at, but he'd been fired for pulling a gun on a patron. He was even arrested for it. We'd hung out and drank several times, so I didn't think it was strange when he called. After exchanging pleasantries, he asked, "What're you doing right now?" I explained that I was with my little brother, but we weren't doing anything. He asked me to meet him at a sports bar, and I agreed to go. I didn't want to leave Joey, so I brought him along. Ramiro was already sitting in a booth with a pitcher of beer when we arrived. We took a seat and I introduced him to Joey while I poured myself a drink. Joey was only nineteen years old and couldn't drink, so he ordered some food. We all laughed and joked for a while. We drank a couple of pitchers of beer while Joey ate. Ramiro suddenly became very serious after we finished the second pitcher and asked if I'd help him go and get some money. I didn't know what he was talking about, so I asked him to explain. He told me some guy had owed him some money for some time and he needed me to go with him to get it. I agreed to help him. I guess a part of me wanted to prove I was a good friend, and another part wanted my little brother to think I was tough.

After leaving the sports bar, Joey and I followed Ramiro to his house. We left my truck there and jumped into Ramiro's Suburban. We drove to a parking lot and parked facing the street and overlooking a bar across the street. He shut his car off and explained that the guy he was looking for was a bouncer at the bar. The plan was to confront the guy when he got off of work. If he didn't have the money, we'd pull him into the Suburban and take him to an ATM to get his money. I didn't think it was a good plan, but I kept my opinion to myself. I didn't think it'd get that far.

The bar closed at three A.M. We waited across the street for the longest three hours. Ramiro drove to the bar's parking lot at three A.M. sharp. We were bored and tired of waiting there. I spotted a truck that had a mini-refrigerator sitting in its back bed. For some reason, I got it in my head that I wanted it. I thought it'd be perfect to keep our beers in at home. "Let's grab that fridge!?" I told Joey, as I started to get out of the Suburban. Joey jumped out with me and together we lifted the fridge out of the bed of the truck. "Hey! What're you doing?!" I heard someone yell. I turned to look, and there stood a guy dressed in all black standing with two other guys. We dropped the refrigerator and ran back to the Suburban. "Let's get outta here!" I yelled to Ramiro as we jumped into the back seat. Ramiro quickly turned the ignition and started the truck, but before we could drive off the windows of the truck began exploding.

I immediately realized we were taking fire. My first thought was of Joey. I pulled him down to the floorboard and placed my body over him. The shooting seemed to last forever. Joey was beneath me screaming "Stop!" but the shooting continued. As quickly as it began, it stopped. I sat up and realized I couldn't breathe. I looked down at my stomach and saw that I was covered in blood. I'd been shot. I got out of the truck and collapsed.

I awoke in the hospital with nobody around. There was a phone on the table next to me, so I picked it up and called my cousin Chris in El Paso. He was surprised to hear my voice. He told me Joey had already called our mom and told her we were in jail. Not fully understanding what had happened, I told Chris to sell my bike and truck in order to bail him out. Chris explained that Joey's bail was $500,000, and my bike and truck wouldn't be enough to get him out. A detective came into the room as Chris was talking and forced me to hang up.

The guy dressed in all black at the bar turned out to be an off-duty police officer. He was working security for the bar and was the one who'd fired all the shots. He shot the Suburban twenty-one times—meaning he must've reloaded—despite the fact that we'd never threatened him. I was shot seven times, and Ramiro was shot four times. Joey escaped without a scratch because

I shielded him. Unfortunately, Ramiro died at the scene. It turned out the cop's blood alcohol level was .17—more than twice the legal limit to be considered drunk. He'd been caught on video drinking just minutes before the incident. Despite that, Joey and I were charged with first-degree murder, three counts of aggravated assault, and burglary.

I was confused and shocked when I learned of the charges. After all, I was the one who'd been shot, it was my friend who'd been killed, and my brother and I hadn't killed anyone. I panicked when the police tried to talk to me, so I refused to speak with them. I asked for a lawyer, and it didn't take long for one to show up. She came into my hospital room and explained how I could be charged with first-degree murder without having killed anyone. What she told me freaked me out.

My attorney explained that first-degree murder is not just premeditated murder in the state of Arizona. There is a thing called felony murder under the Arizona statutes. It says that felony murder occurs when a death results during the course or commission of committing a felonious act. Apparently, when Joey and I attempted to steal the refrigerator from the back of the truck, which was felony burglary, and the off-duty officer shot at us, killing Ramiro, it was our actions that set forth the series of events that led to his death. That's what made us liable as if we'd killed him ourselves. The punishment for being convicted of felony murder is either life in prison, with no chance of parole, or the death penalty.

I was taken from the hospital and formally charged in March 2013. I was totally embarrassed when they read my charges at arraignment. I was ashamed and felt as though I'd lost all my honor and integrity. To make matters worse, I'd involved my brother and had gotten someone else killed because of my actions. All I could do was cry. I even contemplated suicide. I had nobody in my corner either. My mom wouldn't speak to me because she blamed me for my brother's incarceration. I had nobody to turn or talk to. It became the lowest and darkest point in my life. I truly felt more like the victim because I was being treated as if I'd pulled the trigger. It seemed as if no attention was being given to the drunk off-duty cop who fired twenty-one times, killing someone.

The prospect of facing the death penalty, and life without parole, for basically trying to steal a refrigerator weighed heavily upon me. I realized for me to be convicted, all the state had to prove was I merely tried to steal the refrigerator, and that scared the hell out of me. So Joey and I accepted it when the prosecutor offered us a plea bargain for second-degree murder.

I would have killed myself without some semblance of hope. Carla became that for me. She frequented the nightclub I worked at. Although we never met outside of my job, I thought she was very attractive each time I saw her. We were always friendly and professional whenever we interacted with each other, so I never thought there was a possibility of us being together. It wasn't as if we'd ever flirted with each other, so I was surprised when I received a letter from her. I'd been in jail for nearly a year and a half and I'd just been offered the plea bargain when her letter arrived. She offered me some words of encouragement, and I wrote her back. We started writing to one another and a relationship blossomed from there. We were married in October 2016. She became my saving grace.

Joey and I entered a plea of guilty to second-degree murder in April 2014. The court allowed me to wear my uniform and medals to my sentencing hearing. They took my military record under advisement and sentenced me to ten years in prison. Joey was sentenced to fourteen years, so my military record knocked off four years in prison.

We've been in prison for a couple of years now. Joey was sent to a different facility than me, but we're both on medium-custody yards. Surprisingly, adjusting to prison hasn't been that difficult for me. It's kind of like the military without any of the fun stuff. I was sent to East Unit, in Florence, Arizona. I'm thankful I was sent here because there's not much violence or racism. My biggest concern about coming to prison was dealing with the Mexican prison gangs. I was worried how it'd be around them because I don't think like them. Thankfully, I've only had one minor problem. I just hope it stays this way. I'm scheduled for release in March 2023, and Joey's release is in 2027. Until then, I'm just trying to do my time as best as I can. In the meantime, I'm a convicted murderer who hasn't killed anyone.

Part 2

Progression
_____

Oso

But she wasn't accepting that, so I left.

My mom gave me up when I was two months old. I was born in San Bernardino, California, in October of 1989. My mom was a Mexican "Cholla" girl who smoked crack and was an alcoholic. My dad was an old school "Chollo." They met as kids who lived in the same neighborhood and began partying together. My mom was a "neighborhood girl"—the type of girl who'd have sex with anyone from the neighborhood for drugs or alcohol—so she and my dad were never really boyfriend and girlfriend. Mom became pregnant by him at eleven years old. She gave birth to my brother Daniel at twelve years old. She had two more sons—Marcos and Renee—by two different guys when she was seventeen and nineteen. Mom had me when she was twenty, and she gave birth to twin girls at twenty-two. Daniel, the twins, and I had the same dad. My mom made it clear, on several occasions, she never wanted any of her kids.

Mom loved partying. Only, her kids seemed to get in the way of that. The fact I was born with symptoms of fetal alcohol syndrome shows just where her priorities were. I continue to have learning disabilities because she partied while pregnant with me. She didn't want the responsibility of raising her kids, so we were given to her parents to raise. She told them she'd send us to an orphanage if they didn't take us in. Thankfully, my dad's parents came and picked us up from them because her parents didn't want anything to do with us. They took us to Tucson, Arizona, to live with them. Soon after my coming to Arizona, my mom was sent to prison for five years. She gave birth to my twin sisters while incarcerated—they joined us in Arizona shortly after their birth.

My dad's mom was great. She was the most lovable woman I've ever encountered. She was a devout Catholic and was very strict, but she was a great lady to be around. We called her Mom, but her name was Juanita. My dad's father passed away, so she was remarried to Grandpa Enrique. Still, I looked at Grandpa Enrique like he was my real grandfather, and he always treated me like he was. They lived on a huge ranch in Tucson that was built by Grandpa Enrique. They had horses, goats, cows, and chickens. For me, it felt like living in a zoo, and I loved it.

I helped with the chores from the first day I was there. With all of the animals there was plenty of work to go around. At five years old, I was assigned the task of making sure that all of the animals had water each morning before I went to school. After school, I helped to clean the horse stables. It was hard work, but I enjoyed doing it with Grandpa Enrique. He became like a surrogate father to me. He taught me how to ride horses, fish, and hunt, because my dad was hardly ever around.

Mom was released from prison when I was around seven years old. When that happened, she came to the ranch and attempted to reclaim her kids. Until then it was normal for me to call Grandma Mom, but something happened the day Mom showed up that caused me to begin referring to her simply as Grandma. I started feeling sorry for my mom. That is, until she began to argue with Grandma for refusing to let her have us. Ultimately, Mom was asked to leave. She refused and called the police. When they arrived and began to investigate, they talked to Grandma, Grandpa, and the five of us kids—by that time my brother Daniel had moved away. They let Mom talk with me, and I remember her saying, "I never wanted you. It was supposed to be a one-night stand with your father. I didn't love you at first, but I thought about it and I do now. I want to be a part of your life now." What she said and how she said it seemed weird to me, even at that age. I talked with Grandma after listening to Mom, and asked her why my mom left me. Her response was, "Your dad didn't want you and she was too busy doing her drugs." When the police asked if I wanted to go with my mom, I refused. "I don't wanna go anywhere," I said. That time was really confusing for me. I refused to go with my mom because the reality that she'd given up on me really hit me that day.

My dad moved to the ranch when I was about eight years old. At first, I thought it'd be cool to have him around. I learned pretty quickly after he began coming home drunk that it wasn't cool. He turned out to be a weird drunk. Sometimes he was a happy drunk, and other times he was a mean drunk. Whenever he'd come home drunk, I didn't know if he was going to hit me or hug me.

I told myself my dad was only trying to make me tough whenever he hit me. He had no problem hitting anyone around him when he was drunk. One night, my grandma waited for my dad to come home so she could talk to him about one of my school field trips. She needed money from him so I could go. He was drunk when she tried talking to him, and I heard him say, "F-ck that motherf-cker! I never wanted him!" My grandma began to yell at him, and he slapped her so hard she fell to the floor. I ran and hid under the bed until Grandpa Enrique grabbed the both of us and attempted to take us to his truck to leave. As we were getting into his truck, my dad struck him in the back of the head. My grandpa turned around and hit my dad so hard that it knocked him unconscious. The next day, as usual, my dad was apologetic, but I didn't want to go near him.

My grandpa developed a heart problem and became sick when I was nine. I didn't really understand how serious his sickness was. I merely thought he had a cold, so I was devastated when he passed away. I immediately regretted not taking his illness seriously and not spending more time with him before he passed.

Grandma took Grandpa's death really hard. She cried a lot and rarely got out of bed. His absence meant someone had to step up and take care of the ranch, so I began staying home from school in order to help with the chores. I didn't mind the work because it kept me away from Dad and school. School had always been frustrating for me because I had a hard time with reading and writing. Learning never came easy to me like it did for the other kids. Watching the other kids grasp the material before I did made me feel like I was dumb and discouraged me from even trying. I now know I'm dyslexic, but back then nobody paid close enough attention to discover that about me. So working on the ranch was the perfect excuse to avoid school. Besides, I was at peace working with the animals, so it was a bonus. I came to love them like they were my family, because they made me feel like they needed me.

My grandma took ill when I was twelve years old. When that happened, my aunt—mi tia—and cousins—mis primos—moved to the ranch to help take care of her. My aunt began to question why it was that I rarely went to school. She convinced my dad to make me go. I think the stress brought on by my grandma's illness combined with my dad's abuse, and my inability to perform in school, all became too much for me to handle. I began acting out in school and started getting into fights, which led to me being suspended.

My cousin called me stupid after I was suspended one day, and I snapped. I began hitting her. My aunt called the police on me and had me arrested. My grandma tried to talk the police out of taking me away. She even pleaded with them, but that didn't help. I was sent to juvenile hall. My aunt told the judge during my first court appearance that I was a "problem child." She said I was just too much for my grandma to handle in her condition. I felt betrayed, because I never gave my grandma any problems. It was all I could do to not yell, "You're a liar!" when my aunt told the judge she feared for her safety and the safety of her kids if I was allowed to go home. From that moment on, I no longer considered them as my family. On top of it all, I found out my dad had been arrested and was charged with DUI and vehicular manslaughter. He later received an eight-year prison sentence.

The judge sentenced me to a boys' ranch called Vision Quest. It turned out to be a pretty cool program. Although I didn't like being away from home, I did have some good experiences there. They took troubled kids and had them drive cattle while living like early pioneers. Each kid had his own horse, and each day we drove cattle for ten to fifteen miles before breaking for camp. After camp was set up, school began. Not only was basic school curriculum taught there, but they also taught life skills. Each cattle drive, called quests, lasted about three months, and each day was jam packed with activities designed to teach us something. I enjoyed riding horses. I found peace around animals, so I didn't mind that aspect of it. There were a few rough times in the program, but I enjoyed it.

I found out my grandma had passed away four months before I was to be released from the program. That was the hardest thing I endured up until that point. I was crushed. I blamed my aunt for keeping me away from her, and I felt like I should've been there for her. She was the only "mom" I'd ever known. I've never really gotten over her passing.

I was allowed to attend the funeral, but I was made to feel like an outsider the entire time. People I'd never seen before were treated better than I was. I had to sit in the back of the funeral home and was largely ignored. After the funeral, my aunt's son, Gilbert, walked up to me. I could see he was upset, and I figured he wanted to make amends with me, because of the lie his mother had told. Instead, he told me it was all my fault Grandma was dead. I couldn't believe he said that. I was caught off guard as he continued to tell me about how our grandma would cry and say how much she missed me and wanted me home. He told me I caused her so much grief, and that's what'd made her sick. I lost it when he said that and began beating him down right there at the funeral. Of course, I was arrested for that, and my aunt pressed charges on me again.

I was sent to a group home instead of prison. My brother Daniel stuck up for me in court. He asked the court to grant him custody of me, and the judge initiated a custody hearing. My brother was given a list of things he needed to show he'd done before I could be placed with him. I was told the process could take up to six months. My brother became my hero that day.

In the meantime, I was sent to Regina House group home. It was filled with a bunch of kids who turned out to be bullies. I hated it there. I learned pretty quickly I had to be the hardest bully. We not only lived there but were home-schooled there, too. I went stir crazy after a week! Between being bullied for my learning disability and missing my grandma, I hated that place.

I survived nearly six months in the group home before the court awarded custody of me to Daniel and his girlfriend Arlette. I was ecstatic! I understood

Daniel had to change his lifestyle in order to prove he could be my guardian. To do that, he had to get a job, a house with a bedroom for me, and take several drug tests. I loved him even more for doing all of that, because nobody else cared enough about me to do it.

Daniel had been on his own since he was sixteen. He grew up in the streets and earned his nickname, "Demon." At six feet eight inches tall, and weighing 250 pounds, he was the biggest Mexican I'd ever seen. He was dark-skinned, muscular, and had tattoos everywhere. On top of all that, he was a handsome man, so chicks dug him. He dressed in a typical Mexican style of Nike Cortez shoes and tan Dickies. He belonged to a Blood gang, and nobody wanted to mess with him because of his size.

We lived on 12th Avenue and Valencia. It's a gang-infested neighborhood on the southside of Tucson. Our house was a small three-bedroom, one-bath place in the middle of the hood. I didn't mind that it was run down. I didn't even care that my room didn't have nice things. What mattered to me was that I was with family. I attached myself to Demon whenever he wasn't at work. He became my "ace" (best friend). Just being around him meant everyone respected me, and I liked that. Soon the whole neighborhood treated me like I grew up there.

I started my freshman year at Sunnyside High and immediately hated it. I didn't grasp the schoolwork like the other kids, and that was the main excuse for me not to be there. It was also full of Crips—the main rival to Demon's gang—and everyone knew where Demon was from. So everyone believed I was from there too. I was unable to convince Demon I shouldn't go there, so I sucked it up and went. It didn't take long for me to begin getting into fights, which ultimately led to me being suspended. Demon wasn't too happy about that, but I tried to tell him what would happen. That was my secondary excuse to not be there.

I began inviting people to our house each time I was suspended. We'd have a "kickback"—a small party during school hours—while Demon was at work. I started smoking weed and drinking alcohol at those kickbacks. I even began having sex with some of the girls that came. I learned pretty quickly that everyone had to be gone and everything had to be cleaned up before Demon came home. That way he'd have no clue as to what I'd been doing. Everything went well for several weeks. That is, until the school notified Demon about all my absences. He beat my ass when he found out what I'd been doing. That didn't deter me, though. He eventually came to understand it was my choice to go to school or not.

I began selling weed to have weed to smoke and to make money. Being able to hang out all day, smoke weed, and make money was fun. It allowed me to meet all sorts of people. I met a girl named Alyssia who became a real close homegirl. There wasn't anything sexual between us, she was just cool to be around. Plus, people always called her looking for drugs, so I'd hang out with her and make money.

I showed up at Alyssia's house to find her smoking methamphetamines with a lady named Donna. I knew Alyssia did that sort of thing, but until then I'd never been around to see her do it. As I sat there and watched, it became more and more appealing to me. Each time they exhaled smoke, I found myself wanting to experience the sensation for myself. "Let me hit that?" I heard myself say before I realized I'd said it. Alyssia protested before Donna could answer. "No! People like you don't do this. It's not for you!" Hearing her tell me that made me want to do it even more. "If I'm gonna do it, then I'm gonna do it!" I responded and reached my hand out to Donna for the pipe. Alyssia said, "No! Don't do it!" as I grabbed the pipe, put it to my lips, and put the flame to the bottom of it.

I held the first hit in for as long as I could. I was surprised by the taste. It wasn't bad at all. My body tingled, and I began to sweat as I exhaled. A rush of adrenaline immediately followed. It was the coolest sensation I'd ever felt. I was instantly wide awake and full of energy. All I wanted to do, from then on, was stay awake, make more money, and run the streets.

I went back to school during the second semester of my freshman year. While I continued to ditch from time to time, I realized how much Demon went through to get custody of me, and I didn't want to disappoint him. I figured the least I could do was not have the "authorities" breathing down his throat because of me. I even tried to participate in class.

I had trouble with my work assignment in class one day. I was having a hard time comprehending what was being said in the textbook. I asked the girl sitting next to me, Stephanie, for help. She was considered to be a nerd because everything seemed to come easy for her in school. It didn't help that she wore glasses and preferred the "natural" look—she didn't wear makeup. All of the girls called her ugly because she didn't place much importance on her appearance, and the boys didn't notice her because she was quiet. But I needed her help, so I asked, "Excuse me, you think you could help me with this . . . ?" She looked at me coldly before I could complete the sentence and said, "No!" I was blown away by her abrupt rudeness. "You don't gotta be stuck up," was all I could think to say. She looked directly at me and asked sarcastically, "Now you wanna talk to me?" I was confused, so I asked her to explain what she meant. Apparently, she'd been sitting next to me during several classes, and I'd never said a word to her before. I missed hearing anything after that because I became captivated by her blue eyes. I apologized once she finished speaking, and that seemed to be all she wanted to hear because she helped me with my problem after that.

I saw Stephanie in a completely different light after that. She was actually very pretty in that plain Jane sort of way. She had a great figure despite trying to hide it with baggy clothes. The thing that appealed to me about her the most was her innocence. Everything about her was good. I even thought she was too good for me. That didn't stop me from flirting with her, though. She surprised me when she flirted back. We started out talking on the phone, and that led to us hanging out. Before I knew it, we were in a relationship.

After seeing Stephanie for a couple of months, she missed school one day. I called to check up on her, and she told me she was sick. Even though it was unlike her to miss a day of school, I thought nothing of it and went about my day. I didn't worry when she missed the second day. I went about my normal routine. I stopped by Alyssia's house after school. We smoked some meth and Alyssia had to leave, so I decided to go home. When I walked into the house I was surprised to find Stephanie sitting on the couch with Arlette—my brother's girlfriend. Both had a serious look on their face and sat quietly as I walked into the living room. "Hey, Oso, you know my friend Stephanie?" Arlette asked jokingly, breaking the silence. I ignored Arlette's question as I focused on the serious look on Stephanie's face. "We need to talk," Stephanie said. I immediately thought she was going to break up with me, and I wondered what I'd done. Oddly enough, I wasn't surprised. I was more surprised our relationship had lasted as long as it had. I took Stephanie into my room and sat next to her on the bed. "What's up?" I asked, hoping she'd get to the point quickly. "I'm pregnant," she said, matter-of-factly. To say I was shocked would be an understatement. I was terrified. She was a week away from turning fifteen years old, and I was fifteen years old. We were kids who were about to become parents.

Stephanie gave birth to fraternal twins, a girl and a boy, in September of 2005. She went into labor while I was at school. It just so happened I didn't ditch that day. I was at home smoking weed after school when I received a call from a friend telling me about Stephanie being in labor. I rushed to the hospital and made it just in time for the birth. That was the first time I'd seen anyone give birth. It was a trip! I was even asked to cut the umbilical cord. Stephanie named the kids Fabian and Ericka. I truly didn't comprehend that I was a father. I mean, I knew the twins belonged to me, but I just didn't grasp that it was time for me to become a responsible parent. To be honest, I was confused as to what that even meant.

Having kids was a drastic change for Stephanie, but I still wanted to be a kid. I visited the kids every now and again, but nothing close to what I should've done. I continued to sell and smoke weed, drink, and smoke meth from time to time. Stephanie and her mom began trying to convince me that I needed to change my life and be there for Stephanie and the twins. Every time I went to see the kids I was nagged by either or both of them. That discouraged me from going by to see them, and that strained our relationship even further.

Stephanie showed up at my house with her mom around March of 2008. I'd taken to smoking meth more frequently and was high when she knocked on my door. When I opened the door and found Stephanie and her mom standing there, I stepped out on the porch to talk to them because I had drug paraphernalia out on the table inside the house. Stephanie told me they were moving to Oklahoma and they wanted me to go with them. Her mom gave me an ultimatum, "If you want to change your ways, be a dad, and go to work, you can live with us in Oklahoma." I didn't know how to do any of that, so I declined. Stephanie handed me a plane ticket and told me they were leaving the next day. She asked me to think about going and told me to be at the airport at nine if I decided to go. I was offended that they'd spring something like that on me on such short notice. That in and of itself made me decide to stay.

The decision to stay remains my biggest regret to date. I haven't seen or heard from Stephanie since then. I don't have any contact information on them, and I wouldn't even know where to begin looking for them. I have one picture of the twins. I often wonder if I'd even recognize them if I saw them. I believe I'd be a whole different person today had I taken the opportunity to move to Oklahoma.

There's a place in Tucson called "A" Mountain. While it's not quite a mountain, it's bigger than a hill. Attached to the top of the mountain is the letter A. The letter is huge and can be seen from miles away. Anyone can drive to the top of the mountain and see the big A. It's considered to be a park and teenagers routinely hang out there.

Demon and I went to "A" Mountain on a regular basis to "kick it"—drink alcohol and smoke weed. He liked watching the sunset there while he drank beer. I was seventeen. We sat at our usual picnic table smoking, drinking, and having a good time. The sun began to set after we were there for about an hour. Demon sent me to retrieve a fresh beer from his truck so he could observe his ritual of drinking a fresh beer while watching the sunset. He parked his truck about fifty yards away from our usual table, but I was happy to make the walk. When I reached the truck, I opened the passenger side door, reached into the crew cab, and grabbed two beers from the ice chest. With beers in each hand, I closed the door with my forearm. A blue Monte Carlo with tinted windows suddenly pulled up and blocked my path as I turned to walk back toward the picnic table. The rear passenger side window rolled down exposing a man with a double-barreled shotgun pointed at me. I stood frozen. I was less than ten feet away from those barrels thinking my life was about to be over. My mind was racing. *What did I do to deserve this?* I thought. *Is this how it all ends?* I wondered, as I expected to see the barrels flash before my life ended. "Naw, that ain't him" I heard a voice in the car say as they began to drive off.

I let out a huge sigh of relief as I watched the car drive away. Suddenly the car accelerated and then slammed on its brakes, coming to a screeching halt about five feet away from where Demon was sitting. I saw Demon stand up and look as if he was trying to see who it was. I heard the gunshot that immediately followed and watched as the blast lifted him off his feet. My first thought was of the .45-caliber pistol Demon kept under the driver's seat in his truck. I ran back to the truck and quickly retrieved it. The Monte Carlo was speeding past the truck as I came out of the cab with the gun. I began shooting, but I only managed to shoot out the back window. The gun made a click sound, signaling I was out of bullets, as the car came to a stop. I panicked, thinking they'd double back and get me. I thought about running. I was out of bullets and had no way to defend myself. To my surprise, the car just sped off.

I prayed out loud as I ran toward my brother. "Please, God, don't let it be that bad!" When I reached him his face was bloody and unrecognizable. I don't remember dialing, but 911 was asking what my emergency was. I freaked out as Demon began making a gurgling sound. "Hurry! He's dying!" I heard myself say. My brother breathed his last breath while I was giving the operator our location. I dropped the phone and held my brother in my arms until the police and ambulance arrived.

The word on the street was Demon had been doing a lot of bad stuff that angered the wrong people. They say he was robbing "pisas" (Mexican nationals) who sold large amounts of drugs. Although I never saw any evidence of that, it wouldn't surprise me if it was true.

The police attempted to question me a few hours later, but I refused to cooperate. I simply told them I didn't know what'd happened. I kept quiet because I wasn't about to be labeled a snitch. Plus, I wanted to be the one who found my brother's killer. I wanted revenge . . . not justice. Unfortunately, I was never able to find out who killed him. His case continues to remain open today.

I became a different person after my brother died. I didn't care about anything. I began drinking heavily to numb the pain. I became so depressed that I wanted to die. Arlette was so worried about my drinking one day that she called my sisters. When they came to check on me I'd already decided to end my life. Seeing my sisters only seemed to make matters worse. I ran into my room and locked myself inside. My sisters were on my heels and pounding on the door yelling, "Let us in!" and "Don't do anything stupid!" I grabbed my .357 magnum, put the gun to my head and pulled the trigger. *Click!*

I opened the cylinder to see if there were any bullets. The cylinder was full. I closed the cylinder, and right as I put the gun back to my head, my sisters broke down the door. I sat frozen and couldn't do it with them in the room. They took the gun from me and stayed with me for several days, until they were sure I wasn't going to try and harm myself again.

Sometimes I think about the gun failing to fire when I pulled the trigger. I've fired the gun since so I know it works. I now believe God had a hand in it. It wasn't my time to go. I was in such a dark place at that point in my life, so it didn't occur to me at the time why the gun didn't fire. I'm now thankful it didn't.

I began smoking meth on a regular basis after my brother's funeral. I was angry all the time. I was like a time bomb waiting to explode. I fought anyone and everyone who angered me. I even shot at a few people over the smallest things.

My dad was released from prison around that time. He'd heard about what happened to Demon, and what was happening with me. He came to see me and apologized for how he'd treated me as a kid and for not being around while I grew up. He told me about his commitment to sobriety and his desire to be my father again. He attempted to persuade me to take on sobriety with him. To be honest, I enjoyed the conversation with him, but I wasn't looking for him to be a father to me. It was too late for that. Plus, I damn sure wasn't looking to be sober, but I was excited to establish an adult relationship with him. He understood my way of thinking and became like a homey to me.

I was fixated on getting revenge for my brother's murder. I figured if I couldn't find the pisas who killed Demon, then I'd rob everyone I could. Taking their money and dope made me feel as if I was doing something to make those who killed him pay. I didn't really care about the money. In fact, I gave most of the money to my sisters so they could put it away for school. All told, I must have given them about $20,000. What I cared about was the drugs I gained from my heists.

My dad became increasingly worried about me. One day he told me, "I've already had to bury one of my kids. I'm not about to bury you too." He suggested that I leave Tucson and move to Phoenix. He found an apartment for me there and offered to pay the rent if I agreed to move. There was one catch: he wanted me to enroll in an alternative school called "Summit." I agreed because I thought a change of scenery would be good for me.

At eighteen years old, I finally had my own place. My dad and uncles—mis tios—helped me move in. Once they were gone, and I was on my own, I celebrated by getting high. It felt good not to have to worry about anyone walking in on me.

My dad helped me to get enrolled in Summit. I told myself going in that I was going to work hard in order to graduate as soon as possible. I wanted to get school over with. After two weeks in school, I showed up one day wearing a University of Arizona T-shirt. Some guy made fun of my shirt, so I hit him in the mouth and was kicked out of school.

I was then placed in a high school for troubled kids called "Career Success." I lasted a whole two months before I was kicked out of there for, you guessed it, fighting. It was then that I decided I was done with school.

My dad was unhappy with my decision to quit school. He'd been paying the rent on my apartment and threatened to quit when I told him about my decision. I guess he thought that'd change my mind. It didn't. He even had his sister drive up and try to convince me to go back to school. She realized pretty quickly my mind was made up. "What are you gonna do, mijo?" she asked. I told her I'd figure it out, but in my mind I thought, *I'm gonna run and gun.*

My uncle Chuy was heavily involved in the drug trade. He lived in Mexico and always told me to give him a call if I ever wanted to make money. So that's exactly what I did. He happened to be in Tucson and gave me the address to meet him at. I hopped in my '97 Tahoe and hit the road as soon as I hung up with him. I was surprised when I arrived at the address he gave me. It was the nicest house I'd ever seen, in an equally nice neighborhood. Uncle Chuy was standing outside when I pulled up. I assumed he lived in the house and was surprised to find out it was only a stash house—a place where drugs are stored in bulk. The house was nicely furnished and everything! When I asked why he used such a nice place, he said. "Who'd think this was a stash house . . . you didn't even know?" When we sat down in the living room he asked, "You sure this is what you wanna do, mijo?" I explained to him why I needed the money and he understood.

He explained the rules I needed to follow. He told me I couldn't drive while I was drunk. He said, "You have to keep your mind right and stay focused at all times." He told me I had to drive the speed limit. He said, "You can't be driving like a bat outta hell cuz you'll draw attention to yourself." He taught me that drugs were a business and one never puts pleasure in front of it. The only rule that troubled me was the one that said if I were caught then I'd have to pay for the product. He said, "Don't get caught. It doesn't matter you're my nephew." I didn't expect to get caught, but that still made my heart skip a beat because I knew what would happen if I couldn't pay. The most important rule was, "No snitching!" That I didn't have a problem with.

There was a knock on the door while Uncle Chuy was running the rules down to me. He stopped mid-sentence, walked to the door, and opened it. A short Mexican dude who was about my age stood there. Uncle Chuy acted as if he'd been expecting him and invited him in to join us. "This is Junior," he said, introducing us as he sat down on a plush leather recliner. "This is my nephew, Oso." He told Junior, "You'll be tailing him." Anytime drugs are transported there's always a chase car that trails the transport vehicle. Junior took a seat next to me as Chuy gave us the instructions for our first drop.

I never had a problem with any of the drops, and the money turned out to be great. Junior and I became fast friends. We transported loads from Tucson to Phoenix, Phoenix to Flagstaff, and Tucson to Winslow. We were all business each time. However, once we were finished we partied hard.

Transporting the drugs was the easy part, but it was never far from my mind what would happen to me if I were ever caught. The thought made me realize the job was only temporary, as luck eventually runs out for everybody. So I saved up enough money to walk away after about a dozen transports. Uncle Chuy was cool with my decision, and Junior and I continued to be friends.

I had enough money to pay my bills for about six months. I bought a pound of meth. I put some meth to the side for myself and began selling the rest. I was careful not to use too much at first, and I thought I was doing a good job not being controlled by the dope.

My homegirl, Alyssia, moved to Phoenix. I was happy about that because, other than Junior, I didn't have many friends. It was nice to have an old friend around. We began to party together again, and it was like we'd never been apart. After only a few months Alyssia called and informed me that she'd had a falling-out with her roommate and would have to return to Tucson. She had no place to stay. So instead of letting my friend move back to Tucson, I let her and her three kids come and stay with me.

After Alyssia moved in, her sister Constance started coming to visit with her three kids. I didn't mind because she seemed pretty cool, and I loved playing with the kids. I enjoyed having them around and started looking forward to them coming. Constance came by one day, and asked Alyssia to watch the kids while she went to work. Alyssia wasn't there, so I volunteered. Constance reluctantly agreed and left. Grace (age nine), Alex (age six), and Xavier (age five) began playing games, and I helped build them a fort. I gave piggyback rides, swung them around, and played hide-and-go-seek until lunchtime. I asked the kids what they wanted to eat and Grace talked me into taking them to McDonald's. Once there, we ordered our food and ate while making jokes and acting goofy. The kids decided to play in the Funland, so I took them out and watched while they played. Out of nowhere, Grace began complaining about a stomach ache. I remembered being told about her serious kidney disease, but I was never given instructions about what she could and couldn't eat. I decided to call Constance to see what she wanted me to do. She freaked out when I told her I fed the kids McDonald's. "She can't eat that!" she yelled, and instructed me to take her to the hospital. "I'll meet you there!" she told me as she hung up. Feeling like a terrible person, I piled the kids into the car and began to drive away. I paused when I realized I didn't know where the hospital was, so I ran back inside and asked the manager for directions. After receiving directions, I jumped back into my car and drove there like a crazy person. The whole time I was thinking about how much of a screw-up I was and kicking myself for thinking I could take care of kids.

Once at the hospital, I rushed Grace to the front desk and tried, unsuccessfully, to explain what was wrong with her. When the nurse found out I wasn't the parent or guardian of the kids, they began acting as if I'd kidnapped them. Hospital security showed up and attempted to take the kids from me. I tried to tell them I was babysitting, and their mom was on the way. I wasn't getting through to them, though. In the meantime, Grace was getting worse and moaning in pain. I was squaring off to fight security when Constance showed up just in time and calmed the situation by explaining everything. They ended up treating Grace and pumping her stomach while I sat with the boys in the waiting room. Afterward, Constance came and reassured me. "Everything's gonna be fine," she said. "It's not your fault. Grace knows what she's not supposed to eat and took advantage of you." Grace then asked to see me. When I went into her room I was sad to see her in a hospital bed. When I walked to her bedside, all I could manage to say was, "I'm sorry, Gracey-girl, for getting you sick." She looked up at me and said, "It's not your fault, Oso. I knew I couldn't eat McDonald's, but I just wanted it." "Was it worth it?" I asked. Her eyes opened wide and a smile appeared on her face while she shook her head, yes.

I became close with Constance and the kids after that. The next few times Grace went to the hospital, I was there. Constance was impressed by that. "Their dad doesn't even come to the hospital for her," she once told me. Soon after that, she asked to be with me. A few months later, I moved in with her. After living with her for only a week she told me she was pregnant.

Hearing that I was going to be a father again brought about emotions I forgot I'd had. I was sure I could be a father, yet I was afraid I'd screw it up again. On top of that, I didn't know if I could contend with my drug addiction. I didn't know if I could stop. I didn't even know if I wanted to stop. I had a home life and a street life, so I felt like as long as I kept both separate then everything would be fine.

I began buying all sorts of baby things before Constance even began to show. I guess it was my way of showing her I was committed. Maybe I was trying to show myself, too. I don't know. I went to her doctor's appointments and was even there when she found out the baby was a boy. I went out and celebrated by doing drugs.

Constance gave birth to our son, J.R., in October of 2008. I was out tweaking—using meth—when she went into labor. My phone was turned off, so they were unable to reach me. I checked my voicemail two days later and learned of the birth. I felt like a dirt bag for not being there. When I walked into the hospital room, Constance was holding the baby. I started to feed her the lie I'd concocted on the way there, but she shushed me. She signaled that J.R. was asleep. I joined her at her bedside and could sense her disappointment. Without saying a word, she handed my son to me. I was high when I held J.R. for the first time, and Constance knew it.

Things changed between me and Constance after that. She didn't say a word to me when I drove her and the baby home from the hospital. At home, she began acting as if she didn't want me to leave the house so much as to go to the store. We started getting into arguments over the smallest things. Then she asked me to stop partying. I told her flat out I wasn't going to change. I wanted both of my lives, but she was unwilling to allow that any longer. I left when she told me that.

Looking back on our relationship, I realized all Constance ever tried to do was love and build a family with me. I guess I ran away from that because I wasn't used to it. I convinced myself that I didn't need a woman's love after my grandma died and drugs allowed me to not think about that. I now yearn for that love.

I went to a client's house, Jayce, to sell her some dope, shortly after leaving Constance. When she invited me into her home, and I made the transaction, she began preparing to use the dope intravenously. Until then I hadn't seen anyone shoot up meth. So I became curious about the process. I watched as she put some dope on a spoon, mixed it with water, and began heating the bottom of the spoon with a lighter. She looked at me and said, "You should try it." I was curious as to what it was like, but I was afraid of using a dirty needle and contracting AIDS. "I'm good," I replied. I watched as she injected, and the look of euphoria that immediately came over her became appealing. When the initial rush began to subside, she looked at me and said, "If you do it, you'll get more lit then you've ever been." That sounded really good to me, but my concern about sharing needles was all that stood in the way. "You got a clean needle?" I asked, and watched as she went into the kitchen. When she came back, she handed me a brand-new syringe that was still in its package. After making sure it was new, I said, "Alright, let's do it." I was excited as I carefully watched her prepare the dope. I became a little nervous as the needle found a vein, but no sooner was the dope shot into me than the nervousness was replaced by an intense rush. I felt like I could fly, and in that moment I knew how I was going to get high for the foreseeable future.

I continued to sell dope, but it wasn't enough to support my new habit. To supplement my income, I started stealing cars and driving them to chop shops in Tucson. I began staying up for weeks at a time, and my behavior became erratic. I decided to stop by Junior's house one day on my way to Tucson with a stolen car. I spotted his sister, Jess, arguing with some guy in front of their house as I pulled up. I'd always been attracted to her, but out of respect for my homey I never pursued her. I knew she was married and with kids, but I also knew her husband hadn't been around. She sold dope as a means of taking care of her kids, and I admired her for that. I sat back and observed the argument to determine what it was about before I decided to intervene. I concluded the guy had owed Jess money for some time, and he was trying to give her the runaround about paying her. I grabbed my shotgun, got out of the car, and crept up behind the guy as he talked. I hit him in the head with the butt of the shotgun, causing him to fall to the ground. I racked a shell into the chamber, for effect, and put the barrel to his face. "What are you doing!" screamed Jess. "What? I'm helping you," I replied, confused by her reaction. Jess pulled out her own gun, pointed it at the guy, and asked, "Do I look like I need your help?" Seeing how angry she was about coming to her aid, I began to second guess my decision to help. "Sorry!" I responded, as I began walking back to the car. After returning the shotgun to the car, I had to shake my head at the sight of Jess taking her money from the guy's wallet as he laid on the ground. Jess didn't say a word to me for the rest of the night.

I returned to Junior's house a few day later. While we were kicking back on his couch, Jess walked in and said, "Hey, Oso," with a smile and walked away. Once she was out of the room, Junior asked me why I hadn't tried to pursue her. I explained to him that I'd thought about it, but I never tried out of respect for him. He appreciated that. He told me Jess had been talking about me, and she told him she liked me. He then gave me his blessing to be with her, so I went and talked with her. We ended up getting together. We were only together for a few months when she told me she was pregnant.

Meanwhile, I continued to steal cars and drive them to chop shops in Tucson. A homey of mine asked me to take a black 2007 Chevy Impala that'd been stolen to my chop shop. He promised to split the money with me. The thought of an easy payday excited me, so I accepted. The car needed gas, so I stopped at a gas station before getting on the freeway. After buying enough gas to make it to Tucson, I pulled out of the gas station and out of nowhere a cop appeared behind me. I tried to play it cool and drive as normal as possible in hopes he'd just ignore me. My hopes were dashed when his lights came on and he attempted to pull me over. I panicked and stepped on the gas. The only thing on my mind was, *I can lose him!* I soon found myself in a neighborhood I was unfamiliar with, and many more police cars were behind me. I didn't even know where they came from. I made a left, and I turned right. But no matter what I did they were still there. The last turn I made was on a street that ended in a cul-de-sac. The police blocked the street off, and I realized I had no place to go. I surrendered.

Apparently, the car had been reported stolen two weeks earlier. Had I known that, I never would have accepted it. Everybody knows the longer the car has been reported stolen the greater the chances of getting caught. My mistake was trusting my "homeboy."

I was charged with theft of means and transportation. I was twenty years old, and it was my first offense. I was given a plea bargain after spending six months in jail. The plea was for time served and two years of probation. I quickly accepted it, because I needed to get out and get high. Once I was sentenced and processed out of jail, the first thing I did was put a needle in my vein. The fact I'd been forced to be clean while in jail meant that the first time I shot up was even more amazing than I'd remembered.

I violated my probation about four or five times. I kept shooting up and failing drug tests, I was never at the address I said I lived at, and I never checked in with my probation officer. I was put on intense probation (IPS). I gave the IPS people a fake address and went on the run. I knew IPS would only cause me to end up in prison, so I decided to have some fun before I went.

I ran into Jess at a party, and we began to talk. She told me she'd miscarried while I was locked up. I was saddened to hear that, and I apologized for not being there for her. After she accepted my apology, I filled her in on everything that'd happened and was happening with me. I told her about my drug use, and the fact I was currently on the run. She sat and listened to me. We talked about everything for hours. That was the first time I'd ever been that open with anyone. We ended the night by "hooking up," and we went our separate ways the next day. I was arrested for having a fugitive warrant a few days after our tryst.

I was sentenced to a year and a half in prison. Because I'd already spent a year in jail, I only had to be in prison for a little over three months. I was cool with that. The nearly four months I had to do flew by quickly, and before I knew it I was being released.

The first stop I made after I was released was to see my parole officer. He told me he wasn't going to be that strict with me on account I'd only had a month to do on parole. The only rule he gave me was to "stay out of trouble." He warned me that if I had any contact with the police, then he was to be informed. He gave me his card, and I was sent on my way. The process was easier than I was told it'd be. I was pleasantly surprised. I went straight to Junior's house. It was good to see him, too. He embraced me like a brother. "C'mon, man, we've gotta celebrate!" he said as he motioned me to his car. He took me to the store, and I purchased beer, legally, for the first time. We went back to his house and smoked weed and drank until the middle of the night.

It felt good to be out, but toward the end of my sentence I made the decision to leave the street life alone once I was released. So for the first time in my life I decided to get a job. I quickly found out how hard it was to land one. I had no work history, no references, and I even struggled to fill out the job application. Plus, I had two felony convictions. Each time I handed an application to a prospective employer, I could swear the first thing they looked at was the box that asked, "Have you ever been convicted of a felony?" My answer always drew a look of condemnation followed by the words, "We'll give you a call if something opens up." Each time I walked out of the business feeling more defeated than the last time.

My job search went on for weeks until I went to a party one night and met a guy named Toney. He and I began talking while drinking beer, and it turned out he was a foreman for a landscaping company. He was sympathetic when I explained to him the frustrations I'd faced with my job search. He offered me a job and a chance to prove myself. I was ecstatic. I never thought I'd ever be happy about getting a job.

Toney started me off doing all of the crappiest jobs. I did them without complaining, though. I showed up to work on time, worked hard, and eventually earned Toney's trust. I finished my parole and gradually learned each task assigned to me. Working was cool, but it did start to become pretty monotonous after a few months. Little by little, I began to sell meth and run the streets again.

I continued to work with Toney. I even became his backup foreman after nearly a year. I smoked weed and drank beer while off work, but my time was largely spent being a father. Even though Constance and I weren't together, I made it a habit to go by and pick up J.R. and the kids and take them places. I sold meth as a means of helping Constance support the kids. After about a year of doing that, the lure of the streets began to draw me back.

I balanced my work life, my street life, and my family life for several months. It wasn't until I was able to get a few buddies hired that everything began to unravel. My buddies smoked meth, and at first I resisted smoking with them. However, running the streets at night began to take a toll on me. I started to oversleep and show up to work late. That affected my performance. My buddies convinced me that smoking with them would improve my work performance. I told myself I'd do it just once, as a pick-me-up. It quickly became an everyday thing.

It must've been obvious to Toney that I was high at work, because he started asking questions, such as, "Is everything alright?" and, "What's going on with you?" I responded with a lie each time. After a few months, I arrived at work to learn from Toney there was a new "company policy" that called for everyone to be drug tested. Instead of going through the motions of taking the test when I knew what the results would be, I quit. I remember the look on Toney's face as my buddies and I left that day. He was not just disappointed . . . he was hurt.

I was an uneducated and unemployed twenty-three-year-old man who slept on a homey's couch and sold meth. To make matters worse, I was an absentee father. These realities seemed to overwhelm me with a sense of hopelessness that seemed insurmountable. Doing drugs allowed me to withdraw from the reality of my worthless life, and withdraw I did.

I met up with Junior one day so we could kick it. He convinced me to go to Jess's house to party. I hadn't seen her in nearly four years, so I was excited to see how she was doing. She greeted me with a huge smile and a hug. The three of us talked for a few before we began smoking meth. Afterward, I got up and went to the bathroom. When I came out of the bathroom there were three kids running around the house, playing. I recognized the two bigger kids as Jess's, but the smaller kid, a little girl who looked to be about three, caught my eye. *Who is she?* I wondered. When I looked closer at her, she looked just like my son J.R. I just sat there watching her play, and when she glanced at me with the cutest smile, it hit me. "Who's that little girl?" I asked Jess. "Oh, that's my daughter Theresa," she said nonchalantly. "How old is she?" I asked, remembering our last tryst four years earlier. "She's almost three." She replied, and before I could finish doing the math in my head she continued, "Yes, you're her father." I sat stunned by that. Jess broke the silence by apologizing for taking so long to tell me. It was all so sudden and a lot to process. "I don't wanna sound like a jerk, but I'm gonna need a DNA test. I'll pay for it," I told her, and she agreed.

The result of the DNA test was conclusive. Theresa was my daughter. I was formally introduced to her after we received the results. She was shy at first. She looked at me like I was some kind of monster, but she slowly began to warm up to me. I started bringing J.R. over to get to know his little sister. He really enjoyed playing with her and being a big brother. I really enjoyed seeing my kids play together.

There had always been something between Jess and me. Being together around the kids meant we couldn't avoid it. We eventually got back together and became a team. We did drugs and sold them together. I moved in with her, and it just felt right.

It all fell apart one night when Jess's ex-boyfriend showed up at the house and wanted to see Theresa. Apparently, Jess didn't know if she belonged to me or him while I was locked up, and he stepped up as her father. I took offense when he showed up and asked to see my daughter. I stepped outside and calmly explained to him that we'd had a DNA test done, and it turned out I was Theresa's father. I told him I thought it'd be best if he didn't come around anymore because it'd be too confusing for Theresa. He tried to protest, but I cut him off. I thanked him for stepping up and being there when I was gone as I turned and walked inside the house. A few seconds later I heard a loud *crash!* I opened the door and found that he'd smashed the window of my truck. I pulled out my gun and began shooting at him as he drove away. I then jumped into my truck and tried to chase him, but he got away.

Once I explained to Jess what'd happened, she wasn't too happy. She told me I had no right to tell him not to come around, but I disagreed. She was mad that I shot at him, and her attitude changed after that. The next day she began complaining about how tired she was of getting high. She started talking about how she wanted more out of life. We began arguing all the time. She wanted me to stop selling and using drugs. She also wanted me to find a job. We had the same arguments that Constance and I used to have. It was like déjà vu! I tried to make it clear that I was stuck in my ways and refused to change, but she wasn't accepting that, so I left. I was gone for a week in order to allow things to cool down. When I came back, she tried to physically fight me. She started yelling and hitting me, so I packed my things and left. When I walked out the door that time, I was sure we were done.

I didn't see Jess or call her. I went down to Tucson and stayed with my dad. I stayed down there for a few weeks hanging out with family. I hung with my sisters, cousins, and uncles. By then my dad had purchased his own ranch, so there was plenty of room. One day while sitting on the porch with my dad and uncles, a Crown Victoria drove up. At first we thought it was the police, so my dad stood up and walked out to meet them. I was surprised to see Jess exit the vehicle. My dad gave her a hug and opened the rear passenger door and helped Theresa out of the car. Theresa ran right into my arms as soon as she saw me. "Daddy!" she yelled as she hugged me. "Hey, mija," I said, as I hugged her back. My attention was on Jess as she walked up with my dad. I wondered what she wanted. "Can I talk to you?" she asked as she stood there looking nervous. My dad put his hand out to Theresa, and breaking the awkward silence, he said, "C'mon, mija, let's go inside so mommy and daddy can talk." My dad gestured to my uncles to follow him, and they all went inside. Once alone, Jess proceeded to explain to me that she wanted to sober up and start a new life, but she wanted to do it with me. She told me she worried I'd either die or end up in prison if I didn't change. She told me she decided to move to North Dakota, and she wanted me to go with them. *Here we go again!* I thought, *First she turns into Constance and now she's Stephanie all over again!* I started to wonder if all three of these women had spoken and were all working together. I didn't want to go to North Dakota, and I told her so. "Besides . . . ," I told her, "you expect me to leave J.R., and what about Constance's kids?" Jess left and took Theresa with her when I refused to go.

I stayed with my dad for another two weeks after Jess left. I couldn't believe she'd actually left. I'd hoped she would end up staying once I refused to go. I felt guilty for not going, and my dad made it worse, because he thought I should have gone. He wasn't shy about his feeling, either. I went back and forth in my head about whether I made the right decision. It stressed me out, so I decided to go back to Phoenix and get back into the game.

I stayed with my homegirl Roxanne. I kicked back at her spot and sold dope. She was cool with me being there as long as I gave her some dope from time to time. For the next few months, I shot up as much dope as I sold.

One day, two young guys showed up at Roxanne's house. As usual, she introduced them to me, and I sold them some dope. Over the next few days they continued to come and buy dope from me at least two or three times a day. They preferred to smoke the meth, so they used more with that method. Of course, I didn't mind because they were steady customers. I started to take a liking to them and started kicking back with them.

We decided to go to Circle K one afternoon to buy some cigarettes. After purchasing the cigarettes, while we were on our way out of the store, I received a text from Roxanne asking me where I was and if I had some dope for sale. She asked me to wait there because she had someone who wanted to buy some from me. While waiting in front of the store, the two youngsters began to joke around and drew the attention of the store clerk. Before I could tell the youngsters to calm down, the clerk furiously pushed the door open and yelled, "You little wetbacks need to leave! You can't be standing out there!" In an attempt to avoid provoking him into calling the police, I said, "No problem, man. We'll leave." As we began to leave the property, the two youngsters started to rib me for allowing the clerk to "disrespect" me. I let them get into my head and incite me. I became furious and decided to teach the clerk a lesson. I turned around, followed by the youngsters, went into the store, and sprayed the clerk in the face with a can of pepper spray. I hit him in his jaw when he grabbed for his eyes, knocking him unconscious. I don't know why I did it, but I dragged his unconscious body into the freezer and left him there. The two youngsters took the opportunity to begin stealing the store's cigarettes. When I came out of the freezer and saw what they were doing, I became aware of what I'd just done. Suddenly, I realized we were on camera. "C'mon! Let's go!" I yelled. One of the youngsters handed me a few bags full of cigarette cartons, and we left.

We made it back to Roxanne's house, and before we went inside we could hear sirens. The youngsters were obviously proud of themselves. They had smiles on their faces as they emptied each bag and began to divvy up the booty. Roxanne walked into her house and saw all of the cigarettes. She'd been by the Circle K to meet me and saw all of the police there, so she immediately understood that we'd robbed the place. She began to panic and urged us to get rid of the "evidence" as quickly as possible. I had to calm her down, so I threw some dope at her. That seemed to do the trick. I assured her everything was going to be alright, and that we'd get rid of the evidence once the police activity died down. However, I really didn't believe it because I kept thinking about those cameras. I shot up some dope to take my mind off the whole situation and began making phone calls to try and find someone who'd buy the cigarettes from us. The next day we traded all of the cigarettes for an ounce and a half of meth.

The youngsters smoked their dope over the course of the next few days while I sold mine and shot up. Apparently, Roxanne told her friend about the robbery and my trading the booty for dope. So Danielle showed up and wanted me to front her some dope. She became angry when I refused and started insulting and threatening me. She told me she was going to "kick my punk ass," and that pissed me off. I pulled my double-barreled shotgun out and stuck it in her face. "If you don't leave I'm gonna blow your head all over this room!" I yelled.

With that said, she left. I later found out she went and called the police and told them about the robbery.

I decided to leave after Danielle left. I needed to get out of the house for a while, so the youngsters and I went to their place. We had to stop at the gas station to put gas in the car. One of the youngsters went inside to pay while the other one pumped the gas. I stayed in the back seat and prepared to shoot up. As one of the youngsters got back into the car, several police cars pulled in and blocked the exit. The cops jumped out of their cars with their guns aimed at us. "Driver! Put your hands out of the window!" was all I heard from a loudspeaker. The two youngsters immediately put their hands up. My only thought was about the dope in the syringe. I wasn't about to let it go to waste, so I quickly shot up and became oblivious to what was happening. The next thing I knew, the back seat windows were smashed in and I was being pulled out of the car.

I spent a year in jail before I was offered a plea bargain for five years in prison. The two youngsters made it seem as if I was the ringleader, and that I made them take the cigarettes. They only received probation for their role, as it was their first offense. I faced eighteen years because it was my third conviction, so I quickly signed the plea bargain when it was offered. I was almost twenty-six years old, and I'll be nearly thirty when I'm released from prison in 2018.

Dee

His beatings did ignite in me one trait
of his that I did possess . . . spitefulness.

I've thought many times about how best to describe my childhood, and it's not an easy thing for me to do. Both of my parents had violent sides to them, and I know that I inherited it from them. I have good and bad memories, so I couldn't say that my childhood was either good or bad. I guess that you could say that I decided at a young age that I was grown, so the best way for me to describe my childhood would be to say that it was . . . brief.

I was born in Mesa, Arizona, in May of 1977. Both of my parents came from traditional Catholic families, but my mom was more "Catholic" than my dad was. My dad was born in September of 1950. His parents emigrated from Poland, making him a first-generation Polish American. He was a slim six feet tall and weighed about 175 pounds. His dark hair and mustache made him look more like he was Italian, if you didn't know any better. My dad was a good man. He was smart, hard-working, and law-abiding. He took responsibility seriously. In a way, he took responsibility too seriously. He was full of anxiety and tended to keep it bottled up. He had a bad temper and blew up over the smallest things. He also had big expectations. He expected things to be a certain way, and if his children didn't conform to that, then he believed he could beat them into conformity.

My mom was the complete opposite of my dad. Born in August of 1954, she was a half-Polish and half-French church girl whose family had been in America for over a hundred years. My mom was a good mom and wife. She was smart and had a good sense of humor, but she was socially awkward and had a tendency to be overbearing. She stood about five foot nine inches tall and was very slim. Her reddish-brown hair and green eyes made her look more Irish than anything. She was a sweet person . . . until she wasn't.

My parents met in a grocery store located near my mom's childhood home. My dad had been stocking shelves there since he was sixteen years old. My mom was seventeen years old and a senior in high school. My dad was twenty-two years old when they bumped into each other in the store. They'd admired each other from afar over the years but never had a chance to converse until that day. Eventually, my dad asked her out and later ended up marrying her. I suspect he married her because she was a "nice Catholic girl," and it made his mom happy.

My parents tried to have kids for six years before Mom gave birth to me. Apparently, she kept having miscarriages. I believe her miscarriages were due to the strain of their unhealthy marriage. Mom went on to give birth to my sister, Lauren, in August of 1979. She turned out to have my dad's personality traits, coupled with my mom's social awkwardness. She quickly became the favorite child. It's almost as if she was the only child and I was the black sheep.

My earliest memory occurred when I was between the ages of three and four years old. My mom had an argument with her sister over the phone. I remember Mom yelling and slamming the phone down. She put me and my sister in the car and began to drive. We were oblivious as to what was going on. It was raining outside when we pulled up to my aunt's house. My aunt came outside when we pulled up, and my mom began to chase her. My aunt ran inside her house and locked the door before my mom could get to her. Mom ended up breaking the window in my aunt's door, and she tried to stab my aunt with a shard of glass. Mom came back to the car with her hand bloodied and wrapped up. She got into the car and drove us home using only one hand. She still has a scar in the palm of her hand, and a story she concocted that is contrary to the truth about how she got it. My mom tends to lie about things like that because she's in denial about the things in her life that she thinks people will judge her for. That's the difference between her and my dad. While my mom would concoct a lie and deny any instance of her snapping, my dad wanted everyone to remember his brutality.

I started kindergarten at a private Catholic school when I was five. I was treated differently there and I hated it. You see, while Mesa, Arizona, looked like an affluent city, it had a huge economic divide. By all outward appearances, my family was middle class; however, we didn't quite have middle-class money. In private school, I was surrounded by kids whose parents were doctors, lawyers, and judges. The kids at school knew my parents didn't have money, and some kids' parents wouldn't let their kids play with me because of it.

After a few years of being tested and ostracized, I became fed up. I began to stick up for myself. Unfortunately, this caused me to get into fights. I was smaller than the other kids my age, so I became a target for the bigger kids. I learned pretty quickly that if I used violence, then the bigger kids would learn to leave me alone. The problem was, I got into trouble when I used violence, and violence was then used on me as punishment from my dad.

A kid set fire to a dumpster when I was in the third grade. Even though I wasn't there when he did it, for some reason he blamed me when he got caught. His name was Paul, and he was a troublemaker. His parents were lawyers, and he felt as if he could bully, tease, and do whatever he wanted with no consequences. He told the school officials that I made him set the fire after he was caught red-handed. He told them that I made fun of him for being adopted, which I wasn't even aware of, and that he felt I'd continue to tease him if he hadn't done it. The fire department put the fire out, and the cops were called. It became a whole thing, and his parents called for my expulsion. Everyone believed Paul, but nobody believed me. My punishment was to sit in the principal's office for the rest of the school year. Once school was over, I never went back there again.

I was enrolled in a public school in Tempe, Arizona, called Thew Elementary, for the fourth grade. The school was located in the "barrio." It was a predominantly Mexican neighborhood called La Victoria, home to a large street gang. By then, I was used to not fitting in or being liked, but I was picked on mercilessly there. It was my first experience with people who generally didn't care, and I became a target because I was small and white. Despite my size, I was never one to back down, so I kept on getting into fights; with each fight came more "trouble" from my dad.

The severity of beatings from my dad became worse as I got older. You see, you couldn't be a screw-up with my dad. All he expected from his kids was that we went to school, got good grades, and didn't cause problems. Yes, I could've had thicker skin when kids teased me. Yes, I could've walked away instead of fighting, but I didn't. That wasn't my personality, and I don't think my dad could accept that. He thought his beatings would cause me to be more like him, but they had the opposite effect. His beatings did ignite in me one trait of his that I did possess . . . spitefulness.

After literally fighting my way through Thew Elementary, I started the sixth grade at Conner Junior High in Tempe, Arizona. I was optimistic about going to school there because the kids were more racially and economically diverse. By then, the previous years of being picked on at school, fighting, and being beaten by my dad made me leery of people. That caused me to be on edge all the time. I learned how to calm myself down and relate to people better at that school.

Each year it was the same cycle that continuously caused me and my dad to butt heads. I'd get into trouble at school and get detention. Whenever I got detention, the school would send a notification paper home with me that my parents had to sign. Instead of having my parents sign the paper, I'd forge their signature. Each time I did that, my parents ended up fighting about it. Of course, that led to me getting beaten. The cycle repeated itself each year through the seventh grade.

I started smoking cigarettes with my friends when I was twelve. We either stole them from our parents or from the store to support our habit. That is, until my friends and I found out about a bar that had a cigarette vending machine. Of course, we had to check it out. When we went to see for ourselves, it was perfect. The vending machine wasn't inside of the bar. It was next to the doors going into the bar. As long as we were quick about it, nobody would ever catch us. We devised a plan, too. We had lookouts, and a guy whose job it was to drop the coins and get the cigarettes. We were organized. Each time we went to replenish our stash, we made a mission out of it, and not once were we ever caught.

We went on a cigarette mission one day, and I was the coin guy. I opened the set of doors and went to the machine. Before I could put the coins in the slot, I spotted a partially smoked cigarette sitting on top of the machine. It was a hand-rolled cigarette that had barely been smoked, so I decided to take it. I dropped the coins, retrieved the cigarettes, and completed another successful mission. We went into the desert to divvy up the smokes, and I decided to smoke the cigarette I'd found. To my surprise, it didn't taste like any cigarette that I'd smoked before. I lit it and inhaled, "What the hell is that?" I wheezed, while I coughed out my lungs. My friend took the cigarette from me, smelled it, took a drag, and began coughing. Once his coughing fit had subsided, he told me he thought it was weed. By that time, I was feeling the beautiful effects of the new thing I'd smoked. And I liked it a lot.

I began to smoke weed on a semi-regular basis. At twelve years old, I didn't really have the money or the supplier to smoke regularly, so I smoked when and where I could. When I was thirteen, a friend and I came across a guy in an alley, of all places, who offered to sell us some weed. I happened to have ten dollars on me, so the guy sold us a quarter ounce of weed. It was the most weed I'd ever possessed, and I was excited to start smoking. We walked to another friend's house and we all smoked together. We didn't know that a house in the area had been burglarized, and the police were patrolling the area. A cop pulled up on us while we were walking through the alleyways. We were high and not paying attention until we saw the cop coming our way. My instinct told me to run, but I decided to stay and play it cool. The cop stopped us and decided to pat us down. He found the weed in my pocket, and I was taken to juvenile hall. I was released with probation thirty days later. Of course, when I returned home, my dad made me realize the severity of my actions.

I smoked weed soon after I was placed on probation and subsequently failed a drug test. I had to go to court, and my probation officer (PO) recommended

I take a drug class. Once I successfully completed the drug class, I had to go back to court. By that time, I'd begun to fight back whenever my dad tried to beat me. That caused more friction around the house. I guess my mom got tired of me and my dad being at each other's throats because she asked her father to take me in. He showed up at my court hearing and formally asked the court to allow me to live with him. Everyone agreed living with him would be better for me, so the judge granted him guardianship of me.

The court didn't know about my grandfather. Had they known, they never would have granted him guardianship. My grandpa had two houses, one in Mesa and another in Mexico. He rarely spent any time at his house in Mesa. Also, he was a hedonist, so his vices were big league compared to mine. Living in Mexico allowed him to do certain things without getting into trouble. He liked to drink, do drugs, and sleep with prostitutes. He liked to beat prostitutes, too. I also got the impression that he liked underage girls. In any case, that was the man the court gave guardianship of a twelve-year-old boy to.

Whenever my grandpa was sober, he was the coolest; however, he was rarely sober. He was usually drunk, and he was a mean drunk. I had no parental guidance with him whatsoever. I didn't mind it because that meant I could do whatever I wanted. He was the one who taught me not to snitch. He gave me cocaine, weed, and alcohol. I just learned to stay away from him when he was drunk.

We went to his house in Mexico after a couple of weeks of living with him in Mesa. Grandpa waited until I'd seen my PO a couple of times before going. I have to admit, I was excited to go with him, and I was pleasantly surprised when we arrived. He had a nice five-bedroom, three-bath ranch house in the countryside of southern Sinaloa, Mexico. I had my own room and everything. I met his girlfriend, Candy, and I didn't like her from the start. She was a filthy stripper with a vulgar mouth. Even though she tried to be cool with me, I could tell from the moment I met her that she didn't like me or want me around. I went into town with her one day, and while we were there I overheard her badmouthing my grandpa. I confronted her about it on the way back to the ranch, and we got into a huge argument. She kicked me out of the car, and I had to walk the remaining few miles back to Grandpa's house. When I arrived back at the ranch, she tried to act as if nothing happened. She gave me lines of cocaine so as to bribe me to keep my mouth shut. Of course, I took the coke and kept my mouth shut because I felt as if telling Grandpa about her would've been "snitching," and I knew how he felt about that. I wasn't about to be labeled a snitch.

One day, Candy refused to give me some coke. She just ignored me. She put the remaining coke into her purse and attempted to walk away. Enraged, I grabbed her purse and a tug-of-war ensued. One swift wrench of the purse caused the strap to break and cut her hand. With blood pouring out of her hand, she ran into my grandpa's room and cried to him. Grandpa was passed out in his drunken stupor when she woke him up with her tale of woe. He became furious. I don't know if he thought I'd abused his "woman," or if he was just angry about being woken up. In any case, his response to the situation was to grab me and begin beating me.

I heard the door shut and a car start. I looked out of the window and saw her and my grandpa drive away. I stayed in my room and contemplated my next move. I decided to have a conversation with him about her. I was determined to inform him about who his girlfriend really was. When they came back, I walked out of my room and began telling him everything. We argued, and before I knew it he was on top of me. He was strong, and there was nothing I could do to get him off me. With one hand, he took his cigar out of his mouth and put it out on my stomach. The pain was excruciating, and it caused me to shriek. "You're gonna learn, boy, never to mess with another man's shit!" he snarled at me, then punched me in the mouth before he got off me. Mouth bleeding, out of breath, and feeling betrayed, I laid on the ground while he went into the bathroom. I spotted a shotgun hanging on the wall over the walkway to the kitchen. A lifetime of rage came over me as I stood up and grabbed it. I checked to see if there were any shells in it, but there weren't. I didn't know where he kept them, and I didn't care. The gun would suffice. I walked to his bedroom and there he sat in his chair with her by his side. I took a few steps into the room before they noticed me, but by then it was too late. I cracked my grandpa in the face with the butt of the shotgun, causing a geyser of blood to erupt. He collapsed with both hands cupping his nose. I dropped the shotgun, grabbed my possessions, and began walking to town.

I called my uncle and explained what'd transpired between Grandpa and me when I reached town. He was sympathetic because he knew how his father was. He wired me enough money so I could fly back to Arizona. He met me at Sky Harbor Airport and took me to his house. My uncle's wife didn't like me. They had two kids together, and she didn't want me around them. I respected that. I didn't want to cause any friction between her and my uncle, so I called my mom. She told me that my PO had been looking for me, and she agreed to pick me up and take me to see him. I gave my PO some manipulative song-and-dance about why he hadn't heard from me, and he bought it. Afterward, Mom took me home with her.

I was tired of the same cycle with my dad by the eighth grade. I knew that something had to give, so I figured it was up to me to change so as to avoid repeating the same cycle. One day, my teacher, Mrs. Howard, sat me down and talked with me about why it was that I didn't do my homework. I made up some story about how overbearing my dad was and how he made me do so many chores after school. I gave her a sob story about how my dad would flip out if I didn't complete the chores, so I did them instead of my homework. I told her that my dad flips out if I get bad grades too, and that I was just too tired to do my homework once I completed my chores. Mrs. Howard set up a quick little program for me to see her after school to go over the curriculum with me in place of homework. I successfully manipulated her, and that motivated me to do the same with other teachers. By the end of eighth grade, I had straight As, and I'd learned how to work the system. My teachers were happy; my dad was happy; and, most importantly, I wasn't getting beaten. That made me happy. It also taught me a great lesson about the power of manipulation. It was my first attempt at criminal behavior, and it was easy. I decided to roll with it.

After I'd finished the eighth grade with straight As, my parents gave me a lot of leeway to do whatever I wanted during the summer. I went to Mesa Community Center one day and found a bulletin board that posted job listings. I found there were odd jobs I was capable of doing, so I took the listings and started making money. My dad seemed to like that. If there was a job I didn't know how to do, like repairing drywall, my dad was more than happy to show me how to do it. He also showed me how to charge for equipment and labor. I began working several odd jobs per day and was making pretty good money. I was on the go all the time and only went home each night to sleep. I established my own independence that summer.

I answered an ad to paint an apartment one day. The apartment was in a small complex that was full of activity. There was a bunch of bikini-clad girls hanging out at the pool. Their ages ranged from thirteen to twenty years old. After I completed my job, I was invited to hang out at the pool with the girls. It was an offer no thirteen-year-old boy could turn down. They had weed, beer, and pizza. It was the first time I smoked weed and drank at the same time. More importantly, it was the first place I felt completely at ease. I loved hanging out there because there was no structure. At home, everything had its place, and everyone did what was expected of them. At the apartment complex, all that was expected of me was to just show up and have a good time. I did that and was openly accepted for it. The place became my sanctuary. For the first time in my life, I wasn't being scrutinized or judged. I wasn't expected to be anyone other than myself. I hung out with a group of girls. All of them were related. Misty and Marzina were sisters, and their cousins were Sherry and Tammy. Their ages ranged from eighteen to twenty-three years old. They took a liking to me and kept me with work. They all sold dope, so people would go to their apartment to buy from them and see me working. I'd end up doing work for their customers, too. I benefited by hanging out there. I mean, it was also an added bonus to be around a bunch of half-naked women every day, too.

Sherry was married to Michael. They always fought, so I constantly repaired things in their apartment that'd been broken. I repaired everything from broken tables to holes in their drywall. Sherry's brother showed up one day while I was painting a patch of recently repaired drywall. I tried to pretend I wasn't watching them as they sat in the living room snorting lines of speed. When Sherry's brother noticed me, he asked if I wanted to do some. I thought, *What the hell*, and agreed. He fixed me a small line, and I snorted it like a pro. It wasn't as if I thought it was the best thing ever. To be honest, I didn't care much for the taste, and I didn't even realize I was high. All I knew was it gave me a lot of energy. I thought that was cool. I went home later that evening and found I was unable to sleep that night. I stayed up all night watching TV.

My high went away by the morning. Even though I'd stayed up all night, I knew I had to keep to my usual routine to avoid my parents' suspicion. Although I was deathly tired and wanted to sleep, I left the house the same time as usual. I went back to Sherry's place and continued working, but I secretly hoped that someone would offer me some more dope. That way I could quit being so tired. I had jobs lined up, and I couldn't imagine getting them done in the condition I was in. Thankfully, I hadn't been working for long before Sherry's brother showed back up. He was with his buddy, and when he saw me he recounted to him how he'd gotten "the kid" high the day before. His buddy was thoroughly entertained by the story. He was probably picturing this five foot four inch kid, who weighed a hundred pounds soaking wet, doing dope, so I went along with the story and described how it made me feel. I even told them that I hadn't slept all night, hoping they'd offer me some more dope. As soon as I said that, they offered me some more, and I was all too happy to accept. They gave me twice as much as I'd been given the day before, and I snorted it quickly before they could change their minds. I completed my entire list of jobs and more that day. When I was counting the money I made, I thought to myself, *This stuff is awesome!*

I was too high to go home, so I called my parents at ten P.M. and told them that I was spending the night at a friend's house. My parents had no problem with it. When I went to my friend's house, his parents wouldn't let me stay. I knew I couldn't go home, so I went to Sherry's house. Her husband worked the graveyard shift, so she was all alone. She invited me to go to the store with her, and I explained to her why I couldn't go home on the ride there. I was happy to hear her tell me I could stay at her place. When we got back to her place, she asked me if I wanted to watch a movie. I agreed, and she told me to go and find a movie I wanted to watch. While she unloaded her newly purchased groceries in the kitchen, I went into her bedroom where the VCR was located. There was already a tape in it, so I just pressed play thinking it was a movie. I was surprised to find that it was a porno movie. Sherry came into the room and caught me. I was astonished when she didn't say anything. She just sat down on the bed with me and began watching the movie. It didn't take long before we were having sex.

I thought I was the MAN. I was fourteen and having sex with a twenty-three-year-old woman. We continued with our affair for months. Each night, we'd get high and have sex for hours. One night, Sherry's husband came home while we were having sex, and I was forced to climb out the window to avoid being caught. The next day, their neighbor told Sherry's husband they'd seen me climb out of his window half-naked. Needless to say, I was banned from their house, and that was the end of my awesome affair.

I started my freshmen year of high school after that summer. I was still doing dope, and I saw an opportunity to sell dope in school. So I really only went to school to network and sell dope. While I disliked most of my classes, I did take a liking to a chemistry class. It was the best. I loved that we actually did stuff instead of just reading through a book. We had labs three times a week, and I enjoyed learning about chemical compounds. I discovered that I actually liked science, and I learned a lot in that class.

I went to Marzina's apartment and babysat for her each day after school. Marzina's boyfriend, Jerry, showed up while I was sitting and doing homework. He saw my chemistry book and took an interest in it. We started talking about chemicals and he really began to get into the conversation. Before I knew it, we were getting high and talking while we went through the book. Afterward, he took me to a house in Apache Junction, Arizona, and showed me how to pull ephedrine out of cold pills. He demonstrated how raw ephedrine was made into meth. All I could think about while I was learning was how much money and dope I was going to have.

Jerry cooked methamphetamines. People who do that consider the task of having to get a regular supply of cold pills too tedious and risky to do. To them, they considered it to be grunt work. Cooks prefer to just get the raw ephedrine, so they can cook it up and produce meth. I was all too happy to be the grunt, so I set up a system. I had a crew of females who did dope go into stores and steal cold pills for me. I'd give them some money and get them high depending on how good of a job they did. When I got the cold pills from them, it was time for me to do my thing. I took the pills, broke them down, and pulled the ephedrine. Once I was done, I sold the raw ephedrine to Jerry. At first I was only able to do my thing every other week because I had to find places to steal the chemicals I needed. I ramped up production once I found a steady supply and had a batch of ephedrine every week. I'd end up with about a half quart to a quart of pseudoephedrine each week. A quart typically sold for up to $5,000. I'd sell it to Jerry for $1,000. I didn't care if Jerry was taking advantage of me. I was just a kid who was having a good time. Besides, Jerry always gave me some pretty cool stuff. He gave me a mountain bike and a Sony Discman, which cost a lot of money back then. He even gave me guns. For a fourteen-year-old, I had everything.

I started to transport dope for Jerry on my mountain bike. He paid me $200 per delivery. That was good money, and I fell in love with the lifestyle. The freedom I felt was invigorating compared to my home life. Yes, I was surrounded by a bunch of degenerate people at the age of fourteen, but I thought those people liked me. I was secure with the fact I fit right in with them. Plus, I had fun. I knew the guy who had all the dope, so I became "the dude." Everyone came to me for dope. I wasn't the average naïve kid, either. I knew I couldn't trust anyone in that lifestyle. And I didn't. People got a kick out of the "street smart little white boy," and I became known in many different circles. That was my lifestyle until I went home.

My exploits began to keep me away from home and school for longer periods of time. I once stayed away for like ten days. By that time, I really resented my dad, so I figured there was no point in even going home if I was going to be late. I wasn't going to fight my dad for being ten minutes late. I might as well fight over being ten days late. That was my thinking. I decided to go home after about a week, though. I did it for my mom, but when I got home my dad and I began to argue. I jumped on my bike and left rather than fight with him. He called my PO after I left and told him I hadn't been home in a week. While I rode my bike down the street, the cops pulled me over and arrested me.

My dad came to visit me while I was in juvie. I told him that I was tired of the beatings and butting heads with him. To my surprise, he admitted that he was tired of it too. We talked for a while, and I finally realized that my dad did love me. I realized he saw me going down the wrong path, and beating me was the only way he knew to try and fix me. He never considered that his beatings only made me rebel even more out of resentment toward him. We came to an understanding in that visit. We agreed I was going to have to change in my own time and not his. My dad came and picked me up when I got out of juvie, and he never beat me again.

I met Jay when I was in the fourth grade. He was two years older than me but had been held back a year. He was in the fifth grade, and we rode to and from school together. While I was small for my age, he was the complete opposite. He was taller than most kids his age and had an athletic build. He always acted as if he was better than everyone, too. He was a bully. I didn't like that one bit. He tried to bully me once, and we fought. I lost, but I sent a message that I wasn't an easy target. He moved to Seattle, Washington, shortly after our fight.

Jay moved back to the neighborhood when I was fourteen and in the ninth grade. I was surprised to see him back in the neighborhood after I was released from juvie. His buddies brought him to me to buy some dope. To be honest, I was surprised to find out he even did dope. I thought he'd think he was too good for it. I got a kick out of selling it to him because it was like he was admitting that I was better than him. For some reason, I liked that feeling.

Jay started seeing my buddy's girlfriend's sister. One day, she claimed that he'd raped her. Apparently, they were making out and it got pretty hot and heavy. She claimed that he pushed it too far and raped her when she tried to stop him. The cops were called, but no charges were filed. We didn't see him for a while after that. He must've skipped town or just laid low. About a month later, my buddies and I were hanging out when my buddy's girlfriend showed up. She began talking about how Jay was back in town. The news got me and my buddies all riled up.

We received word that Jay was hanging out at the pool hall. We decided to go and find him. I hate child molesters and rapists, so I was down to go and hurt him. We spotted him walking down the street as we drove to the pool hall. We drove ahead of him and pulled into an empty parking lot. I had a wooden club, and my buddy had a knife. We waited in the parking lot for him to walk by us. When he did, we ran up on him. He heard the footsteps at the last second. The look on his face told me he knew why we were there. Before he could say a word, I hit him in the head with the club. *Crack!* The blow to his skull caused him to fall to the ground. My buddy stabbed him in the pelvis as he struggled to get to his feet. He screamed as the knife sank into him and became lodged in his pelvic bone. A car stopped in the middle of the road just as my buddy was trying to dislodge it, so we ran away before he could pull it out. The attack must've only lasted a minute.

I was stopped by the cops while I was walking to a girl's house later that evening. They asked me my name, and I gave them a fake one. That didn't work because they called me by my real name and forced me to get into the back of their car. I was taken to the police station and thrown into an interrogation room. After about an hour, detectives came in and started to interrogate me about the assault on Jay. Of course, I denied knowledge of everything. "Why'd you stab him?" they kept asking me. The fact that they thought I'd stabbed him confused me. They never brought up the fact that there were two assailants in the attack, and I thought that was weird. The detectives told me Jay had implicated me in the stabbing, and it all began to make sense. Jay had lied on me. I just couldn't figure out why he'd try and pin the entire thing on me. In our lifestyle, snitching was a no-no, but there is nothing worse than a lying snitch. I vowed to get revenge in the future.

I was charged with attempted murder and remanded to a juvenile detention center pending trial. Everyone there belonged to some gang. Well, everyone except for me. That meant I had to fight. Meanwhile, the district attorney was talking about trying me as an adult. I knew I had to do something to prove I didn't stab Jay, and I had to do it quickly. My attorney suggested we get our own fingerprint analysis to examine the knife. He said it could take several months before the state got around to it, and I didn't like hearing that. I had to have my buddy sell all of my dope and my possessions to come up with the money I needed to pay for an independent fingerprint analysis. Thankfully, he came through for me and my attorney was able to prove conclusively that my fingerprints were nowhere on the knife. The charges had to be dropped, because the evidence we presented contradicted the statements Jay gave to the police.

I was beyond happy when I heard the charges were dropped. My happiness turned into shock when my parents began to push for me to stay in jail. They stood up in court and asked the judge to keep me. I couldn't believe what I was hearing. I felt betrayed by them. I was relieved when the judge declined. I was due to be released at six P.M. that night, and I guess my parents refused to come get me. I was taken to a foster home and dropped off when they didn't come.

I refused to live in a foster home, so I walked away from it. I knew I couldn't go home because it was clear to me that my parents didn't want me there, so I went to an abandoned apartment complex. I'd known people who'd squatted there before, and I knew there'd be at least one apartment I could stay in. I broke into a house on the way there and found a wad of cash. It was more than enough for me to buy some dope and food. I was too young to rent a hotel room, so the only thing left for me to do was invest the money. I made about $2,000 off the dope I bought.

After being on my own for a few weeks, I went to the store one day to buy some hygiene products and food. I'd been on drugs the entire time and hadn't had a proper shower or meal. As I placed some items in my cart, I could feel someone watching me. I turned and looked toward the end of the grocery aisle and found my mom standing there watching me with tears running down her cheeks. I suddenly became aware of my unkemptness and was embarrassed to have her see me like that. She walked up to me without saying a word and embraced me. Her crying brought tears to my eyes, and in that moment nothing else mattered. She looked me in the eyes after she released me and said, "Come home." I was worn out from being on the streets and wanted to go home, but I declined out of spite, remembering the feeling of betrayal in their attempt to keep me in jail.

I left the store and went back to my vacant apartment. I laid in my make-shift bed of old clothes and blankets that night and contemplated that day's events. Suddenly, I heard pounding and screaming coming from the apartment next door. I pulled out my gun and went to check on my next-door neighbor. I found him lying in a pool of blood. He'd been beaten and robbed. He was in bad shape and in need of an ambulance. I knew if I called for an ambulance, the cops would come. If that happened, I wouldn't be able to squat there any longer. On the other hand, I knew that if I didn't call for an ambulance, then my neighbor wasn't going to make it. I placed all my belongings into my backpack, walked to the store, and called 911.

I had no place else to go, so I went home the next morning. My mom was about to leave the house and go to work when I showed up. She immediately embraced me. "Go take a shower," she told me. "I have to go to work, but don't worry. I'll talk to your father." She gestured toward the bathroom, as if to tell me I stank. I turned and walked into my bedroom as she left for work. I placed my backpack on my bed and looked around. I felt as if I hadn't been there for years. Even though I was only fifteen, I felt as if I'd outgrown the place.

I placed my gun underneath the mattress, went into the bathroom, and jumped in the shower. It felt so good to take a real shower. I realized I hadn't had one since before I was locked up. I watched in amazement as the dirt from my body turned the water brown as it rinsed from my skin. I must've been in the shower for ten minutes when something told me it was time to get out. Having learned to listen to my intuition in the streets, I didn't hesitate to turn the water off. I heard my dad's voice. I realized as I walked back into my room that he was talking to someone on the phone. I walked into my room and found my backpack open and my belongings sprawled across the bed. I checked my bag and found my money was missing. Anger and panic overwhelmed my senses, and I quickly dressed. I looked to see if my gun remained in its hiding place. I was relieved to find it.

Gun in hand, I followed my dad's voice and found him in the kitchen talking on the phone. His back was turned to me, so he didn't hear me approach. "Who are you talking to?!" I yelled, knowing he was talking to my PO. He turned toward me with a startled look on his face. My money was in his hand. I pointed the gun at him and calmly said, "Put the phone down." The look on his face told me he couldn't believe this was really happening, but he did as he was told. "Why are you doing this?" he asked as he hung the phone up. All I could think to say was, "Why'd you steal my money?" "You're going to prison," he warned me. "No, I'm not," I replied and told him to drop the money. He complied, and I picked it up. I ran to my room, grabbed my things, and left before the police arrived.

I started to rely on friends whenever I needed a place to stay. I was tired of the lifestyle I'd been enamored with. At that point, I was tired of moving from place to place. There was no stability in my life. I lived my life day to day and hour to hour. It was no life for a fifteen-year-old.

I spent a lot of time at my buddy's apartment in Mesa. One day, while standing in front of his apartment, I watched as a truck pulled into the complex across the street. I thought I recognized the guy driving the truck. He looked like someone I knew who cooked dope, but I couldn't remember who. I watched as he parked the truck under a carport, got out, and disappeared into the complex. I knew he didn't live there, but I didn't think anything of him being there. I thought he was probably just dropping off some dope or something. I went about my business, and the next day the truck was still there. I watched the truck for three days, and nobody touched it. It was an old Chevy truck with a camper shell, and I became obsessed with having to know what was in it. So I decided to break into it. It didn't take me long to get in. Once inside, I discovered it was a mobile meth lab. It had everything needed to cook dope. I got out of the truck and watched in anticipation for one more day. In the meantime, I called around and tried to find someone who wanted to buy its contents. I didn't have anywhere to store its contents, so I had to have everything sold before I stole it.

Eventually, I found a buyer. Once I did, I stole the truck and quickly sold or traded all of its contents. I took the truck to an isolated spot in the desert and torched it. I made about $15,000. Plus, I traded for a bunch of dope. Of course, I shared the wealth with my buddy, Shane. His car needed a transmission, so I traded some of the truck's contents for a new one. Over the course of the next few days, all we did was install the new transmission, get loaded, and party with chicks. I had a blast!

Three weeks later, a van pulled up next to me while I rode my bike to Shane's house. Suddenly, the side door slid open, revealing a burly man wearing a ski mask. I remember looking at the masked man and thinking how weird it looked that his beard was so big that it stuck out from underneath his mask. Before I could even be scared, I was yanked off my bike and pulled into the van. There were two other guys in the back of the van, also wearing masks. One of them threw a tarp over me, and I was thrust into darkness. They began to beat me as the van sped off. Each punch brought immense pain. Sound faded with the impact of each hit. I considered if that's what it felt like to be beaten to death.

I came to in the middle of the desert. I couldn't move, and I could barely see. My face was bloodied, and I felt as if my entire body was broken. It took me a second to realize that I was duct-taped to a fence post. "Where's our shit!?" I heard someone yell. A hand grabbed me by the hair and yanked my head back. A short, angry-looking bald white guy stood in front of me. "Where's our shit, you little bastard!?" He repeated the question, and I realized he was talking about the contents of the truck. My heart began to pound, and I was overcome with fear thinking about what they'd do to me in order to extract the information they wanted. My next thought was about what they were going to do when they heard the truth. In a split second, I decided to tell the truth, and if they killed me then so be it. "I sold it," I managed to say. My mouth was so dry that I could hardly speak. I could see my captor get angrier in response to my answer. He punched me in my stomach so hard that it caused me to puke on myself. "To who?" he asked once my coughing began to subside. "All over the place," I replied, hoping they wouldn't force me to name names. I didn't want to get anyone else in trouble because of my dumb decision to steal the truck. He hit me in the stomach again, and I threw up once more. "What should we do with you?" he calmly asked in a half-whisper. My lips were burning from the vomit, and I gasped for air. *This is when they kill me*, I thought. It was unsettling to think about my scrawny body being left tied to a fence post after I was killed. "I don't know. Don't kill me," I pleaded with him. He hit me in the head with a blunt object, and everything went black.

There was a bag over my head when I came to. I had no idea how long I was out for, but I could hear bugs buzzing around. Singing crickets revealed that it was nighttime. I could tell I was still attached to the fence post. I tried to move, but with each movement came a sharp pain. Suddenly, the thought of my torturer coming back to finish me off brought fear and panic. Disregarding the pain, I began to struggle to get loose. After what seemed like forever, I felt the tape begin to loosen. My panic turned to hope. I became even more determined to get free. It must've taken me several hours of twisting and turning before I finally broke loose.

I collapsed into an irrigation ditch. I tried to get up and walk, but my legs wouldn't work. The thought of never walking again popped into my head. I quickly dismissed the thought and replaced it with the reality of the situation I was in. *I needed to make it out before my torturer came back*, I reminded myself, and I began to crawl out of the ditch and through a field. I crawled until the sun came up and continued through the morning. Sometime in the afternoon, the thought occurred to me that I could die in that field. Adrenaline washed through my body, and I began to crawl again as something inside of me refused to die. I crawled for the better part of a day before I finally made it to a road. I felt as if I'd won a race when I made it to the street. That is, until I realized it still wasn't over and passed out.

The sun wasn't quite down when I woke up. It was evening, and I was thirstier than I'd ever been. I struggled just to sit up and look around. When I did, I spotted a ditch that held standing water. In desperate need of a drink, I decided to crawl to it. Once there, the water looked disgusting, but I knew I had to drink it. I drank several handfuls before I laid back and dozed off.

I woke up the next morning to a pisa (Mexican national) standing over me speaking Spanish. I was so thankful to see him and not my torturer. He picked me up, put me in his truck, and took me to the hospital. It turned out that I had several cracked ribs, a busted wrist, lacerations to my face, and CAT scans revealed severe head and neck trauma. My spleen had been severely damaged and had to be removed. My entire body was badly bruised and swollen. My arms and legs were also covered with lacerations from crawling through the desert. The doctor told me that I was hours away from death. I was severely dehydrated, and the water I drank gave me dysentery. I spent three weeks in the hospital. It took another two months for the lumps on my head to heal and six months for my ribs to heal. I was in pretty bad shape.

I was determined to find out who sold me out after being released from the hospital. I found out the truck belonged to an outlaw motorcycle gang called "The Dirty Dozen." I'd done business with them several times and knew they were nothing to be messed with. Had I known the truck belonged to them, I never would've taken it.

I set out on a mission to find out who sold me out and had nearly gotten me killed. I came across a Mexican dude named Angel. He told me "the Dozen" had questioned him, but I believed him when he said he hadn't given them any information. I felt as if he knew more than he was telling me, so I kept on hounding him. Eventually, he told me the Dozen had talked with my old nemesis Jay, and it was him who told them about me. I became furious when I heard Jay's name. He'd lied about me stabbing him and testified in open court. Now he'd almost gotten me killed. I became obsessed with finding him after that.

Looking back on my conversation with Angel, it could've been him who gave me up to the Dozen. You can't really trust anyone in that world, but he was convincing. Until this day, I can't say definitively that Jay gave me up, but you couldn't tell me he didn't do it at the time. I let my hatred for him cloud my judgment.

The Dozen spread the word that nobody was to do business with me, so I had to go out of my normal circle and do business with people who didn't know me. And I was robbed a few times. I blamed Jay for each time I was robbed.

I found out Jay had been arrested for dope and was locked up. I heard about a girl who lived in his neighborhood who'd been writing to him, so I made it a point to befriend her. She didn't know about my history with him, and I didn't tell her about it. I found out through her when he was due to be released. By that time, I heard he'd snitched on some other people to get a reduced sentence.

I had a buddy drive me by Jay's house the day after he was released. I saw him standing outside, but I told my buddy to keep driving. I went and got high. Afterward, I went and gathered all the materials I needed to accomplish my mission. I went back to his house around four o'clock in the morning. I walked into his backyard and found that it had no fence to separate it from the desert. I journeyed into the desert and found an isolated area and left a shovel behind to complete the first phase of the mission. Then I returned to my buddy's house and waited.

I went back around seven o'clock in the morning. I hid in some bushes across from his house and waited until his mom left for work. His mom came out of the house around eight o'clock, got into her car, and pulled out of the driveway. I waited a few minutes before I left my hiding place. I walked to the front door and turned the handle to see if it was unlocked. It turned. I felt as if what I was about to do was destined to happen as I walked inside the house. I went down the hallway and into his bedroom. He was asleep in his bed, so I jabbed him with the barrel of my shotgun, causing him to wake up. He stretched and yawned, thinking it was his mom waking him up. When he opened his eyes and discovered me standing over him, he was jolted awake. "What the f-ck are you doing here!?" he yelled, still dazed from his sleep. "You and I have unfinished business," I calmly told him. "Get up." "Get the f-ck out of my house!" he yelled. He noticed the shotgun in my right hand resting by my side. His face registered the seriousness of the situation before he asked, "What's this about?" "You know damn good and well what this is about," I told him. I couldn't believe he was audacious enough to play dumb. We went back and forth for the next few minutes, and he tried to convince me I had it all wrong. Of course, I was unmoved by his attempt to persuade me. I made him put his shoes on, and I walked him out of the house and into the backyard.

He continued to try and convince me he hadn't done what I thought he did as we walked out of his backyard and into the desert. Finally, I'd had enough. I told him his friend Jimmy had given him up to me. Of course, I lied to see his reaction. He suggested we go and talk with Jimmy. Coincidentally, Jimmy lived in the same direction as I planned on taking him, so I agreed to take him to "talk" with Jimmy. When we arrived at the isolated place that I'd chosen, Jay stopped when he saw the shovel. "Pick it up and dig," I told him, as I pointed the shotgun at him. He slowly picked the shovel up and began to dig. He dug four scoops of dirt before he stopped. He looked at me and said, "You're not gonna kill me!" "You know what you did. You deserve this," I told him. I saw the look on his face. He looked as if he'd decided to hit me with the shovel. I squeezed the trigger.

The blast was louder than I expected. His body jerked back before he fell to the ground face first. My adrenaline kicked in, and it was as if I couldn't hear a thing. It took a second before my hearing came back. In that moment, I realized the permanence of what I'd done. I instantly knew I'd messed up and gone too far. I felt as if time stood still as I gazed at his body. My mind shifted from guilt to say, *What's done is done. You've gotta get through this situation now.* I picked up the shovel and started to dig.

People talked about his disappearance a few days later. Anytime he was brought up, I acted as if I knew nothing. After a few weeks, people started to treat me differently. Everyone seemed to be cagey with me. In my mind, nobody knew what I'd done; however, in reality, everyone suspected that I had something to do with his disappearance.

Four months later, an off-duty cop was walking his dog in the desert when his dog ran up to him with a jawbone in its mouth. I watched the story unfold on TV. I was doing so much dope that it seemed surreal to see the story on TV. I'd heard people talk nonchalantly about taking a life. My soul felt as if it ached all of the time, so I increased my dope intake to numb the sensation. It seemed as if I was having a bad dream each time I watched my crime scene on TV.

I was walking with my girlfriend, Rachel, down the street about three days later. It was a nice evening out, and we were holding hands as we walked. I stopped to light a cigarette. Suddenly, two cop cars sped by us. They were driving in the direction of Jay's house. I thought of Jay's mom calling the police to report the possibility of the body that'd been found as being that of her son. Overcome with regret and remorse, I smoked my cigarette in silence for the rest of the walk.

People really began to avoid me. I thought it was strange, but I kept dismissing it. At the time, I didn't know the police were talking to people about me behind the scene.

It was a normal day in May of 1993. I was living with Rachel at her parents' house. I went with her stepdad, Dave, to sell some dope to one of his friends. We hung out with his friend and did some dope before we returned to his house. I began washing Rachel's mom's car around three o'clock. Rachel came home before I had finished washing the car, and I playfully sprayed her with the water hose. That led to some sexual banter, which caused us to go inside and have sex. We came out of her room around five o'clock. Her mom was preparing dinner. We were all in the kitchen when there was a knock on the front door. Dave went into the living room and opened the door. I heard him ask, "Who are you looking for?" I went to see who he was talking to and found three cops standing in the living room. "What's your name?" one of them asked me, as the others turned toward me. I instantly became defensive and replied, "What does that matter?" I could feel the tension begin to build, so I gave them a fake name. They told me they knew who I was and asked me to go outside with them. I didn't want to bring drama to Rachel's house, so I went with them. I was surprised to find about ten more cops outside. "We're gonna need you to come with us to the station and answer some questions," one of the cops said, and I knew that he wasn't asking me. I complied with them, and that was the last time I saw Rachel's parents' house.

They asked me about everything but the murder at the police station. They asked me about drugs, burglaries, and people I knew. They painted a picture of me to let me know they knew who I was and what I was about. They knew way too much about me, and that shocked me. I began to wonder if I was even there because of the murder. Then they started to ask me about Jay. For the next two hours, they talked about my history with him. A detective came into the room and asked me, "Would it surprise you to know we found his body?" I stayed silent. The other detective broke the silence when he said, "We know that you shot him, and we have your gun." I denied everything.

I was charged with forty-four felonies and first-degree murder. They charged me with crimes I had forgotten about. They also charged me with crimes I hadn't committed, but I knew the people who committed them. My court-appointed attorney later explained to me why I had so many charges. He told me that some of the cases were put on me by the people who implicated me in Jay's murder. Apparently, they felt as if they could put their case on me and kill two birds with one stone. Other charges were piled on by the cops in order to close some of their open cases.

The only actual evidence they had on me was my gun. The forensic report came back from testing the gun and proved conclusively that it was the murder weapon. I kept the weapon because I believed forensics couldn't be done on a shotgun. Unfortunately, I happened to have my shotgun repaired prior to the murder. Unbeknownst to me, a new firing pin had been installed that had a square head instead of the usual round one. The square head acted like a fingerprint, and that's how they got me.

I was transferred to adult court, and remanded to Madison Street Jail. That's where I was introduced to a real dog-eat-dog world. I was put with the worst juveniles Maricopa County had to offer. There was nothing but gangs in there, and white boys were the minority. At five foot six inches tall and 110 pounds, I was a target. People tried to take my stuff, so I had to fight in order to show people that my possessions and I were NOT a free meal. I had to send a message that I wouldn't go out without a fight; however, anytime I began to get the best of someone I fought, then their friends jumped in. To make matters worse, the guards were worse than the prisoners.

I spent seven months in jail before the prosecutor offered me a plea bargain. I accepted it.

I walked into the courtroom. I immediately noticed my mom, dad, and sister sitting in the front row. I noticed Jay's mom too. She was sitting behind the prosecutor's table. The prosecutor presented my attorney with a copy of the plea bargain for review. My attorney showed it to me, and I read it. I found two things wrong with it. First, the description of the crime was brief and wrong. Last, I didn't like the fact that I was going to have to pay restitution. When I asked what I was paying restitution for, the prosecutor sarcastically replied, "To bury the victim." His patronizing tone angered me, so I responded loudly with, "There's no way I'm paying for the burial! I already buried him once!" The entire courtroom gasped for air in astonishment. My outburst angered the judge, so she pulled me and my attorney into the hallway. "Do you have any idea what you just did in my courtroom?" the judge asked, as if trying to scold me. "I didn't do anything to you," I replied, not understanding what the big deal was. The judge had the audacity to try and explain to me that I should have tact in her courtroom. Astonished, I waited for her to be done before I responded by saying, "You're about to sentence me to life in prison. How much 'tact' do we really need to have right now?" The judge looked as if she understood my point. She just asked that there not be any more outbursts in her courtroom, and I agreed.

I was fed up in that courtroom. I was fed up with my sixteen years of existence. I was fed up with living like a prisoner of war in jail. I was fed up with getting beat on every day. And I was fed up with those adults in the courtroom who were trying to tell me something. I felt justified in my actions at that time, and to hell with everyone who wanted to judge me. I was sentenced to life in prison that day, with parole eligibility after twenty-five years.

I was sent to prison a couple of weeks later. I was still a minor, so I was sent to Rincon minors unit on Tucson complex. I was nervous, but I knew I had to endure it. I was stunned to see manicured grass and trees when we pulled into the unit. Aside from the razor wire and fences, the place looked more like a college campus. That is, until I was escorted into the building.

Prison guards were walking around everywhere. The cell blocks were full of disembodied voices and screams. It was different than jail. I was assigned to a cell. As usual, I was the smallest kid on my tier, so I was quickly singled out. Anytime someone felt as if they needed to prove to their homeboys that they were tough, they ran up on me to fight. I felt like I was a ball getting kicked around everywhere.

A Mexican guy was assigned to my cell, even though the prison was segregated. As soon as the guards put him in my cell and walked away, we began to fight. We fought for ten minutes, but it felt like it was forever. When the guards returned, blood covered the entire cell. The guard called for backup and took us both to medical. After we were sewed up, he and I were questioned about why we'd fought. We acted as if nothing happened. As a consequence, we were placed in "the hole."

While I was in the hole, the guy I'd fought continued to talk shit to me through the door for three days straight. We were housed in separate pods when we were released from the hole. I wasn't in my pod for five minutes before I grabbed a padlock, attached it to a belt, and snuck over to the pod that housed my tormentor. I saw him before he saw me. I took aim and swung the belt and lock. The lock hit my tormentor dead in his face. I continued to hit him in the face over and over. By the time the guards came and pulled me off of him, his blood was everywhere. That earned me an assault charge, but it also earned me something more precious . . . respect.

Things got better for me after that. I learned that I had to be heavy-handed when it came to violence. I learned that I had to be willing to use whatever I could get my hands on to hurt those who wanted to hurt me, simply because I was smaller than everyone. Every now and again, someone new would show up and try me, and I'd have to make an example out of them too. This was the life that was forced upon me.

On my eighteenth birthday, I was transferred from minors to adult prison. I thought my life was about to become more violent. I was scared, but I knew I was prepared to meet violence with violence.

Part 3

Permanence

Oakland

So that meant I had to sell dope in order to make the kind of money I felt like I needed.

I was a premature crack baby born a month and a half early in Berkeley, California, in the mid-1980s. I had so many medical issues that I was forced to stay in the hospital for the first two years of my life. I don't recall much from that time. I do remember my mom would come visit me from time to time toward the end of my stay there, and I remember feeling lonely whenever I didn't see her for days. I don't recall ever seeing my dad there, though. I've never had the courage to ask my mom about why or when she began smoking crack. I've never talked about it with my dad either. My best guess would be she started smoking after my older siblings were born because neither of them were born addicted to it.

My earliest complete memory is of the day I was allowed to go home from the hospital. I was two years old, and it was a day of firsts for me. My mom and dad came with my brother and sister, and we were all together for the first time. I remember my room was filled with a lot of balloons, and there was a cake for me. I remember blowing out the candles on the cake and sticking my entire face in it. It was the first time a party was thrown in my honor. To say I was happy or excited would be an understatement.

After the celebration, I was put into a wheelchair and escorted out of the hospital to a waiting car. It was the first time I recall being outside, and it was definitely the first time I rode in a car. I can still remember watching all the people and places pass by from inside the car. When I stepped foot into our home for the first time it was different. It was so unlike the hospital. The walls were not white, it had a funny smell, and there was carpet. I'd never seen carpet before, so that was a first. My older sister and brother were so excited to have me home. I must've seemed like a new toy to them because they refused to leave me alone. It was the first time we were able to interact without me being hooked up to a monitor. They took me around our Oakland neighborhood to meet our cousins and "play-cousins"—a term used by Black people to describe kids who come from families that are longtime friends of their family. Everyone seemed to know where I'd been and showered me with a lot of attention. That day of firsts continues to be one of my best memories.

I guess people would label my mom a "functioning addict" back then. I don't recall her looking like the typical crackhead, but I was too young to know anything about her being an addict. She was a beautiful Black woman who stood about five feet eight inches tall with a beautiful milk chocolate complexion. She wasn't "crackhead skinny," nor was she overweight, and she had a steady job cleaning airplanes. When she wasn't high, she was the most loving and caring person anyone could meet. She was second to none.

My dad has always been a strong figure, especially back then. He's always been a big, heavyset man who exudes strength. He's a light-skinned Black man who stands about six feet tall. He worked at some construction place that rented out heavy equipment. Years later, I found out he sold large amounts of weed. At the time of my birth, my parents had been together for approximately ten years—they were high school sweethearts.

I began to understand that my mom was on drugs when I was around five years old. I started noticing that whenever she went to the bathroom she'd come out a different person. At first, I thought she was just happy, but a few hours later she'd become angry for no reason. I also noticed she and my dad began to fight more frequently. Each time they fought, my dad would give my sister money and send us to the corner store to buy candy. While on our way to the store one day, I noticed a bunch of older guys standing on the side of it. I was curious as to why they were just standing there, so I asked my sister about them. She told me they were selling crack. I was too young to know what that meant, so it wasn't a big deal when she told me our mom smoked it. I just thought she was sick and it was some kind of medicine that made her happy.

The fights continued between Mom and Dad until I was six years old. One day they told us they were getting a divorce. Dad explained that he was leaving Mom, moving to Antioch, California, and encouraged us to go with him. Each of us were given a choice as to who we wanted to live with. I didn't think it'd be right to leave Mom while she was still sick, so I chose to stay with her. My siblings decided to go with Dad and pleaded with me to change my mind. "Why do you wanna stay? Our clothes are dirty all the time, and the kids at school make fun of us!" my sister said, but I refused to abandon our mom. *Besides,*

I thought, *someone needed to stay with her until she got better.* I later told the judge, in court, that I wanted to stay with her, but I was just too young to understand what I was getting myself into.

Mom's addiction really began to get the best of her, so I took care of the both of us. By this time, she was getting a disability check, but it wasn't enough to feed her addiction, pay the bills, and buy food. We had to get on food stamps, and, at one point, my aunts and uncles showed me how to pay the bills and buy food. I knew my childhood was unlike that of the other kids, but I also knew I was helping my mom for the right reasons. It didn't matter to me that I was being neglected. I guess I didn't know what "neglect" was. It was just normal for me.

I stopped going to school and started hanging out with the guys on the corner at the age of eleven. I became tired of all the kids making fun of me because my clothes were dirty and had holes in them. I thought, *At least on the corner I could make money to buy new clothes so nobody would make fun of me anymore.* I started smoking weed with the older kids. We'd skip school and just hang out and smoke. It was way better than going to school. Unfortunately, because I stopped going to school, Child Protective Services (CPS) removed me from Mom's custody and sent me to live with my dad.

I grew accustomed to having my independence while with my mom, so I wasn't prepared to live with my dad and his rules. He was strict. My siblings and I were given chores to do, and if they weren't done precisely to his specifications, then we'd receive a beating. I began to feel as if living with him was a punishment, so I started sneaking out of the house every night. It was my way of keeping some sort of independence. Each night I'd sneak out, meet up with some "friends," and learn how to steal cars. We'd steal a car and sell it to a chop shop. We ended up getting caught one night while we were driving a stolen car. That was the first time I was arrested. I was charged with grand theft auto, and after spending a couple of months in juvenile hall, I was let out on probation. My dad was not too happy about having a twelve-year-old son on an ankle monitor.

I began selling weed at school at around thirteen years old, and was making pretty good money. I became known as the "go-to" guy at school. One day, I was approached by a kid I hadn't met before. He wanted to buy some weed, so I tried to negotiate with him to buy more. I preferred to sell all my weed before school began, so I wouldn't have to bring it onto campus. I tried to give the guy a good deal, but he refused it very rudely. So I decided to take his money. I went back to school and was surprised when the police pulled me out of class and arrested me. I couldn't believe the kid I'd robbed had called the police on me. He told them I had weed on me in school, and I was sent back to juvie and spent six months inside before being released to my dad on probation. When I was released, I didn't look forward to going back to my dad's house.

Things were not welcoming at my dad's house when I arrived back from juvie. I felt like he was simply putting up with me because I was his kid, so I decided I wanted to see a loving and welcoming face the first night out. I snuck out and went to my girlfriend's house. I only wanted to spend a few hours with her, and I knew my dad would never let me leave the house. Well, he caught me sneaking back in around four A.M. He was so furious that he beat me down, kicked me out of the house, and called the police on me. I was on probation and out after curfew, so I was arrested while walking down the street, bruised and bloodied. I was sent back to juvie for six more months.

After six months in juvie, I was to be sent to a halfway house in Los Angeles until I was eighteen years old. I wasn't scared about living in a halfway house. I was scared about living in L.A. You see, Northern California and Southern California don't exactly get along. So, aside from the fact that I didn't know anyone in L.A., I knew what was in store for me if I went down there. I wasn't about to subject myself to being hurt or killed, so I decided to run the first chance I got.

When my probation officer (PO) arrived to take me to the airport, I acted as if I was excited to be going to L.A. and was placed into the back seat of his car without handcuffs. That's when my search for a window of opportunity to escape began. As we drove toward the airport, I noticed we were close to my neighborhood. I began pretending as if I had to go to the bathroom. My PO insisted I hold it until we reached the airport, but I convinced him to pull over. I told him I'd go on his back seat. He decided to pull over at a gas station. He let me out and escorted me to the bathroom. We discovered that in order to gain access to the bathroom we'd need a key. He took me inside the gas station and watched as I received the key from the attendant. He escorted me back to the bathroom, and I looked for an opportunity to run the entire time but wasn't given one. That is, until I unlocked the bathroom door and opened it. My PO began walking toward his car as I began to enter the bathroom. I slowed down and watched him walk away. Once he was far enough away that I knew he wouldn't be able to catch me, I made a break for it. It was the middle of the morning and there was a lot of traffic, so I ran full speed into the street and across the intersection. I heard my PO yell something, but when I glanced back I was pleased to see he wasn't trying to chase me. I knew once I made it back to my neighborhood I was home free.

I realized I was a fugitive, so I went straight to my cousin Lil-D's house. He was surprised to see me and happy to take me in. I ended up calling my mom because she'd recently remarried and was living with her husband. As far as I knew, the police didn't know where to find her either, so I asked to stay with her. Her new husband turned out to be pretty cool. He was a cocaine dealer, so he gave me some coke to sell and make money. He also taught me how to sell it and turned me loose. I stayed with him and my mom for several months selling dope, and mom benefited by having two dope dealers around. She was able to get the crumbs from whatever leftovers her husband had so she could smoke, and I helped out with the groceries. One night, after I'd just purchased a quarter ounce of coke from her husband, Mom asked me to go to the store to buy some alcohol (neighborhood stores regularly sold alcohol and tobacco to neighborhood kids). When I returned home from the store, I discovered my mom had stolen some coke from me. She was high and the only one in the house, so I knew it was her. I couldn't believe she'd stolen from me. I was hurt. I remember yelling, "If your addiction is so bad you have to steal from your own son then it's too bad!" before walking out of the house. My mom was crying as I left, and she hasn't smoked crack again since that night.

My mom's husband got busted soon after that incident, and everything changed. His incarceration meant I had to step up and help pay more bills. Mom ended up having the phone switched to my name and, before I knew it, I was staring at a $1,600 phone bill because her husband kept calling collect from jail. When I confronted her about it, we began to argue. I told her I didn't have that kind of money to pay the bill and refused to pay. She responded by telling me if I didn't pay the bill, then I couldn't live there anymore. I don't like ultimatums, so I didn't pay the bill. Mom was true to her word because once the phone was cut off, she kicked me out. With no place to go, I took what belongings I had and began walking down the street. I came to an old family friend's car and decided to crash in it. I hopped into the car and fell asleep. I awoke to find flashlights and guns pointed at me. I was pulled out of the car and arrested. As it turned out, after I left the house, my mom went to the neighbor's house and called the police on me.

I was sent to a boys' camp in Tracy, California. They sentenced me to nine months for running away from my PO a year earlier. I decided to go to church one night after a few months there, and I met a man named Reverend Tinsley. I immediately liked him. He was an older, light-skinned Black man but he knew how to talk to us kids. After a few months of going to his service, he sat down next to me one evening and told me he knew my sister. Apparently, he'd mentored her a few years earlier and even helped to get her a scholarship to some college in Tennessee—although she never went because she didn't want to leave Oakland. Reverend Tinsley also offered to mentor me. I was surprised by his offer, but I accepted because he seemed to be a good man.

Reverend Tinsley had a way of encouraging me. He always knew exactly what I needed to hear. When I was released from the boys' camp, everyone was shocked to hear that I intended on going to church with him. He even encouraged me to play football during my freshman year of high school. When I did sign up, he came to every game. I turned out to be pretty good at football and fell in love with the sport. I played defensive end that year and did very well, too. I had eleven sacks, four forced fumbles, and a ninety-nine-yard interception return for a touchdown. Not only did I fall in love with football, but that love forced me to apply myself in school.

I was selected to play on the varsity team my sophomore year—a huge honor because varsity is for juniors and seniors. During the previous summer, I grew to be six feet one inch tall. The varsity coach took one look at me during practice and told me to play wide receiver for him that year. I ended up with 1,176 yards and fourteen TDs for the season. Reverend Tinsley continued to come to each game; my dad began coming as well. My grades improved to a B average, and I started receiving recognition from the media.

One day after football season had ended, I went off campus for lunch. Across the street from my school was a place called the Snack Shack, where many of the kids would go for lunch each day. On this particular day, a bunch of Asian kids showed up as I was eating, and I was caught in the middle of a race riot. Apparently, the Asians were angry about being cut out of the drug market by a Black gang. One person was left dead and several others were injured. I was able to escape uninjured before the police showed up. The riot really opened my eyes as to just how serious the drug game was, and it made me realize football could take me away from it. I decided football was what I wanted to do, so I quit selling weed to focus on it.

I worked out consistently during the summer in anticipation of football season. It was my junior year, so I wanted to bulk up for varsity football. I also started dating the head cheerleader. While my dad and I didn't have the best relationship, we were getting along better than ever. Unfortunately, when things begin going good in my life, it's usually just the calm before the storm. I went to meet up with my girlfriend one day during our first week of school, and as I approached our meeting place, I spotted a guy who looked to be harassing her. I could tell she was frustrated and attempting to get away from him. I'd seen him around school, but I didn't know who he was. I sped up, and as I arrived behind the guy, I heard him call her a "bitch." The next thing I knew, people were pulling me off of him. I beat him so badly they kicked me out of school. I couldn't understand why. I'd only been protecting my girlfriend. The thing that hurt me the most was being kicked off the football team. I felt like I didn't do anything that warranted such punishment.

I enrolled at Antioch High School. Football season had already begun, so I wasn't able to be on the team. I felt like there was no point in going to school if I couldn't play football. I got into another fight and was kicked out of there after only a couple of weeks. I wasn't mad about that one, though. I didn't like that school anyway.

My dad seemed to understand why I was kicked out of the first school. He even respected the fact that I'd stuck up for my girlfriend. However, the same couldn't be said for the second school I was kicked out of. After riding home in silence with him from school that day, as soon as we were inside of the house, he hit me so hard with a left hook that all I remember was waking up. It seemed like the older his sons became, the harder my dad hit us. I was tired of his abuse and decided to leave, but the only place I knew to go was back to my mom's house.

The one good thing about being back at my mom's house was being close to Reverend Tinsley's church again. He had me enrolled in Oakland High School so I could finish my junior year. And he tried to keep a close eye on me. He went out of his way to pick me up as often as he could and take me places with him. He made sure I kept up with my schoolwork and always encouraged me to do better. I finished with a B average and was eligible to play football during my senior year—all because of Reverend Tinsley's guidance. I worked out with members of the football team every day that summer and became close with a few guys on the team. We pushed each other in the weight room by turning our workouts into a competition, so when football season began I'd already been accepted as one of the guys. It turned out to be a breakout year as a receiver. I had 1,380 yards and seventeen TDs that season. However, colleges were scared away from recruiting me because of my criminal history. My past came back to haunt me.

I had a great season my senior year, and I thought for sure I'd get all kinds of offers from college recruits. Several PAC-12 schools contacted me, but none of them offered me a full scholarship. I became disheartened by that and sought advice from Reverend Tinsley. I poured my heart out to him and he listened. He offered some words of encouragement, but it didn't help much. Several weeks later, Reverend Tinsley came by my house to pick me up for church. When I climbed into the passenger seat of his car and closed the door, he placed a big manila envelope on my lap and began driving. The letterhead on the envelope had the name of a college I'd never heard of before. I curiously opened the envelope and withdrew its contents. On top of all the papers and brochures was a letter explaining that they were a Division II school, and they'd received a video of my games. What got me was toward the end of the letter they offered me a full scholarship to attend their school. I couldn't believe what I'd read. *How did they get a video of my games?* I wondered. When I looked over at Reverend Tinsley, he had huge smile on his face, but continued to drive as if he had no clue what I was reading. "You sent them a video of me playing?" It was a rhetorical question, but Reverend Tinsley quickly replied, "You bet I did!" That night I thanked God while I was in church.

Being offered a scholarship was a dream come true. It didn't matter to me that it was a Division II school. The scholarship wasn't just a means of paying for college; it was a validation that I was good at something. I could have attempted to walk on at a PAC-12 school or accept a partial scholarship, but that would mean I would've accepted that they didn't think I was good enough. I knew I was good enough. Besides, I thought if I worked hard at that school, then the big schools would eventually come running to me with offers. I had a legitimate path that could take me down the road I'd been dreaming of, so I quickly replied and accepted their offer. I was invited to view their campus, and I couldn't wait to see the school and check it out. I counted down each day in anticipation until the day finally arrived.

The campus turned out to be everything I'd imagined and more. It was bigger than I'd anticipated and more beautiful than the pictures in their brochure. Everywhere I looked seemed perfect. The buildings, the bushes, and the people all looked like they belonged there. With that thought, I began to feel out of place. As I toured the dorms I couldn't help but notice they were co-ed. That excited me. The women were beautiful and abundant, but they seemed like they were out of my league. I walked out of the dorms and noticed the parking lot was full of brand-new cars. It convinced me that I couldn't show back up to school broke and be around all those rich kids—at least, I perceived them as being rich kids. I wasn't about to have them laugh at me for being ghetto and broke. So I knew I'd have to go back to Oakland and make enough money to hang with the kids at my new school. It was either that or be humiliated once again. And I wasn't about to have that.

My knowledge consisted of three things: selling dope, football, and God. I realized God gave me the talent to play football, but making money was up to me. My mom and dad didn't have money for me to live on while at school, so that meant I had to sell dope in order to make the kind of money I felt like I needed. I tracked my cousin Lil-D down the second I returned to Oakland and explained my dilemma. He and his older brother Bubs were happy to help me by giving me some dope to sell, and they volunteered to have my back on the block while I "slanged." Where I'm from, you can't just go out on any street corner and sell drugs alone. You always had to be in groups of threes to avoid being robbed or arrested. I figured it would take me at least a week of selling dope to have enough money to last an entire semester. The fact Lil-D and Bubs were willing to help me was much appreciated. They helped me with everything I needed to get started.

My cousin's neighborhood is called "Sixty-Five Village," so they already knew the layout of the spot they regularly sold dope at. I set up shop in front of a neighborhood store, and things went well for the first few hours. I was making a lot of money and was happy with my decision. I didn't know my cousin's neighborhood was at war with a rival gang for turf. That is, until someone began shooting at us. I thought Lil-D had been hit because he fell to the ground. I ran over to check on him even though bullets were still flying. Thankfully, he only fell to avoid being shot. I helped him up and we ran back to his house.

The whole incident probably lasted ten seconds, but it seemed like ten minutes. We arrived back at Lil-D's house to find Bubs waiting for us, and we decided to call it a night. We were just thankful none of us were shot. We nervously joked about each other's reaction during the incident, but neither of us wanted to admit how scared we really were.

Lil-D decided to take his car out with us to sell dope the next night. He figured we'd at least have something to hide behind if someone shot at us again. After about five hours of selling dope, we were surprised to find that nobody shot at us. We were nervous the entire time, but after three or four hours we began to relax a little. Finally, Lil-D suggested we go and get something to eat. Things had been going so well that I wanted to take advantage of it, so I decided to stay. Lil-D understood and asked Bubs to stay with me while he went for food and promised to bring some food back for us. He jumped into his car, started it, and as he leaned down to turn the music, the first shot shattered his driver's side window. I didn't hear the shots at first. I just saw his window explode. "Run!" I heard Lil-D yell as he put his foot on the gas to escape the line of fire. I stood there frozen while Bubs yanked on my arm to get me to run. Finally, I snapped out of my shock and ran back to Lil-D's house unscathed. We once again met up and nervously joked about the night's events.

The third night was much the same as the first two. We were shot at after only being there for a few hours. The difference between this night and the previous two was that we'd had enough of looking over our shoulders. We'd done nothing to provoke the shootings, but we were well aware by not responding we'd only be encouraging them to continue to shoot at us. We all agreed we had to retaliate.

Lil-D took me to a neighborhood called "Sobronte Park" the next night. We arrived at a house I didn't recognize. Lil-D told me it belonged to his homeboy Tommy. Apparently, Tommy would be helping us, but I didn't know what that meant. So I kept quiet. The front door swung open before we could reach it, revealing a towering figure. "What up, big homey?" Lil-D said as he embraced the stranger. He introduced me to Tommy, and after shaking hands we were invited into the back room of the house. Lil-D lit a blunt and passed it to me while we waited. Wondering what it was we were there for, I just smoked the blunt and sat in silence. We didn't wait long before Tommy appeared from the back room holding an AK-47 assault rifle and handed it to Lil-D. Lil-D took the rifle and handed the blunt to Tommy. "That's what I'm talking 'bout!" Lil-D said while taking the rifle and giving it a once-over. Satisfied that the gun was good, Lil-D handed it to me. "Here, hold that," he told me while pulling out a 9mm Ruger from his waist and handing it to Tommy. "Good lookin' out, big homey," he told Tommy, then nodded toward me and said, "Let's go." As we began to leave, I understood what it was we were there for. We were preparing to retaliate.

Once inside the car, Lil-D grabbed the rifle from me, chambered a round, gave me a few instructions on handling the weapon, and then gave the weapon back to me. Lil-D began driving while explaining our plan of attack. By this time, I realized I was going to be the shooter. I became more and more nervous with each passing block. I didn't want to be the shooter, but I didn't want to disappoint Lil-D either. I kept my mouth shut even though I just wanted to get out of the car and go home. My mind was racing when I heard Lil-D yell, "Alright, cuz, here we go. They're gonna be on the left. So get ready!" I rolled down the window, stood up in it, and positioned the rifle on the roof of the car. Lil-D drove slowly as I spotted about five or six guys huddled together on the street corner. "Shoot!" I heard Lil-D yell. I took aim, closed my eyes, and pulled the trigger.

We sped off as soon as the gun was out of bullets. I sat back down in the passenger seat, put the rifle on the back seat, and began to realize what I'd just done. I was shaking uncontrollably, my heart was racing, and my mind was all jumbled as we drove back to Lil-D's house and parked the car. I sat speechless as he turned the car off, pulled out a blunt, and lit it. "Here, smoke this and calm down," he said while handing it to me. As I grabbed it from him, I noticed an Astro van slowly pulling up beside us. Lil-D turned to see who it was and was shot in the face. I saw his head jerk back and a red mist before I heard the gunshot. I could feel the bullets travel past me, and I sat frozen until I heard a voice tell me to *Run!* I opened the car door and began running. *Pop! Pop! Pop!* I heard the bullets whizzing all around me before I felt an incredible pain and fell to the ground. I tried to get up and continue running but I couldn't. All I could do was crawl as the shooting continued. The voice told me, *Play dead!* When I did, the shooting stopped. I heard a car door slam, the sound of a car speeding off, and then silence. Frantic voices and screaming penetrated the silence and the next thing I remember is waking up in the hospital.

I awoke to find my left leg in a cast. I'd been shot in the leg twice, and my ankle had been shattered. To repair my ankle, the doctors had operated on it and placed screws and plates in it to hold it together. No sooner had I woken up than the police attempted to question me, but I refused to cooperate. I learned the only fatality that night was my cousin, and I instantly regretted his death. I was also thankful I hadn't killed anyone or been killed myself. I was told I wouldn't be able to play football anymore due to the severity of the injury. My cousin was gone, I'd been shot, and my football career was over. A deep depression overcame me and all I could do during the next week in the hospital was cry and sleep.

I went back to my mom's house the day I was released from the hospital. To my surprise, she had my bags packed and told me about a friend of hers who was moving to Phoenix, Arizona. She wanted me to go with her. Apparently, she'd already talked with her friend, and the lady agreed to let me go with her and her family. My mom believed if I continued to live in Oakland I'd end up getting myself killed. She thought I needed a fresh start in a new place, and after everything that had just happened, I couldn't disagree with her, so I agreed to go.

My mom's friend was a middle-aged French woman named April. She had three kids, and the reason why they were moving was because her eldest—an eighteen-year-old named Pierre—had been getting beat up by a group of Samoan guys. April was tired of her son being in danger, so she decided to move to Arizona, where she had family. April also had two daughters—ages six and thirteen. They'd already taken a trip to Phoenix and rented a small apartment, which meant five people would be staying in a two-bedroom. I wasn't too excited at the thought of living in such a cramped space with strangers.

When we arrived and began moving into the apartment, the manager appeared and inquired about the number of people who'd be living there. When the manager found out five people would be occupying the apartment, he quickly shut it down. My first thought was that I'd be told I couldn't stay and would be left homeless. April ended up calling some family members and found out her cousin was in the process of moving in with his girlfriend. He had a two-bedroom apartment, and a week left on the rent, so he agreed to let me and Pierre stay there and even take over the rent. I wasn't too sure about living with Pierre, though.

Pierre was eighteen years old and, from what I could tell, he wasn't very mature. While he stood six feet three inches tall, he acted like a child. I could tell he'd been sheltered his whole life, but the one good thing he had going for him was his good sense of humor. I figured I'd have to work with that because if I wanted to stay in the apartment, then I'd have to agree to live with him. We agreed to split the bills fifty-fifty. We had to pay the first and last month's rent plus security deposit. I had about a thousand dollars left from selling dope in Oakland, so I was almost broke after I paid my half. I was in desperate need of a job, so I hit the pavement in search of employment. I was hired at Jack in the Box while still on crutches, and I began to think everything would work out just fine.

Pierre and I decided to go to Walmart to buy a few household items after a few days in the apartment. I spotted a couple of pretty girls getting out of their car as we parked. They were a few cars down from us, so I made a point to hurry out of the vehicle so as not to miss them. One girl in particular caught my eye. She was a light-skinned Black girl who stood about five feet tall. She was beautiful, and as I slowly passed by, she spotted me checking her out and said, "Hi." She bent down and pulled a baby out of the back seat of the car when I responded. That caused me to be apprehensive, so I just walked away. I ran back into her in the movie section of the store. Only this time she didn't have the baby with her. "Are you following me?" she playfully asked with a smile. "Only if you want me to be," I responded in kind, trying to be cool while looking around for the baby. She told me her name was Stephanie, and after inquiring as to the whereabouts of the baby, she explained that the baby belonged to the girl she'd come to the store with. Relieved at this information, we began talking for a short period of time before she gave me her phone number. I called her the next day and was with her the entire time I was in Arizona.

Living with Pierre was cool for the first few months. We ended up getting along pretty well. He began meeting girls and bringing them to our place to party. This was the first time either of us had our own place, and we acted like it. We'd party all night long and go to work the next morning. Pierre did have a problem, though. He always tried to act like he had money to blow every time females were around. He began spending money recklessly, and I didn't say anything because I figured he was aware of the amount of money he could spend. As it turned out, I was wrong in thinking he could be responsible enough not to blow his rent money. After paying his half of the rent for two months, I'd had enough of his antics and was ready to find another place to live.

Once my living situation began to deteriorate with Pierre, I decided I couldn't wait to leave. I had no credit, so I realized finding a place without credit would be next to impossible. I thought about getting a place with Stephanie. After all, she had two jobs, which would enable us to rent a nice place. When I proposed the arrangement to her, I found out she was only seventeen years old and couldn't rent an apartment. She had two jobs and went to Apollo College, so I never asked about her age. I was only nineteen years old so it wasn't a big deal. However, now that she couldn't rent an apartment I had no choice but to go back to Oakland.

I couldn't stay with my mom or dad once in Oakland. Thankfully, my grandma agreed to let me stay with her. Unfortunately, my grandma lived in the hood, and I wasn't too enthusiastic about going back there. I was depressed because it seemed like something would always pull me back every time I began to move forward in life. I was back to square one again, but at least this time I had my granny. She loved having me around, too. She was getting old and having me around to keep her company was enjoyable for her. I benefited by having her wisdom and guidance around me.

I found a job pretty quickly selling Kirby Vacuums in Fremont, California. Usually the commute would only be about thirty minutes by car, but I had to take the bus, which more than doubled the commute time. It didn't matter to me, though, because I was determined to work. I proved to be a pretty good salesman, too. It was tiring work going door-to-door, making my pitch, and demonstrating how the vacuum performed on potential clients' carpets, but my pitch delivery became great. My sales increased, and I began making $700–800 a week—almost as much as if I were selling dope; only this was legitimate money, and nobody was trying to shoot at me for it—a fact that made me really like the job.

I passed by an E-recycling plant while selling vacuums one day and something told me to go in and pitch them the vacuum, so I did. When I walked inside the place, I quickly noticed there was no carpet, but I pressed forward anyway. "How can I help you?" I heard a voice ask from behind me. I turned around and faced a man in a dirty jumpsuit and replied, "I'm looking for your boss." From the look of the man, he didn't look as if he was in charge. "Up those stairs and to the right," he said as he nodded toward the stairs. I walked up the stairs and went through a door. I found myself in an office that had no carpet. I tried to hide my disappointment when I came face to face with a lady who looked to be a secretary. "Can I help you?" she asked with a smile. "I'm here to see your boss," I replied as if I had an appointment. "Right through the door," she told me. I couldn't believe how easy it was.

I entered a very nice office with beautiful carpet. I instantly became excited thinking the place would need a few good vacuums and felt as if the day may become my biggest sell yet. Sitting behind a huge desk was a middle-aged man who seemed to be writing. He looked up at the sound of his door opening and quickly asked, "What can I do for you?" The man stood up as I went into my pitch. He listened while I began hooking up the vacuum and just stood there and watched as I began vacuuming his office. As soon as my pitch was completed, I looked at him and could tell he was amused. He asked me, "How much do you make a week?" Surprised by the question, I took a second before I said, "Between $700 and $800." He immediately replied, "How would you like to come and work for me, and I'll pay you that plus a ten percent commission on anything you sell?" Without even knowing what it was the man wanted me to sell, I agreed.

The man who offered me the job turned out to be the CEO of the company, named Andy. His company had contracts with several big retail stores to pick up electronics that were broken or deemed defective and recycle them. Andy also had a store that sold office equipment, and that was the job he hired me for. He told me he liked how fearless I was at selling and how I'd reminded him of himself at my age. He told me I was to be his sales manager, and I immediately became motivated to work hard for him. I started making $4,000 a month. Having that kind of money at twenty years old made me feel like I could do anything. I had the money to fly back and forth to Arizona on my days off and spend the weekend with Stephanie. On the weekdays, I partied in California. I felt as though I'd finally made it.

I spoke with Andy's wife, Cindy, one day. She told me about a house they had for rent. It was a three-bedroom, two-bath home with a guest house and a four-car garage. It sounded too beautiful to ignore so I went and checked the place out. It had a beautiful front and back yard, but what mattered the most was how nice the neighborhood was. It was perfect timing, too, because my sister and her son needed a place to live, so each of us would have a room. The rent was $1,500 a month. I couldn't turn that down.

Everything was going great at that point in my life. The new house needed some painting done to it, so between painting and work I became too busy to fly to Arizona to see Stephanie. She called me one day and informed me she was pregnant. The news was shocking, but I was also excited. I wanted her to move to California so we could be a family. I was making plenty of money, and the house had plenty of room, but she insisted I move to Arizona. I didn't want to have the conversation on the phone, so I took the next flight to Arizona so we could talk. I believed I could persuade her to come back to Oakland with me. To my surprise, she refused. I was forced to leave because I had to go back to work, but I couldn't understand why she was being unreasonable. I had a good job and a nice house. I stood to lose both while she only had a job in the healthcare industry, which would allow her to transfer anywhere. Her refusal to listen to reason forced me to choose my job over her.

I knew my decision to go back to Oakland was the practical one, but I felt guilty about it because I was going against my moral obligation. No matter how I rationalized it, I knew I was being selfish, but something wouldn't allow me to give up what I felt I'd earned. I tried to avoid the guilt by partying. I began drinking and smoking weed more. I also started snorting cocaine and popping ecstasy pills. Before I knew it, I needed more money because my habits increased. I started to sell office equipment and not write the sales down so I could pocket the money. I didn't do it often at first, but as my habits increased, so did my thefts. After a few months, Andy noticed something was going on. He compared the inventory with the sales receipts and found some anomalies, so I was fired.

Andy's wife chose to allow me to keep renting the house, provided I continued to pay the rent. My sister couldn't afford to pay the bills on her own, so I had to go back to selling dope. My sister noticed how unhappy I became each time I hung up with Steph, so she told me to go back to Arizona because she didn't want me to stay in Oakland for her. I was relieved to hear her tell me that, so I called Steph and took the next flight back to Arizona.

Steph and I rented our own apartment the day I arrived in Arizona. She had a good job and established credit. As for me, I was broke, had no job, and no prospects. I began selling weed so I could contribute to the household while I looked for a job. By the time I found a job at Circle K, I had built up a nice clientele, so I decided to do both—sell weed and work—because I didn't want to quit making the easy money. By the time Steph gave birth to our daughter, I was making pretty good money. Our combined incomes allowed us to put a nice amount of money away in a savings account, and I was even able to set up a trust account for my daughter's college tuition. I was pleased by that.

A friend of mine sold dope out of an apartment complex, and he convinced me to set up a weed spot there. He had pretty much taken over the entire complex and wanted to make it a one-stop shop kind of place—a place where someone can buy any drug. I had two apartments there: one to sell weed and another to store weed. Business was going well, and everyone liked what I had to sell because it was a type of weed that wasn't sold in Arizona. I had the market cornered. One night, after finishing my shift at Circle K, I was about to go to the apartment complex when I received a call from my friend telling me it was raided by the police. I wasn't too concerned about the cops being after me because my name wasn't on any rental agreement for either apartment. As long as I wasn't there when the raid happened they had nothing on me. I was more devastated because I'd lost all of my product, and that really set me back.

I was forced to take a trip to Oakland to secure more inventory to sell, but the lack of money only allowed me to purchase two pounds of high-grade marijuana. Soon after returning to Arizona, I was contacted by one of my best customers. He gave me a story about being robbed and needed me to front him some weed to sell. I've always been apprehensive about doing business that way, but I decided to make an exception for him. I thought, *He's always been straight up with me. Plus, I stand to double my money while he did all of the work*. However, things didn't go as planned. Once his two-week deadline to pay me expired, not only didn't he pay me, but he began avoiding me. I'd call him and get no answer. He knew my work schedule, so when I went by his house, he wouldn't be there. I played that game with him for two weeks. My frustration mounted, and I became determined to get my money back from him.

Drunk and high, I decided to call him using Steph's cell phone instead of my own, so he wouldn't recognize the number. He answered after only a few rings, and I kept my cool as I spoke to him, even though I was furious. He acted as if he'd been trying to get a hold of me, then told me he hadn't sold all of the weed. He owed me $6,000 and claimed he only had $2,100 for me. I told him to bring me half of what he owed me. I was tired of his games and wanted to show him I was serious. After telling him where to meet me, I waited for him. He showed up with some guy I didn't know, and I pulled my gun on them both as soon as they walked up. "Where's my money!?" I asked angrily. "In my pocket!" the guy replied with his hands up. I allowed him to take the money out of his pocket and hand it to me only to find out he only had the $2,100. "I told you to bring me half!" I yelled, feeling like he wasn't taking me seriously.

I took them back to their apartment at gunpoint and duct-taped the both of them to chairs. I looked around the apartment for anything of value to take, and the rest of my weed. I found $300 in cash and that only made me angrier. "That's all the money you have, huh?" I yelled while waving the money in his face. Determined to prove a point, I began grabbing electronics, video games, and jewelry, filling two garbage bags I'd found. After the bags were full, I decided not to search the bedrooms because I could barely carry what I already had. I decided to take the bags to a girl I'd known for some time who lived in the same apartment complex, and asked her to hold them for me. She agreed, took the bags, and I left. I went to another apartment of a guy, Ryan, I knew in the complex. He let me into his apartment, and no sooner had the door closed than we heard sirens. I went and looked out the window and didn't see any cops. Ryan had a concerned look on his face when I turned back from looking out the window. He asked me what was going on, but the police began banging on his door before I could answer him. They called out my name and told me to come out with my hands up. I just stood there stunned. I didn't want them to kick Ryan's door in, so I did as I was told and gave up.

As it turned out, there was a third person in one of the bedrooms while I robbed the apartment. The guy hid when he realized what was going on, and as soon as I was gone, he undid the duct tape binding the two guys and called the police. They knew where I was because they watched me walk to each apartment while they were on the phone with the police. Within five minutes of leaving the crime scene, I was in handcuffs.

I was looking at fifty years in prison after being charged with three counts of armed robbery with a deadly weapon, three counts of aggravated assault with a deadly weapon, and kidnapping with a home invasion. The thought of doing fifty years in prison blew my mind. Until then, I'd only done time in juvenile, and for no longer than six months at a time. Now I was looking at doing more years behind bars than the twenty-one years I'd been alive.

My court-appointed attorney came to see me after a few months of being in jail, and handed me a paper with a look that suggested he was pleased with himself. "I gotcha a plea bargain," he said with a smile on his face. One look at the plea bargain told me my attorney was crazy. "Fifteen to thirty years?!" I replied in shock. I stood up and handed the paper back to him and said, "If you think that's a plea bargain, then you can't be my attorney," and walked out of the room. I went back to my cell and prayed.

The next time my attorney showed up he had another plea bargain. This time it was for ten to twenty-one years in prison. I refused to sign that too, because I didn't feel as if what I did warranted that much time in prison. Besides! Nobody was hurt, and the "victim" received all of his property and money back. I thought the victim made it out of the ordeal pretty well, but I knew I needed a real attorney after seeing that plea. I had Steph call my brother and together they came up with enough money to retain me an attorney. After spending thirteen months in jail, my new attorney brought me a new plea deal. The deal was for five to twelve years in prison, but the sentence would be suspended and I'd be on intensive probation or IPS. I'd never heard of IPS before, but I didn't care what it was. I just heard I could get out of jail as soon as I was sentenced; so I signed. When I returned to my cell after signing the plea, everyone began telling me I shouldn't have taken the deal. They told me IPS really stood for "In Prison Soon," and that it was set up to make you fail. I didn't believe it. I was just ready to go after spending fourteen months in jail.

I was thankful to be able to walk out of the jail into the arms of Steph and my daughter. I was immediately rehired at Circle K, and that allowed me to begin paying my probation fees. My probation officer wasn't bad. He'd check up on me and give me a drug test every now and again. I quickly recognized his pattern of when I was to be drug tested. I realized I could smoke a little weed after each drug test, and I'd show up clean by the time the next one came around. It worked a couple of times, too. After eight months in the program, I received an unexpected knock on the door in the middle of the night. When I opened the door, I was greeted by a surveillance officer (SO). An SO's job is to spy on those on IPS and do drug tests. She handed me a drug test and told me to produce a urine sample. As soon as I did, and the SO left, I began packing a bag because I knew I was dirty. The look on Steph's face was of pure hurt, as I explained to her that I was going on the run. I wasn't about to go to prison anytime soon because they'd have to catch me first.

Steph continued to encourage me to turn myself in, but I didn't feel like going to prison. I went back to Oakland to live, and when Steph told me she was pregnant with our second child it was even more incentive to stay out of prison. I wanted to be there for the baby's birth. That didn't happen, though, because she went into labor a week early, and I missed it.

My brother came home from working overseas the previous year and wanted to party with me. He picked me up in his rental car, and we smoked weed and drank while on our way to the club. He jumped on the freeway and was driving erratically. I tried to get him to slow down but he wasn't trying to hear me. Before I knew it, we were being pulled over, and, of course, I had a fugitive warrant and was arrested. The judge appointed me an attorney and was going to schedule an extradition hearing to send me back to Arizona; however, I waived my right to the hearing. I was tired of being on the run and was just ready to go to prison and start doing my time. I'd been on the run for a year and a half, so I signed the papers and Arizona picked me up and took me back.

I resigned myself to the thought of going to prison while in California. Once I was back in Arizona, I refused to allow my attorney to try and get me reinstated on IPS. I felt like I wouldn't be able to complete it anyway. I figured I'd rather go to prison and get it over with so I could get out and live my life.

The judge sentenced me to four years in prison and gave me fourteen months of back time. Steph found someone else and gave up on me. I wasn't mad at her because I really gave her no choice. She had two kids to raise, and I had to focus on the fact I was going to prison.

I was released from prison in August of 2015. I had no place to go, so I paroled to Tucson, Arizona, on the advice of a guy I'd met in prison. I was sent to a halfway house called Transitional Living Communities, or TLC. My brother sent me $300 and my dad sent me some clothes, so I was ready to begin the next phase of my life. I'd never been to Tucson before and had no knowledge of exactly where I was in the city. The thought of walking around a strange new city crippled me with fear—something I hadn't experienced while in prison— so I just decided to stay at the halfway house until they found me a job. On my second day, a few of the other residents invited me to smoke spice, a synthetic marijuana, with them, and I accepted. Afterward, I was expected to attend a "mandatory" house meeting, which they held each night to address the next day's events. I hadn't realized how high I was until I sat down in the meeting. I thought I was being cool, but the manager noticed something was wrong with me. He incorrectly assumed I was drunk so he escorted me into his office and gave me a breathalyzer test. To his surprise, I passed.

After four days, I still didn't have a job. I was tired of sitting around the halfway house, and, once again, I was offered more spice to smoke. Someone inside the house snitched on me to the house manager after I'd smoked. Before I knew it, the manager escorted me to his office and accused me of being on heroin. I was given a drug test and passed it, but the manager continued to accuse me of being on something. He chastised me after passing the test and made me feel as if I had to defend myself. The more he insisted I was on something the angrier I became. I felt disrespected, so I punched him so hard that he fell flat on his back.

I figured I'd be sent back to prison, so I went into my room and packed my things. My parole officer was at the door no sooner than I was done packing. She escorted me out of the house and into her car. Once inside her car, she asked me to tell her my side of the story as she drove. Soon after explaining what had happened, we pulled into a strange-looking facility. I figured it was where they brought those who had violated before being sent back to prison. My PO explained that the manager didn't want to press charges against me. She told me the facility she brought me to was a different kind of halfway house, and it was where I'd be staying. I was shocked when she showed me where I'd be sleeping. The place looked just like a prison dorm! They had the same metal bunk beds, metal lockers, and ugly gray paint. She began to tell me there would be no phones, TVs, music, or electronic devices whatsoever. It was actually worse than being in prison. The last straw came when she told me that on the weekends I couldn't leave the facility, and on the weekdays I had to be out of the facility by six A.M. and had to be back by two P.M. In my mind, it was worse than being in prison because they were dangling freedom in my face. I wasn't about to play that game, so I decided I wasn't staying there. I took my things and left the first chance I was given.

I found a hotel in a neighborhood that looked pretty ghetto and rented a room. I stood around outside and watched the drug traffic, and I figured out who was selling dope. I approached him and we talked business. The guy gave me a pretty good deal, too. I began selling dope in the motel and became pretty cool with the guy. He even sent me some of his clients, which I appreciated. I traded twenty dollars of dope for an unused laptop and even made enough money to enroll in Pima Community College. I began taking online courses in pursuit of an associate's degree that I began while in prison. My days consisted of eating, selling dope, and doing schoolwork online. One night, I heard a commotion outside while doing schoolwork. I looked out the window and saw the police everywhere. Thinking they were there for me, I hid my dope, grabbed my belongings, and left. Halfway down the street, I was stopped by the cops and arrested. I was only out for fifty days.

I was sent back to prison and given a parole hearing with a judge via videophone. I expected to be given additional time in prison until my PO was caught lying to the judge about me. He tried to tell the judge I'd been using heroin and had failed two drug tests for opiates. I quickly told the judge how untrue that was given the fact I'd never used opiates. The judge asked my PO to submit the records of the failed drug tests to the court. The PO responded by pretending to look for the records in his paperwork until he stopped on a piece of paper and pretended to read it. He then apologized to the court for "misspeaking," saying, "Apparently I was mistaken, Your Honor, my documentation says they failed to test him for opiates." The judge saw right through that and reinstated my parole. My only request was that I be reinstated to a halfway house in Phoenix instead of Tucson, and it was granted.

I wasted no time seeking out employment when I returned to Phoenix. I found a job at America's Best Tire. The manager of the place liked how upfront I was with him about recently being released from prison. It was the first time I used that approach, but I was desperate. He hired me on the spot. To celebrate my release from prison, my mom, sister, and brother all came out to see me. I was allowed to stay with them at their hotel for the week. I had a blast with them, too. When I wasn't working, I was with them having fun. It was the first time in my twenty-nine years that all of us were together, sober, and happy. It felt really great but unreal.

The day my family was supposed to fly back to Oakland, they decided to drop me off at the halfway house and view my room. When I brought them into my room, we discovered most of my possessions had been stolen. If it weren't for my family being there, I would have lost it. Thankfully, my brother gave me money to find my own place, and that's exactly what I did. I found a small house, which was nicer and cheaper than most rental apartments. I didn't have much of anything as far as furniture went, but at least I was out of the halfway house. All I did for the next few months was work and take my online classes. When I finished my courses and earned my associate's degree in business management, I felt as if I had just earned a PhD.

I met a guy name Drew, who was also from Oakland, while at work one day. We began talking while I was on a smoke break and he was getting his tires fixed. Drew owned a couple of smoke shops around Phoenix and he offered me a job at one of them. Of course, I accepted. The position he hired me for was at night so I didn't even have to quit my current job. Soon after, I received a new parole officer. She came by the tire shop to introduce herself and told me how impressed she was with me. She pointed out all of the clean drug tests, my two jobs, having earned my degree, and the fact I had my own place. She downgraded my status for being given drug tests from regular—meaning once or twice a week—to random. I decided I could smoke weed in moderation. After three months I was given a random drug test and failed. My PO put me back on regular drug tests rather than violate me. After three consecutive weeks of my THC levels dropping, which showed I hadn't been smoking—the fourth week I received a call telling me to report for a drug test the next day. The problem was, I only had five dollars to my name and that would only allow me to pay for the bus fare to the test site, but not enough to pay for the actual drug test. I called my PO and explained the situation to her. I assured her I was clean and explained that I'd be receiving a paycheck the next day and could afford it then. She reluctantly agreed and allowed me a two-day extension. After two days, I went in as promised and was violated for not reporting to the drug test she gave me an extension on.

I was sent back to prison. At first I was angry about it, but now I think it's for the best. Sure, I lost both of my jobs, but by the time I'm released I will have served my entire sentence. And I'll finally be fully free, with no parole officer to watch over me. I look forward to getting out without having someone there to tell me what to do. For me, that is worth being in prison for a few more months.

Unique

I was institutionalized. I was a mess.

My life was a waste up until I was forty-six years old. I was angry because I never had a childhood, and I felt as if I had the right to blame everyone else for my problems. I believed I didn't have to be accountable for my actions. It was that way of thinking that I believe imprisoned my mind.

I was born at the University of California at Los Angeles (UCLA) Medical Center in April of 1967. My mom was originally from Brooklyn, New York. Her parents were originally from Puerto Rico. Born in May of 1945, my mom became a "problem child" at a young age. She was sent to a boarding school when she was thirteen years old because of her bad behavior. Her parents pretty much abandoned her and moved back to Puerto Rico when she was fourteen. She was able to leave the boarding school and move to Los Angeles to live with her grandmother, who raised her.

My dad grew up in Los Angeles. He was biracial, Puerto Rican and Black, and he grew up in a good home. His parents raised him to be responsible and work for a living, so he was never one to get into trouble with the law. He began installing carpet for a living at seventeen years old and continued to do that for the next forty years. He met my mom when she was fifteen and he was eighteen. They were at a skating rink, and he approached her and introduced himself the minute he saw her. They exchanged numbers and talked on the phone for a week before they began to see each other. Mom fell in love with how he treated her. Before him, she didn't have many boyfriends. Dad waited until she turned eighteen before he married her.

My dad worked hard to provide for my mom. It took a few years of them trying to get pregnant before I was conceived. From what I was told, it was a stressful process that took an emotional and mental toll on him and my mom. Both of them were relieved when I was conceived because they really began to think it wouldn't happen for them. My dad worked day and night in anticipation of my birth. His priority was to provide a better life for his family, but his long work hours took a toll on him and their marriage. He worked so many hours after I was born that he decided to take "uppers," amphetamine pills, to help get him through the long days.

I don't know when my mom began taking drugs. I don't recall a time when she wasn't on something. Her drug of choice was heroin, but she drank and didn't discriminate against other drugs. My dad became hooked on uppers. He did a great job hiding his addiction; unfortunately, the same couldn't be said for my mother. A blind man could see she was an addict, and I detested her because of it.

I was five years old when my mom met Lilly. Lilly was a Black lady who looked just like a man. She used to come over while my dad was at work. They spent a lot of time in the bedroom together. I thought they were just hanging out, but they turned out to be lovers behind my dad's back. He left when he found out my mom was cheating on him. I'm not exactly sure when he left. He wasn't around so often that one day I just realized he never came home. Mom told me he took off and moved to Phoenix, Arizona. He called a few times to talk to me after they split. He'd call every so often and promise to pick me up and take me to such-and-such place at such-and-such time and never show up. I was crushed every time he did that.

Mom and Lilly drank and did drugs together. This made their relationship a volatile one. Each time they got high brought about the inevitable argument. Violence ensued every time, and, even though Lilly won each fight, Mom gave as good as she got.

We lived in the Palms area on Inglewood Boulevard in Culver City when I was ten years old. Mom started seeing a white guy, named Richard, after taking a break with Lilly. I liked him because he used to bring me model airplanes, cars, and trucks every time he came by the house. Mom liked him because he always gave her free dope.

One time, Mom came down with pneumonia. The doctor called it something like pleurisy. It was pretty bad. She was bedridden, so I sat in the living room to let her rest. Richard showed up one time and disappeared into her bedroom. He gave her Demerol and codeine for the pain before they shot up heroin. Mom overdosed and almost died. I was watching TV when Richard calmly walked out of the bedroom. Without even looking at me, he just picked up the phone and dialed 911. He reported my mom's overdose, asked for an ambulance, gave the address, and hung up the phone. I didn't know what an overdose was at the time. I watched as the paramedics gave my mom CPR before transporting her to the hospital. I thought she was dead. Richard drove me to the hospital and waited with me to see if she lived or not. Thankfully, she lived, but sometimes I wondered what would've happened to me had she died.

My grandma lived in East L.A. on 43rd and Avellon. The area belonged to a gang called Four-Tre Gangsta Crips. I used to go back and forth between her and my mom's house, because Mom's house had drug parties from time to time, and I didn't want to be around that. I started hanging out with the guys from the neighborhood while at my grandma's house. They kind of adopted me as their little brother. They always took me to the park, bought me candy, and taught me how to sell weed. I liked selling weed because it allowed me to have my own money. I only made around ten or twenty dollars in the beginning, but that might as well had been a million bucks to me at ten years old. It made me feel good to make my own money and have it in my pocket. My grandma and Mom never had extra money to give to me, so having my own gave me a sense of independence. And I liked that feeling.

Mom was in the hospital for about a week following her overdose. I took care of myself during that time. My grandma had no idea Mom was in the hospital, and I didn't dare tell her. I learned not to snitch from my mom. Plus, I enjoyed being alone. At times, it felt as if I was the parent and not my mom. I was the one who took care of the both of us because Mom would get high and cause drama in the house.

Mom realized when she came home from the hospital that she didn't have the rent money and only had a few days to come up with it. She panicked at the thought of being evicted and claimed to not know what'd happened to her check. But I knew she'd spent it on dope. Sensing her desperation, I told her to give me fifty dollars, and I'd be able to come up with the rest. She seemed surprised, but she gave me the money. I went and bought an ounce of weed and set up in the park. I sold five- and ten-dollar bags of weed until I sold out. I took the proceeds, bought another ounce, and went back to the park. By the end of the day, I went home and handed Mom the $300 she needed for the rent. She didn't ask any questions about where the money came from. She just gave me a hug and thanked me. I felt like a big man for doing that, and I was quite proud of myself. I had thirty dollars left over, so I went and bought a half ounce of weed and began to sell for myself.

I experienced a newfound sense of freedom from having money in my pocket. Even though I was only ten years old, I wasn't scared to get on a bus and go on adventures by myself. I gained more confidence each time I ventured away from home, and that allowed me to go farther the next time. I was so excited when I found the beach. I slept there for a few days. The good thing about selling weed is I could sell it anywhere. That's how I had money for food. Unfortunately, it's also the reason why I was arrested for the first time at ten years old. I was charged with possession and sale of marijuana and sent to juvenile hall for two weeks. I was released to my mom with thirty days of probation.

I hated probation. I was scared to venture away from home as long as I was on it, so I was forced to be at home. Mom got back together with Lilly, so they continued to stay high and fight the entire time I was there. By the time my thirty days was over, I was ready to go. I went back to selling weed and saved all of my money. As soon as I felt I had enough money, I left home.

I found a nice spot on La Brea and Sunset Boulevard and continued selling weed. I learned the police schedules and routes. I realized the cops only flooded the streets to make their presence known at the beginning of their shift. So I learned their shift changes and sold weed all night long until six in the morning. That's when shift change occurred, and that's also when I went to eat breakfast at the Copper Penny restaurant. It allowed me to avoid the initial patrol of the next shift of cops. As soon as I didn't see the cops anymore, I went back out on a full stomach and worked for a few more hours before I slept under a dock for the rest of the day.

I had my own booth in the Copper Penny. It had a perfect view of the entire restaurant and a view of the street. I noticed the same group of well-dressed men who also came in for breakfast each morning. I had no idea the Copper Penny was the hangout spot for a group of Old Original Pimps. I'm talking about legends in the game like Limousine Slim, Pretty Toney, Johnny Dollar, and Memphis Red. I didn't know who they were at the time, but I noticed them for two weeks. They noticed me too. They called me over to their table one morning and bought me breakfast. They were curious about me, so they asked me a bunch of questions. They seemed to get a kick out of every answer I gave them and really took a liking to me. I hung out with Limousine Slim for several hours that first day. He noticed I was tired and asked where I'd been sleeping. He was shocked and impressed to hear I'd been sleeping on the beach. He offered to help me get a room—provided I could pay for it—and I accepted. I was grateful for his help, because having my own room made me feel like I was finally grown.

Limousine kind of adopted me. He started introducing me to everyone as his son. It felt good to hear a man call me that. There was a side to him I didn't like but overlooked, because he treated me good and looked out for me. He was what's commonly known as a "guerrilla pimp." Pimps are given that title when they're violent with their prostitutes. I witnessed many incidents with his prostitutes that I knew were wrong. In a weird way, he kind of taught me how to treat women by showing me how not to treat them.

I never stopped going back to visit my grandma. I hung out with the guys from the neighborhood each time I was there. They were from the Four-Tre Gangsta Crips. I got to know the guys from there, and I was comfortable with them. One day, while hanging out with them, a guy named Midgetman told me, "You hang around here enough, lil homey, you might as well be from the hood." The guys with him all agreed, and another guy named Sinbad asked if I wanted to be initiated. I agreed to it. They went and gathered everyone from the neighborhood, and they all lined up in a parallel line facing one another and told me to walk down the middle and try to make it to the end of the line. They all began to punch me as soon as I started to walk. I didn't make it to the end of the line, though. I was hit so hard that I fell, and they all closed in and jumped me. I later learned it was impossible to make it to the end of the line. The point was, I was beat up to prove I had the heart to face the fear of getting beat up. Afterward, they cleaned me up and gave me a .38 revolver. I was put into a stolen car and taken to a rival gang's neighborhood to complete phase two of the initiation.

We drove through the neighborhood until we spotted a group of rival gang members standing in front of a house. Sinbad parked the car down the street and told me to get out, walk to the rivals' house, and shoot one of the guys. I was eleven years old and scared out of my mind. I didn't want to chicken out because I knew nobody would respect me if I did. I exited the vehicle and could feel my heart pounding with each step I took toward the house. I had to remind myself to breathe. I watched the rivals notice me as I approached. When I felt like I was close enough, I raised the gun and began pulling the trigger repeatedly. I turned and ran back to the car when I ran out of bullets. Sinbad sped off as soon as I was back in the car. Midgetman grabbed the gun from my shaking hand and replaced it with a joint.

My new family became made up of a bunch of pimps and gangsters. Whenever I was with the gangsters, we went around and robbed rival gangs' drug dealers. The pimps taught me how to pick up young girls and talk them into prostituting themselves for me. Limousine took me to the Greyhound bus station in Hollywood, and we sat around and waited until a young girl, Stephanie, who ran away from home showed up. I listened while he talked to her and pretended to be interested until she felt safe with him. He then offered her a place to stay. His sweet demeanor and slick talk eventually appealed to her desperation and caused her to agree to stay with him. Once that happened, the girl was hooked because she became indebted to him and had to "work" to pay him off.

Limousine encouraged me to start talking to the runaways who were my age. By the time I was thirteen, I had young girls prostituting for me. I thought what I was doing was normal. Everything I'd ever seen was done in the open with impunity, so I didn't think there was anything wrong with it. In fact, I became intrigued with the lifestyle to such an extent that it became fun.

Kids frequently run away from home and go to Hollywood to pursue their dream of becoming a big star. Hollywood continues to lure them from abusive homes even today, but reality sets in pretty quickly once they arrive and find they have to do whatever it takes to survive. Many sought refuge in the countless abandoned buildings around the city. I met Willomena in one such building. She was twelve years old at the time. She was a pretty, caramel-colored Black girl with an outgoing personality. She was spunky, and I liked that about her. Her eyes were hazel like mine, and that's what really drew me to her. Originally from Peoria, Illinois, she moved to California some years earlier with her mom. She was an unruly child. Her mom's attempts to discipline her caused enmity and resentment between them, and that led to physical fights. Their volatile relationship caused her to run away from home.

Willomena was down. She was a go-getter like me who'd do whatever it took to get money. She was never my girlfriend, but we messed around from time to time. She was more like my crime partner. She'd stay away from me for a few weeks at a time, but we were never away from each other for long. If we were, it's because one of us was locked up. After we were released, something always brought us back together. She was one of the few people in my life I knew I could always count on—even if we always went our separate ways.

I was with the homies robbing rival gang members when I wasn't with Willomena. I robbed so much I began to see everyone I didn't know but who I thought had money as victims. One day, I went into a Winchell's Donuts and decided to rob the place. I admit it was spontaneous and stupid. I didn't even have gloves or a mask. Not to mention the fact that I was known to the place because I was a regular. One of the employees knew who I was and snitched on me. It took the cops ten minutes to find and arrest me. I was fifteen years old. My punishment was to spend fifty-two weeks in a maximum-custody juvenile facility called "Camp Rocky." I was released after thirty-six weeks of good behavior.

I thought I was grown by the age of sixteen. I'd been on my own for six years, and the streets had hardened me. I quickly found two girls to prostitute themselves for me, soon after my release. One of my girls, Kim, came to me one day and told me about a "client" she had in her room. She believed he had a lot of money on him and suggested we rob him. I took my homey, Fred, to the room and tried to rob the guy, but he didn't want to give us the money. So we beat him up and took it. We also stole his car and drove it to San Francisco with my two girls. The girls worked and brought in the money for us to live on once we were there. Two weeks later, we were double parked and waiting for the girls to bring us money when the cops pulled up behind us and hit their lights. They found out pretty quickly the car was stolen after running our plates and arrested us.

Fred and I stayed in jail for three weeks before we were released. Thankfully, the guy we robbed refused to press charges. The state didn't have any evidence to charge us after that because we kept our mouths shut—meaning we didn't confess during interrogation. After we were released, we met up with the girls and took the Greyhound bus back to L.A.

Willomena and I began burglarizing people's homes when I came back from San Francisco. We started out by scouting neighborhoods for homes that looked as if their owners hadn't been there for some time. Whenever we found such a home, we'd go and knock on the door and break in if nobody answered; however, if someone did answer, we just acted as if we were at the wrong house, only to continue our search. We broke into approximately 300 homes and apartments over the course of the year. Our luck finally ran out when someone spotted us breaking into an apartment and called the police. We were arrested coming out of the house with the stolen goods. Fortunately for us, the lead detective didn't want to take away our lives, because of our age and the fact that we never broke into a place when someone was there. He was convinced we weren't a threat to anyone, so he persuaded the district attorney to be lenient with us. I was given two years in prison, and Willow was given three years of probation.

Willow wrote to me after I'd been in prison for about a month. She told me her mother had moved them back to Peoria, Illinois, where she'd serve out her probation. She wished me the best and hoped I'd look her up when I was released. And she gave me her address and phone number. I didn't hear from her again for the rest of my stint in prison, even after I wrote her back. I wasn't bothered by not hearing back from her. I was just focused on doing my time and getting out.

I only hung out with my cellmate in prison. Everyone called him "Rico" because, like me, he was biracial. Only he was mixed with Black and Mexican. His light-skinned complexion made him appear to be Puerto Rican, which is why his nickname was Rico. He and I became pretty close in our short time as cellmates. We had each other's back like we were brothers. He introduced me to his sister, Carmen, and we quickly hit it off. At twenty-four years old, she was older than me and had two kids from a previous marriage. I didn't care, though. She was a beautiful Mexican woman from Tijuana, Mexico. We wrote back and forth a few times before she started to come and visit me. I really enjoyed and grew fond of her. Though I wasn't in love with her, I decided to give our relationship a shot after I was released from prison.

I paroled to Fontana, California, to be with Carmen and her kids. I realized almost immediately that I wasn't ready to settle down or change my ways, but I didn't know how to tell Carmen. I didn't know how to do anything legitimate and it scared me. I was only out for six weeks and I decided to go back to L.A., so I stole a car. I was on the freeway and on my way out of town when a cop pulled up behind me. I was pulled over, arrested, and taken to jail when the plates on the car came back as a stolen vehicle. Thankfully, my parole officer allowed me to bond out of jail. Carmen came and got me out. I told her I wasn't about to go back to prison and informed her of my plans to run. She suggested we run off to Tijuana together. I was against the plan from the start. I didn't want to uproot her and her kids for a relationship I didn't see working out. I even told her that, but she insisted it was what she wanted to do. Rather than break her heart, I went along with the plan and fled to Mexico.

Carmen's family lived in a small town on the outskirts of Tijuana. There must've only been a handful of families there, but each family was huge. I found it interesting to see an entire town come together to celebrate special occasions such as quinceañeras, birthdays, and weddings. We arrived on one such occasion. It was someone's birthday and the entire town had gathered to celebrate when we showed up. The whole town had a chance to meet me. Everyone was very hospitable and made me feel as if I were at home, but I could tell they didn't get many visitors.

Carmen came from a very conservative Catholic family. In fact, the entire town was the same. Nobody liked that Carmen and I weren't married. I was made to feel uncomfortable whenever I was introduced as her boyfriend. At first, her family simply inquired about the future of our relationship, but as time went on they started to insist that we get married. I wasn't ready for that kind of commitment and couldn't take the pressure being put on us. I decided to leave rather than be forced to marry in order to stay. I spoke with Carmen and she understood how I felt. She gave me $300 travel money, and we said our goodbyes.

I called Willow's house as soon as I made it back across the border. Her mom answered the phone, and I told her I'd recently been released from prison. I asked her permission to go out and stay with them, and as expected she said yes. It came as no surprise to me because her mom always liked me. She knew that as long as her daughter was with me, I'd do my best to make sure no harm came to her. I took a plane to Chicago, Illinois, and a cab from O'Hare Airport to Willow's house in Peoria. Willow dashed out of the house to greet me before I could even get out of the cab. As soon as I was out of the car, she wrapped me up in such a warm embrace that I could feel how much she loved and missed me.

The problem with being a fugitive from the law is you can't just go out and get a job—not without stealing someone's identity. I didn't know how to do that, so I had to resort to getting money the only way I knew how: illegally. So Willow and I started burglarizing people's homes to make money. It was open season in those days because burglary was something that was very foreign in Peoria. People didn't even lock their doors. We then went to an apartment complex and began looking for a place to rob. As usual, we wanted to rob a place where nobody was home. We spotted an apartment, knocked on the door, and nobody answered. We went around to the back of the place and broke in through a window. We went room to room rummaging through the place and setting the loot by the window we entered through. We went into the bedroom together. I chose to ransack the closet while Willow went through the dresser drawers. Suddenly, a woman sat up in the bed and began to scream. She scared the crap out of us. Willow grabbed a porcelain statue off of the bedside table and hit the woman. She screamed even louder. "Hit her until she's knocked out!" I yelled. Willow hit the lady several times until she went silent. We decided it was best to leave. Well, someone had heard the screams and called the police. As soon as we got into the car and attempted to leave, the cops swarmed us and took us into custody.

I was in Peoria for eighty-one days.

Willow and I were charged with burglary and attempted murder. I was thankful to hear that the woman survived. For a minute, I was sure she hadn't. She was in a coma for several days after the attack. She gave her statement as soon as she woke up and told the cops I'd instructed Willow to "hit her." Because of that, I was considered the "ringleader" and was found guilty on all charges. I was sentenced to twenty years in prison in May of 1988. I was twenty-one years old. Willow only received seven years because she was a woman.

I was sent to a maximum-security prison called Joliet. All of the gangs immediately began trying to recruit me. Of course, I didn't know anyone. I was in a state that was foreign to me, and the gangs were unlike any I was familiar with. Each day, a new gang approached me and tried to get me to join them. I thought it was desperate on their part and felt as if I'd be betraying my gang back home if I joined out there. Where I'm from, that's a violation of the "code of the streets." I decided just to keep my head down and do my time.

I was sent to Statesville Prison after a week and a half at Joliet. I was immediately approached by the leader of one of the biggest gangs, Latin Kings, or L.K.s, and his subordinates. They asked me several questions. I told them I was from California and a member of the Four-Tre Gangsta Crips. They seemed to get excited when they found out I was half Puerto Rican. They were convinced I was supposed to "ride with them." They told me about two other Crips they'd recruited in an attempt to convince me. I started to get agitated by the leader's insistence that I join them. "Look, man," I told the leader. "I'm not gonna join your gang. Now, if you have a problem with that then you and I can handle it [meaning we could fight], but win or lose I still won't join you." The leader didn't quite seem to like that. He especially didn't like the fact I'd said it in front of his subordinates. I was sure I'd made an enemy out of him when he walked away. I hadn't even been there for a week.

Illinois prisons are run by organized street gangs. If you're not a part of a street gang when you enter prison, then you have a choice to remain neutral—all the gangs agreed that the neutral guys were "off limits" and immune from extortion, rape, or bullying. The second choice was to choose who you wanted to "ride" with. Only, a gang had to decide to recruit you first, so you didn't necessarily have to join a prison gang. You only had to declare your loyalty to them, and in return you received a position within the organization that came with perks. By declaring your loyalty to a gang, you're expected to fight with them against enemies and you're expected to follow their by-laws and hierarchy.

I was determined to stay neutral. However, the Gangsta Disciples, G.D.s, tried to recruit me next. They were the biggest gang. They weren't as forceful as the Latin Kings were, and I respected that. When I declined them, their leader's right-hand man told me he respected my decision and asked me to walk with him. He took me to meet the leader of the G.D.s—called a minister. I agreed and went with him. The minister was an average-sized Black man named Shot. He shook my hand and proceeded to tell me that the leader of the Latin Kings had put a hit out on me. He warned me to watch my back. He explained that they'd been approached by the leader of the L.K.s in an attempt to hire them to kill me, but they'd declined. He essentially warned me that some guy would be coming to kill me and advised me to watch my back.

I couldn't help but to be scared after Shot told me about my possible assassination, but then he said something that made me skeptical. He went on to say, "If you ride with us, then you'll be under my umbrella of protection and wouldn't have to worry." Hearing that made me wonder if he was just trying to manipulate me. *Was someone actually coming to kill me or was it just a tactic to get me to ride with them?* I didn't know. Hell, for all I knew the G.D.s could've put a hit out on me to get me to join them. I didn't know them, or anyone else for that matter, so I had to assume the worst. There was one thing I knew for certain. I was the only one I could trust.

I thanked Shot for giving me a heads-up and assured him I'd consider all he'd said, but I let him know I needed time to decide. I figured as long as they thought there was a possibility I'd join them then they wouldn't send anyone to kill me, if it was them; however, if someone did try to kill me, then I'd know it wasn't them. It was the only thing I thought to do in order to see if I could trust the G.D.s or not. Shot didn't press the issue. He respected my decision and shook my hand. I parted company with him and went back to my cell.

I was on high alert for the next two days. I developed a system of assessing everyone around me. The first thing I looked at when a person was in close proximity to me was their hands. I figured you can't hurt someone without using your hands, so I checked to see if they had a weapon, clenched fist, or if they were just fidgety. I looked at their facial expression and eyes. I figured someone who was about to kill a person couldn't hide it in their eyes.

I went to the gymnasium to work out with my cellie on the third day. We were lifting weights, and I could tell my cellie was impressed by my strength. I was lifting as much as I could to make a point to the entire prison population that I was strong and a force to be reckoned with. I may have only stood a mere five feet six inches tall, but I weighed 200 pounds of pure muscle. I bench-pressed over 300 pounds. Little did I know, my show made no difference to the one charged with killing me.

I took a break from the workout in order to get a drink from the drinking fountain. A guard tower stood above the fountain, so I didn't think a hit would happen there. I bent over and began to quench my thirst when all of the sudden I felt a blunt object hit me over the head. I saw a flash of light before I realized I was being attacked. I turned to face my attacker and came face to face with a ferocious-looking Black man who was wielding some sort of pipe. I could feel the blood gushing from my head wound and instantly thought I was going to die. My attacker started swinging the pipe in an attempt to finish me off. In that moment, I heard a voice tell me, *You have to fight! He's gonna kill you!* I happened to grab the pipe with my right hand before it could hit me again, and I started hitting my attacker with my other hand. I hit him so hard my left hand split open at the knuckles. It caused my attacker to let go of the pipe, so I pushed him back and stood my ground. I hoped he'd see his attack had been thwarted and walk away, but he charged me. I jabbed the pipe at him like it was a spear, and his momentum caused the pipe to pierce his left eye and puncture his brain—killing him instantly. With a thud, my attacker fell to the ground face first. I stood there in shock and stared at my attacker's lifeless body as blood pooled around him.

Time seemed to stand still as I stood frozen. I didn't hear the guard in the tower yelling at me, "Get down on the ground!" I didn't hear the blare of the siren. I snapped back to reality when I was pulled in a direction by a G.D. named Pookie Slim. "Come on man, walk!" he instructed me and led me into the building and down a corridor flanked by two more G.D.s. They took me back to my cell and Pookie instructed me to take my clothes off and get washed up. One look in the mirror showed just how bad I looked. My head and face were covered in my own blood from my head wound. My right hand was dripping blood, and I could see the knucklebone of my pinky and ring fingers. I was standing in front of the mirror and trying to get the bleeding to stop when several guards appeared at my cell to get me. Despite the blood, they cuffed me up and took me away.

I was taken to the infirmary and given medical treatment. I stayed there for three days and was monitored because of my head wound. I received twenty stitches in my head and had a concussion. I also had several stitches in my knuckles, and my entire hand was wrapped up.

I received a visit from internal affairs on the fourth day. "What happened out there?" I was shocked that they really believed I'd go against "the code" and tell them anything. I would've been branded a "snitch" had I cooperated and wouldn't live another twenty days there, let alone the twenty years I had left to do. "I don't know" was all I could think to say. My unwillingness to cooperate must've angered the guard because he said, "Go ahead and keep quiet. That certainly is your right." A devious smile appeared on his face before he said, "Let's see how quiet you are when you're charged with murder." He and his partner just turned and walked out of the room.

I was put in "the hole"—solitary confinement—while awaiting the murder charge I believed was sure to come. The G.D.s took a liking to me because of how I handled myself and kept my mouth shut. I sat in the hole stressed out, and I imagined I'd spend the rest of my life in a state I'm not even familiar with and didn't know anyone. A couple of G.D.s began looking in on me. They dropped off hygiene products and food for me. I was given a "kite"—a prison note—from the highest-ranking G.D., Big Low. He assured me I wouldn't be charged with murder because I'd killed in self-defense. He also instructed me to sign up for the law library. I did as instructed, and Big Low began meeting me once a week so we could talk. I welcomed our conversation each week because there's nobody to talk to in the hole. I really took a liking to him and appreciated our conversations. He began sending me bags of commissary so I could eat. What I liked most about him was the fact that out of all our conversations he never once tried to recruit me.

I was given an internal disciplinary write-up for an assault that resulted in death. I was found guilty and sentenced to a year in solitary confinement; however, it was only done so the prison could buy time to continue with their "investigation" and "gather evidence" so they could charge me with murder. They held me in solitary even after I'd served my sanctions. Big Low told me the tower guard refused to say what had happened was anything other than self-defense, yet the district attorney kept trying to pressure him to change his story. After thirty-nine months in the hole, I was formally informed that no charges were going to be filed against me.

I was glad to be leaving the hole, but I was relieved to learn I wouldn't be spending the rest of my life in prison. I sat in the hole for another week before I was transferred to Menard Correctional Facility—a maximum-security prison known as "the pit." Big Low knew of my transfer before I did and informed me through a kite. He told me to speak with another G.D. named Sundown when I arrived. He was one of the highest-ranking members of the Gangsta Disciples, called a "board member."

The first person I ran into at Menard, when I went through intake, was a G.D. I told him Big Low had sent me to talk to Sundown. With no expression on his face he simply said, "I'll let him know" and walked away. With any new prison environment comes anxiety, because you don't know who anyone is. I didn't know what was going to come next. The guy I killed turned out to be from a gang called the Four Corner Hustlers. Big Low told me the Latin Kings paid him to assassinate me to avoid using their own guys because it would've traced back to them. Now I had two gangs that had every reason to want to kill me, so I had to consider everyone but the G.D.s as an enemy.

I was greeted by four G.D.s when I came out of intake. They approached me while I walked to my new cell. I tensed up when it occurred to me they could be coming to kill me. "You lookin' for Sundown?" one of the guys asked. I was immediately at ease because their body language suggested nothing was amiss. "Yeah," I responded. "Is that you?" "Naw," he replied. As he turned to walk away he said, "Follow me." I did as instructed and was escorted to a cell that matched the number of the one I was assigned to. "Sundown will be in touch" was all the speaker said, as he and his homies walked away.

Sundown showed up at my cell no sooner than I'd made my bed. He was flanked by two of his guys. I looked him up and down and immediately knew he was Sundown. He was average height and build, but you could tell he was a leader and commanded respect. "I hear you had a bit of a situation at Statesville?" he said. He exuded confidence and emanated intelligence, and I knew he'd said that to show me how fast information travels. "Yeah, a little bit," I responded while looking him in the eye. He introduced himself to me and assured me I didn't have to worry about retaliation behind what'd happened. In an effort to show me how much pull he had, he told me to grab my belongings and come with him. I did my best to appear hesitant as I unmade my newly made bed, grabbed my property, and followed him. He led me to the tier he lived on and to a cell that had someone's property in front of it. We stopped at the cell, and I watched as a not-too-happy dark-skinned muscular man moved his property out. "This is your cell," Sundown said, gesturing toward it. "It's right next to mine." He looked at me in a way that said *I run this place*. I got the message. He left me with instructions to get settled in, and as I began to make my bed, he said, "Oh, there's a box under your bed . . . it's yours."

The box contained a mixture of hygiene products, food, and new shoes—commonly known as a welcome package. Welcome packages are usually given to fellow gang members who arrive at a prison. The fact I wasn't a member of their gang and was receiving one was significant. Over the course of the next week, I went to and from chow with Sundown. We had conversations and went to recreation together. He shared Gangsta Disciple literature and by-laws with me and made me feel as if I was one of them. After a week, I agreed to ride with them.

The G.D.s are highly organized. Everyone within the organization has a job assignment. I was assigned to Sundown's personal security, along with a G.D. named Icky-Red. It was my job to make sure nobody could assassinate Sundown, even if it cost my life. I didn't have a problem with that because I didn't believe it would ever happen, and it never did. I held the job for three years and lived like a king because of it. I had almost everything I needed, but, more importantly, my position gave me status throughout Illinois prisons. Even after I was transferred to other facilities I never had any more problems.

I received a letter from my mom in 1997 after having been in prison for nearly nine years. In it, she told me she'd been clean and sober since May of 1992. She told me how much she loved me and explained how she'd found me. She apologized for how she raised me and promised to keep in touch with me. I hit the floor and cried after reading the letter, because I couldn't recall a time when my mom had been sober. To hear her say she loved me was deeply moving. We started to write each other on a regular basis, and I called her once a month even though I resented and blamed her for the way my life turned out. In my mind, everything was her fault, but I held back my resentment and anger because I was just happy to be in contact with her.

I made parole and was released from prison in 1998. I served ten years of my twenty-year sentence and was released to Peoria, Illinois. I tried to find Willow and her mom but had no luck. I was in a city without any support from family or friends, so I violated parole after being out only thirty days. I was supposed to find a job and report to my parole officer once a week, but nobody would hire me. After three weeks of unsuccessful job searches, my parole officer acted as if my lack of employment was my fault. He became frustrated by my lack of progress and started making subtle threats about violating my parole. He'd say, "If you don't find a job soon. . . ." So when I didn't have a job by the fourth week, I just didn't report to my PO because I didn't want to be threatened. It's not as if I went on the run. I was picked up at the halfway house I was staying at and sent back to prison for a year. I was released back on parole in 1999.

My dad's thirteen-year-old son, Jeff, began to write me sometime in 1995. One day I received a letter out of the blue with a name I didn't recognize on the return address. It was written in a kid's handwriting. The return address was in Phoenix, Arizona, and I realized the only person I knew down there was my dad. When I opened the letter and began to read, it became immediately apparent the letter was not a mistake. Jeff introduced himself as my brother and told me he'd overheard a conversation with our dad about me and that's what prompted him to try and find me. He explained how our dad had found me in prison and talked about how excited he was to write to me and introduce himself as my brother. I remember reading his letter and thinking, *Damn, this kid's bright.* I wrote him back and we began to correspond with each other. I enjoyed his letters. He even encouraged me to get my GED. We forged a bond that had me looking forward to going to Arizona and meeting him.

My dad didn't have a problem with me coming to Arizona; in fact, he even wrote to me and invited me to stay with them after I was released. It was only until I was able to get back on my feet, though. Jeff was seventeen when I made parole in 1999. I caught a bus to Phoenix, Arizona, the minute I was released. Jeff, his mom, and our dad met me at the Greyhound bus station. They took me out to dinner and we had a nice time. I didn't feel as if I was a part of their family, and it kind of bothered me. It wasn't anything they did. They were very hospitable. Everything just seemed fake, and I felt like I was an outsider. I had to remind myself that I was there for Jeff. Unfortunately, I found out Jeff had joined the army and was slated to go to boot camp three weeks after I arrived. That was disappointing, but I tried to make the best of the time we had together before he left. I spent as much time with him as I could and left my dad's house as soon as Jeff went to boot camp.

I heard about Van Buren Street being the place to find drugs and prostitution. I went there and quickly found a guy who sold dope. I spent every penny I had on dope and started selling drugs on the street. I was amazed at how fast I sold out. I went and bought more dope, and by the end of the day I'd turned $200 into $800. I rented a room for the night and got something to eat. I went back out on the street the next day and started making more money—doing it the right way never crossed my mind.

I had an established clientele after being on Van Buren for only a month. I started selling dope out of a hotel room, because being on the street was too high-risk. I had two prostitutes working for me—a white girl named Little Bit and a Black girl named Fast Black. Each girl had her own room to do business out of. Oftentimes, their "clients" bought dope from me to party with them. I became a regular one stop shop for the tricks.

Little Bit ran into my room one day and told me the trick she had in her room had a lot of money on him. I decided to rob the guy, so I went to her room with Fast Black and walked in just as the guy was coming out of the bathroom. He was buckling his pants back up just as we entered. He stopped dead in his tracks when he saw us and had a look on his face as if he'd been caught by either his wife or the police. "What are you doing in my room?" I asked, while doing my best to be intimidating. He just stood there in silence looking at me, so I said, "Where's your wallet? Give it to me!" He removed his wallet from his pants and tossed it to me. "Here," he said as he tossed me the wallet. "I don't want any trouble." I opened his wallet and only pulled out a couple hundred dollars. Fast Black became infuriated when she saw the small amount of money. She pulled out a knife and put it to the man's throat. "Where's the rest of the money, motherf-cker!" she yelled angrily as she went through his pockets. "Hey!" I yelled at Fast Black. "Let him go!" She removed the knife from his throat, and I told him to get lost and never return. He quickly ran out of the room. Happy the ordeal was over, I went back into my room, laid down on the bed, and went back to watching TV.

Men who solicit prostitutes are normally the perfect people to rob. They avoid calling the police because they're usually married and don't want their transgression to get back to their spouse. Unfortunately, that wasn't the case with the guy I robbed. He left, called the police, and returned with them to point us out. There was a knock on the door, and I opened it only to find myself staring at half a dozen cops. Fast Black and I were arrested and charged with armed robbery. We were offered plea bargains for six and a half years in prison for attempted armed robbery. Fast Black took the deal, but I refused mine. I didn't believe the victim would show up at my trial. It turned out I was wrong. Not only did he show up at my trial, but he was a great witness. Hell, I was ready to convict myself after he testified. That's exactly what happened, too. I was convicted and sentenced to ten and a half years in prison. I was thirty-two years old.

I was released from prison on December 31, 2008. I was forty-one years old.

I learned pretty quickly, after my release, that I was institutionalized. I was a mess. Arizona doesn't have "parole." Instead, they have "community supervision." I was allowed to live in a hotel room on community supervision. The problem was, I treated my hotel room like it was my cell. I realized after about a week that I needed to get out and get a job. After a week of rejection, one of my old friends from prison helped me get a job working at a telemarketing company. It felt good to hear the words, "You're hired." I'd never had a job before, so I was excited to get to work and hoped that it made me feel like a normal person. It didn't. In fact, I felt out of place from the very first day. The whole atmosphere made me feel as if I didn't quite belong there. When I received my first paycheck, I decided it would be my last and I quit.

There was one good thing that came from working at the telemarketing company. Her name was Sofia. She stood five feet five inches tall and was biracial—her dad was Black and her mom was Japanese. I saw her on my first day of work. She worked in the same building at a collection agency. I tried to act as if I didn't notice her. I didn't think she'd give me the time of day, let alone get with me, so I went about my business. She was beautiful. Plus, she looked to be significantly younger than my forty-one years of age, so I resisted the urge to talk to her each time I saw her. *Besides*, I thought, *what do I have to offer her?*

I was returning from my lunch break a week after I saw her. I passed by her while she was walking with her friend in the opposite direction. I heard her tell her friend, "He has pretty eyes." I stopped dead in my tracks, turned to her, and asked with a smile, "What'd you say?" My hazel eyes started our first conversation, and had it not been for my job, it never would've ended. We introduced ourselves to each other, exchanged phone numbers, and went back to our jobs. Her beauty compelled me to call her that night. She turned out to only be twenty-one years old and had a four-year-old son named Rey. The age difference made me a bit insecure, so I lied about my age. I told her I was thirty-two. I didn't have much experience with women who weren't prostitutes. Plus, I really liked her and feared my age would scare her off. She found my birth certificate some months later and confronted me about it. I explained to her why I'd lied and apologized. I vowed to never lie to her again. In the end, she decided not to leave me.

I took my pay stub from the telemarketing job to a Pay-Day loan and they gave me a $500 loan. I decided to see how many locations would give me a loan that day. A total of five different locations gave me $500 loans. I took the money and bought an ounce of crack cocaine. I set up shop in a hotel right across the street from the Arizona Department of Corrections intake unit called Alhambra. I used to sit outside of my crack spot and watch the prison guards change shifts.

Sofia didn't like that I quit my job and began selling dope again, but she didn't mind that I bought her and her son nice things and took them places with the drug money. I met her son Rey a week into our relationship and we hit it off. He was the first kid I'd ever been around on a regular basis. He was a cool kid, and it was easy to really like him. His dad was around but wasn't much of a father to him, so I stepped up and tried to be a father figure. I made sure to never let him see any of the things I did. Sofia and I smoked weed, but we never did it in front of him. We usually waited until he was asleep or out of the house. He and I became close over the course of the next few years. Sofia continued to beg me to quit selling dope and get a job, but I wasn't trying to hear her. I couldn't understand why she wanted me to do that when I was making such good money.

Selling drugs and pimping prostitutes was all I'd ever known. I didn't even like the thought of a nine-to-five job. I was stuck in my ways. Sofia used to say, "All the money you make doesn't do us any good if you're not gonna be in our lives." In my mind, I was too good to get caught, so she was talking nonsense. I was making anywhere from two to five thousand dollars a week. I couldn't imagine giving that up to make pennies on a regular job.

After living with Sofia and Rey for about six months, I moved us to a better apartment in Glendale, Arizona. We lived as a family for the next four years, and it was the best time of my life. I felt loved and needed for the first time in my life. Sofia was my "homey" and Rey was my "little partner." It made me realize how much I really liked my life with them in it, so I quit selling dope around the clock. I reduced my days to only eight hours—just like a business. I kept my motel room, and all of my clients knew what time I'd be there. I thought having a more conventional work schedule and being able to spend more time at home would make Sofia happy, but it didn't.

The manager of the motel I sold dope out of was a retired Phoenix police officer. He hated drug dealers but came to respect me because I kept all the riff-raff at the hotel in line. And because I ran a quiet operation. Anytime he needed me to remove people from his property, I came running. He appreciated me for that. One day he pulled me to the side and told me his brother was a narcotics officer, and he'd told him they were close to getting me. He explained that he didn't want to see me get "caught up," so he decided to tell me about it. I'd been harassed by the "narcos"—narcotics squad—for some time. Every time I came and went from the motel they'd pull me over and search my car. I enjoyed the game of cat-and-mouse, but hearing the manager tell me that made me decide to finally take Sofia's advice and quit while I was ahead. Sofia was happy to hear the big news.

One day while I was out looking for work, I decided to steal from some stores. I went in, grabbed some items, and walked out. I convinced myself what I was doing was only a misdemeanor if I stole less than a thousand dollars' worth of merchandise. I don't know where I came up with the amount or the idea, but it seemed right to me. I started going into stores and filling shopping carts up with food and alcohol and walking right out as if I'd paid for everything. I brought the food home and sold the alcohol on the streets. Sofia questioned me about the food and money I brought home, and I just assured her I wasn't selling drugs. She didn't press me for answers, mainly because she knew once my mind was made up nobody could change it. Plus, I didn't think she minded because she enjoyed having everything I provided.

I became more brazen each time I went out to steal. In my mind, I thought I wouldn't be sent to prison if I were caught. I thought I'd probably only pay a fine or do a few months in jail at the most. That thinking only emboldened me. I walked into clothing stores, grabbed things, and walked out. Which stores I stole from or which products I stole didn't matter to me. The consequences paled in comparison with the consequences of the previous crimes I'd been convicted of—at least in my mind.

I went out with a friend of mine to steal, and we decided to hit a JCPenney's. I walked in and went to the suitcase department. I found a duffel bag and grabbed it. I went to the clothing department and casually began filling the bag with clothes until it was full. I didn't realize I was being watched until I walked out of the store with the bag and noticed a lady had followed me. She walked up to me and asked for the bag. Without hesitation, I handed her the bag just as two SUVs pulled up and four cops jumped out and arrested me. I didn't resist. After all, I was committing a misdemeanor, so why make matters worse? I was placed in the back seat of an SUV, and my record was run. After seeing my record, the officer informed me I was going to be charged with three felonies, and my jaw dropped.

I discovered that in Arizona if one attempts to steal a thing while concealing it inside of something else then it's considered a felony. It's called shoplifting with artifice, which is a Class Four felony. I was charged with two counts of organized retail theft because I walked into the store with someone who also stole. I couldn't believe it. I had three felonies for a bag of clothes! When I was asked why I stole, I admitted that I couldn't find work and did it to make money. Turned out, the fact I stole for monetary gain was what got me the organized retail theft. I was shocked! *What else do people steal for if not for monetary gain?* I wondered.

Calling Sofia from jail and telling her what I'd done was the hardest part of the whole situation. It'd be an understatement to say she was angry and disappointed with me. I was more ashamed than I'd ever been in my life. My bond was set at $2,500, but Sofia refused to bond me out. She told me, "You're gonna sit in jail because it's obviously where you wanna be!"

I was considered to be a "career criminal," and that status required a sentence enhancement. I was surprised hearing myself be called that. I just didn't see myself that way. I think I was more concerned about that than the whole sentence enhancement thing, until they began to explain the enhancement process. They call it "roping." I was being "roped" for a non-dangerous bag of clothes because I was a career criminal. I was facing twelve years in prison. I just kept repeating to myself, *For a bag of clothes?*

I sat in jail for fifty-four days before Sofia bailed me out. She made me promise that if she bailed me out I wouldn't do anything illegal and I'd get a job—even if I had to volunteer. I was determined to keep my promises to her. After she bailed me out, I spent the night with her and Rey, but I woke up early the next morning and went job hunting.

We lived down the street from the business district in Glendale. Even though I'd already been down there, I decided to try again. This time I went business to business to see if someone, anyone, would hire me. I was rejected so many times I can't count, but then I saw a construction company I'd never seen before. I walked in and asked the guy at the desk if they were hiring. He looked me up and down, and just when I thought he was about to reject me, he said, "Can you pass a piss test?" That caught me off guard, so I gave a stunned response. I said, "Uh, yeah." I knew I was clean because I'd just spent fifty-four days in jail without smoking weed. He had me fill out an application and told me he'd contact me in a couple of days. I figured I'd never hear from him again and went on with my job search unsuccessfully. Two days later, I received a call from the guy telling me to report to some business to give a urine sample. He told me if I passed, then I'd have a job. Hearing that was one of the best things to happen in my life. I couldn't wait to give my urine sample. I waited for two long days before I heard back from the guy telling me to report to work the next day.

I worked fifty hours a week digging holes. At forty-six years old, it was the most meaningful work in my life. I was surprised to find out how good hard work made me feel. It made me realize how selling dope was a fantasy—it provided money, but deprived you of happiness and contentedness.

My job was a mile away from home. Sofia had to sell my car to bond me out, so I walked to and from work. Even then I was still happy and content. I used to walk by a cop who sat in a parking lot trying to catch speeders. He got used to seeing me in my work clothes and boots, with my lunch in hand, and would wave to me each morning. It was weird at first, but then I began to like it. I understood he viewed me as a working-class man and citizen for the first time in my life. I realized how much I preferred that. It was my "ah-ha" moment.

My relationship with Sofia and Rey became better than ever. I began taking Rey to and from school. I attended his parent–teacher conferences. And I began having regular date nights with Sofia. Other nights we included Rey for a family night out. There were times when I'd be out with Sofia, or hanging with them both, and I'd be reminded of the possibility of going back to prison. The thought of leaving them caused me to break down in tears.

After seventeen months of freedom, I was offered a plea bargain. They offered me six years in prison and three years of probation. My attorney recommended that I take it, but that much time in prison for a bag of clothes just didn't sit right with me. I went and talked with the prosecutor, against the advice of my attorney. I told her, "I understand your point of view. I'd look at me and treat me like a career criminal too, if I were in your shoes." I dumped out a manila envelope containing seventeen months of check stubs from work, along with my income tax returns. While she began looking through them, I said, "I filed my first income taxes and those pay stubs are from the first steady job I've ever had. I've changed. If you don't send me back to prison you'll never see me again." I proceeded to tell her in detail how my life had changed. I told her about Rey and my relationship with Sofia. I pleaded with her, and she listened while wiping tears out of her eyes on occasion. She went and talked with her boss and later emailed me with an offer of four and a half years with no probation. She told me it was the lowest she could go given the law pertaining to enhancements. I took the deal.

I had a month until sentencing, so I spent as much time with Sofia and Rey as I could. It was the shortest month of my life. We took Rey to school on the day of my sentencing and Sofia told him I wasn't going to be around "for a while." He started crying, and it broke my heart. I gave him a big hug, and I knew I'd really changed because prior to that, my instinct would have been to run. But I knew it was time I did the right thing. I went to court and was sentenced, handcuffed, and taken to jail. I looked back at Sofia as I was being led out, and I watched as she sat there crying. In that moment, I realized I'd caused the two people I loved most in the world pain, and I hated myself for it.

I associated with a handful of solid guys in prison who focused their attention on growing in life. They encouraged me to study and exercise. One of the guys offered to try and get me a job in the maintenance department so I could continue to develop "tangible skills" that'd be useful for me once released. I wanted to work there for the opportunity to learn about welding, so I agreed.

After being on the yard for five months, I was introduced to the head of maintenance, and he agreed to hire me.

I was called to the administration on August of 2017. An administrator sat me down and told me the maintenance department had requested that I begin working for them. She explained that based upon "the incident which took another inmate's life, nearly thirty years earlier," I wouldn't be permitted to work in maintenance. I did my best to plead my case; after all, what had happened in Illinois hadn't been a factor during my previous time in Arizona's prison. "They must've made a mistake!" was the response I was given. I calmly told her, "I don't know what your problem is with me, but this isn't right." I proceeded to get up and walk out of the office before I said or did anything I'd later regret. "Don't you walk away from me!" the administrator yelled, but I kept walking. For whatever reason, the administrator called for backup and acted as if I'd done something egregious. I stayed calm as several guards showed up. The administrator instructed the guards to handcuff me and transport me to "the hole" for disrespecting staff.

I'll never allow anyone to cause me to not move forward in life. I'm fifty years old now. I know my time on earth is nearing its end. I'm determined to live the rest of my life the right way. My release date is April of 2018. I'll be fifty-one years old. For the first time in my life, I can truly say I'll never again come back to prison and my mind will never be imprisoned again.

Part 4

Outside + Inside
Solutions

So why include me?

Why, after all of these compelling stories, spoken-word by the people who lived them, would we contaminate them with the voice of someone on the outside looking in?

Why, after the incisive analysis of someone who's lived through and past an imprisoned mind, would we complicate with the outside analysis of an academic?

And why, after the innovative craft of people in prison opening up on their lives to an incarcerated author, would we risk adding this book to the pile of ivory tower proclamations on the subject?

Here are our answers.

I'm white, growing up in western New York. Erik is Black and white, growing up in Northern California. In the year 2000 I received my high school diploma. In the year 2000 Erik received his life sentence. He earned his GED in prison while I earned a master's and a doctorate. And yet with all my degrees, with all my training, I couldn't have written this book. I'd never be able to get close enough to the people and to properly honor the stories that they've lived. It'd be an academic exercise written for an academic audience.

But Erik couldn't have written this book by himself either. He's too close. People often read prisoner accounts with skepticism, expecting to hear from an innocent person about how they've been wronged by the system. Innocent people wronged by the system exist, but as the stories in this book make clear, many people in prison are there due to circumstances and to the decisions they made that were bound by those circumstances. An outside perspective provides the context for these circumstances, and it reframes the imprisoned mind from a fixed, individual deficiency to a malleable viewpoint of oneself and their relationship with others. We hope that the stories of the people in this book are told and retold in a way that retains their authenticity while presenting a balanced understanding of why people end up in prison.

We could write this book together. We couldn't have written it apart.

Erik once told me he thinks of himself as a "ghetto version of me." I don't know what that means, but I consider it a compliment. With complete respect for Erik's voice and the voices of the men with whom he spoke, I join alongside them in sharing my voice.

—Kevin A. Wright

About-Faces

KEVIN A. WRIGHT

I was a three-year-old, jumping off the docks into the waters of Canandaigua Lake in western New York. Dad would already be in the water. I'd launch in and sink, he'd pop me back up to the surface, and he'd return me to the dock to do it again. Over and over again.

I'd be shivering, jumping up and down from the cold and the excitement. Eventually, Mom would envelop me in comfort with a warm towel.

Daddy. Giggles. Jumping off docks. Swimming. Mommy. What could be better? That's my earliest memory. That's the first thing that I can remember.

But here's the thing. I don't remember if this is an actual memory of mine or if it's a memory of someone else, retold to me. And if this isn't my first true memory, I'm not even sure what the next candidate in line would be.

So it was with skepticism that I first read about twenty-month-old Erik's memory of the violent home invasion where an attacker was killed in front of him. It happened again when I read that three-year-old Dee recalled his mom terrorizing his aunt with a shard of glass in her hand. And again when I read that kindergartner Kidd vividly remembered enduring racism from classmates.

How could they possibly have these memories from such a young age? I might believe one extraordinary kid with an extraordinary memory, but all of them?

This nagged at me: if I couldn't believe their earliest memory—the very first thing written about them in each chapter—how could I believe the rest of their story? How could I believe when Oso put a loaded gun to his head, pulled the trigger, and nothing happened? Or when Dee was tied up to a fencepost in the desert and left for dead? Or when Unique put a pipe through another incarcerated man's eye, killing him instantly?

I couldn't stop thinking about it. Erik helped me to better understand.

If you found your mom dead from a gunshot, that is the memory. Not just the earliest memory. THE memory.

If you watch your mom get CPR and nearly die from an overdose in front of you, that is the memory.

If you see your mom shoot your dad in the chest, that is the memory.

These memories, these events, these traumas forever alter the trajectory of your life. They forever change the people and the circumstances around you. They forever alter how you see the world. And they forever alter how the world sees you. *That's the kid whose mom shot herself.*

It doesn't matter if it's a true memory of yours or a memory of those around you. Your earliest memory (or theirs) is when everything changed forever. Sometimes it's just an early memory, and not the first, but it still changed everything forever. There's life before it and life after it.

The stories in this book matter. Reading this book gives you a more complete picture of the men behind the walls. If you were to hear that an "inmate" was abused as a child, you might defensively respond that it doesn't excuse, justify, or rationalize the behavior that put him in prison. But if you were to hear that a child was abused, you might better understand, perhaps even with sympathy or empathy, that his life was forever altered. *How the stories in this book are told and to whom matters.* There's nothing new here—no new theory of the onset or persistence of criminal behavior. But these are men in prison, telling their story to another man in prison. It hits different.

When you acknowledge the full complexity of humanity in these stories, and when you acknowledge the full complexity of humanity in how these stories are told and to whom, it opens up a new world of possibilities and solutions to how we could empower people who are in our correctional system. It allows for the potential of future expectations that go beyond simply being not criminal.

The "mass" in mass incarceration reduces our national incarceration narrative to numbers. Individual people and their life stories are only important in so much as in their aggregation they make up the nearly 2 million people incarcerated in U.S. jails and prisons.[1] They become less than human, they become numbers. And when we do hear the individual stories, it's the horrific snapshot of life that was their worst experience. It's the segment on the news, the mugshot on the website, and the live video of their sentencing. We are provided distance when we reduce people to numbers or to the worst thing that ever happened to them. We are humans capable of good who do no evil; they are not.

Our book is about faces over numbers. It's about the movies of their whole life over the snapshot of their worst days. Our book is about people in all their good and their bad. We see the qualities of regret and despair, forgiveness and hope, that make us all human. And yet we always know how these stories will end. In prison. Sometimes that's hard to expect as you work your way through their lives. You learn of some ordinary human moments. We see Kidd and Oso as fathers holding their babies for the first time. We see Sergeant fighting for his country. Oakland's football career. Seeing these moments humanizes the men in this book. People in prison are people.

Watching this slow-motion movie, we learn that people in prison are also victims. They are yesterday's children of incarcerated parents.[2] We watch the adverse childhood experiences (ACEs) as they happen.[3] It's a painful cycle to read, where you see their parents abusing drugs and alcohol and abusing people. You then see them become parents themselves. And you wonder, *Could we write this book again about their kids?* The men in this book are neglected, abused, and forgotten youth. When we unpack mass incarceration to make it about faces, about people, then we realize the full complexity of being a victim and a victimizer, with a greater understanding of who else is impacted by an imprisoned mind.

Our significant risk in advancing the imprisoned mind concept is that it sounds like it's the individual's fault that they think this way.[4] It sounds like criminal behavior is the result of flawed or deficient thinking that needs to be corrected—a psychological explanation where "inmates" on the inside are fundamentally different from people on the outside.[5] You can even hear the resignation in the men's voices for being at fault for everything that has happened to them, and everything that will happen to them. And if you were to see the faces of the men in this book, you'd see that they are disproportionately Black and brown faces. Our significant risk in advancing the imprisoned mind concept is that it could be taken to represent an individual deficiency disproportionately held by people of color.

These stories matter because you can see that circumstance shapes *everything* for these men from the moment that they are born.

The boys grow up with parents who are absent, drunk, high, abusive, and erratic. The boys grow up with poverty, with inequality, with racism, and with discrimination. The boys grow up with drugs and alcohol. The boys grow up with bullies and with lawbreaking role models. The boys grow up with noxious ideas of what it means to be a man. The boys grow up with guns. The boys grow up with suicide and murder. The boys grow up with juvenile hall, with crummy schools and crummy group homes. The boys grow up without legitimate jobs and with plenty of illegitimate jobs. The boys grow up finding their mother's dead body, seeing their mother get CPR, and watching their mother shoot their father in the chest.[6] The boys grow up with lethal levels of toxic stress that suffocate any sense of healthy development of their brain and their body.[7]

The development, progression, and seeming permanence of the imprisoned mind in men happens when boys grow up in an environment with abundant adversity and scarce support.

Erik has said that each man featured in this book has told him that they found the process of telling their story to be therapeutic. It's likely so because they're able to see the full impact of their life circumstances for where they are today.[8]

These stories that humanize people in all their good and their bad also provide us with glimpses of solutions. Each chapter has moments where you see possibility for something else, something good.

Kidd speaks of the group homes that treated him well, of Miss Bobby and later Rob, who encouraged and inspired him. He tells how it was an incentive to do good in order to live with his father, and how the birth of his daughter motivated him to get a job. Sergeant falls in love with ROTC. Later, he does the same with motorcycle school. Oso recalls his time at a boys' ranch learning life skills and being at peace around animals. Dee discovers he likes science, and later in his life both his mom and dad extend their love back to him. Oakland has Reverend Tinsley on his side, he has football to take him away from the drug game, and later he finds a job that motivates him to do well. Unique gets his mom back in his life, now sober and loving, and he forges a bond with a brother he never knew he had. He becomes a father figure to Rey and feels loved and needed for the first time in his life.

And Erik writes of the positive influence of Arizona State University (ASU) faculty and students who inspired him to do something more than just exist.

In most of these moments, the good thing went away. Sometimes it was out of the control of the men and sometimes it was their decision to squander it away, perhaps due to their imprisoned mind. Oso best recalls the regret: "I'd be a whole different person today had I taken the opportunity to move to Oklahoma."

There are times in my work when I become disillusioned, discouraged, and overwhelmed with the question of whether people can "change." This is especially the case for whether other people or opportunities can motivate people to change. *They have to want to change* is the common refrain.[9] The imprisoned mind sounds insurmountable at times—so much goes into its creation that so much needs to go into its dismantlement. But these full life stories offer me promise that it is possible. I remember first having Erik as a student in my Inside-Out Prison Exchange Program class.[10] He had such a presence in class, an engaging personality with a knack for providing profound class contributions at all the right times. *This is such a waste*, I thought. And so I was immediately onboard when he approached me about the idea to write a book after class ended. It wasn't until after reading his writing in this book that I realized how much that support mattered to him.

These stories matter. They help us understand how people end up on a pathway to prison. They help us understand how to get people on a different pathway.

Erik provided me some advice when I married my wife. He said something to the effect of relationships are like plants that you had to constantly nourish and take care of. And that if you neglected the plant, or the relationship, it would die. It was much longer than that, with many moving parts. At the time I thought it was trite and corny. It is trite and corny.

But how many times have I thought back on that advice? How many times have I thought about Erik having limited opportunity to establish meaningful relationships, and here I am not nurturing my own? It works every single time. I apologize. I make time. I do better. I nurture the relationship.

This experience convinced me that the stories told in this book, to Erik, provide an additional viewpoint and perspective that is of immense value. It matters who is telling the stories and to whom.[11] It doesn't matter if the stories merely reinforce what is already "known" about why people engage in deviant behavior.

And it's true—there's not much new here. Scholars and students of psychology, sociology, criminology, criminal justice, and other disciplines would recognize many theories and correlates of deviant behavior. There's the intense pressure to achieve financial and material success with limited conventional opportunities to do so.[12] There are additional pressures into deviant coping behaviors, when noxious events like abuse are added or positive events like mentoring are removed.[13] There's lack of supervision by adults, perhaps leading to low levels of self-control, and desires for instant gratification, sensation-seeking, and a lack of concern for others.[14] There's fetal alcohol syndrome (FAS), neonatal abstinence syndrome (NAS), traumatic brain injury (TBI), post-traumatic stress disorder (PTSD), and of course, ACEs.[15] There's learning and positive reinforcement of deviant behavior everywhere, especially from parents, older siblings, and older boys and young men in the neighborhood.[16] There are weak bonds with prosocial others and there's a lack of social support provided by prosocial others.[17] There are disadvantaged neighborhoods with weak health and social service institutions.[18] There's outright racism, hidden racism, and differential treatment for people of color.[19] It's all here.

The imprisoned mind concept is the full motion picture rather than these individual snapshots, and here again we see support for well-known ideas about deviant behavior unfolding and persisting over time. We see "criminal careers" from their onset through their escalation and into their continuity.[20] We see men who persist in their criminality into adulthood while others around them leave crime behind.[21] We painfully see a rejection of conventional opportunities and others, where hooks for change could have led the men away from deviance.[22] We see a commitment to "doing masculinity" with little regard for its impact on others.[23] We see identities that are forged in the life of addiction and deviance, with little promise for an identity that is conventional or contributing to others or society.[24] And over and over again, we see the imprisoned mind flourish by justifying and rationalizing the behavior it governs.[25]

This support is important—the stories in this book are valid in the sense that they are backed up by scientific research. They check out. But it would be a missed opportunity to dismiss these stories as applied case studies to validate existing knowledge.

The men in these stories are actively struggling with an imprisoned mind and its consequences while incarcerated. They are sharing their stories with another man who is incarcerated and who has walked down the same pathways as they have. Erik is not an outside, "objective" researcher coming in to conduct interviews on a vulnerable population.

So why does this matter?

The life-history narrative is critical to the foundation and progression of the understanding of deviant behavior.[26] Some of the richest data about who commits crime and how has been documented through the individual stories of men and women caught up in the system.[27] This approach has been lost somewhat in the age of big data where numbers are hallowed. No one tells the life histories of the nearly 2 million incarcerated men and women in U.S. prisons and jails. Part of the challenge in telling these stories is that it is difficult for scholars or journalists to gain access and to establish rapport with people who are incarcerated.[28] It's also difficult for researchers to know whether they are obtaining accurate information from a group of people who may be distrustful of their intentions.[29]

The modern life-history narrative of criminology and criminal justice has shifted away from foundational approaches in an important direction. Those classic works typically involved researchers interviewing people who were *subjects* who played a passive role in how their stories were told and used—any more involvement than this would invite bias. But today we have witnessed a push where people closest to the challenges of the justice system are part of the solutions.[30] Trusted or credible messengers, peer-led organizations and programs, and participatory action research all support the idea that lived experience in the system can be leveraged to produce a better system—any less involvement would risk outsiders producing knowledge and practice that are out of touch with reality.

Erik is a credible messenger. His most powerful writing happens when he uses the collective "we" and "us." It's raw. It's vulnerable. And it's authentic:

It's as if we develop a form of tunnel vision and become hyper-focused on satisfying our desires and needs. The problem with this mentality is its self-deceiving nature: The imprisoned mind causes us to believe that things we simply want are so important that we are required to have them. This inability to differentiate between our wants and needs leads to a sense of urgency and a lack of patience when it comes to acquiring what we feel we must have. We then develop an egoistic attitude. Our imprisoned mind leads us to believe that everything is about us and produces behavior that seems rude or inconsiderate. We lie and manipulate to get what we want. We believe that we have honor and integrity, but in reality they're foreign concepts to us. If there are rules that hinder our ability to do as we feel, then we will attempt to find ways around those rules or just ignore them. It doesn't occur to us that our actions affect anyone outside of ourselves. When faced with the consequences of our actions, we deny culpability, we feign ignorance, and we deflect responsibility. Saying "everybody does it" is a typical excuse, and one that is indicative of the irrationality of the imprisoned mind, yet it is suitable enough for us to justify committing unethical or illegal acts. Once we're caught and suffer the consequences of our actions, the imprisoned mind causes us to see ourselves as victims, virtually blind to our own accountability.

Erik is a legitimate authority among the men, more than any expert or scholar could ever be. When he writes that "our minds are imprisoned," he invites his peers along in a collective understanding with a solution for collective change. It offers a way out: if our minds are imprisoned, then we need to free them.

When people become system-involved, their lives become controlled by the system. Even people with the best intentions decide what is needed for people who are incarcerated. They need cognitive behavioral therapy. They need higher education. They need workforce training. Erik's approach is empowering. It gives people control of their lives. It helps them understand the consequences of the past, the opportunities in the present, and the promises for the future. It helps them decide what they need. Maybe it leads people to want to change.

Credible messenger movements can give people their lives back to understand the challenges that they have faced in order to create solutions.

There is another collective "we" in the writing of this book—Erik and me, us. We have worked on this book together for over seven years now. We've had good times: consistent enthusiasm, support, and even excitement from many potential readers of the book. We've had bad times: rejection after rejection from academic presses who initially seemed interested. We've lost communication through the COVID-19 pandemic and through a prison transfer that relocated Erik. Up until only recently, our entire collaboration and conversation on the book took place through writing that could be shared when we'd be together sporadically in person for other work.

Seven years. We both remained committed to the work and confident in the other's ability to make it happen.

The imprisoned mind development and formulation is all Erik. I agree with and support its principles, but there have been a few times where I've had to remind myself to shut off the academic in me while working on this project. I've wondered what percent of the incarcerated population has an imprisoned mind, what an imprisoned mind index would look like, and how we could measure change in the imprisoned mind. I've wondered about women and the imprisoned mind. I've wondered about empirical support. But all those thoughts dehumanize the idea rather than nurture the idea—it makes it about numbers and not faces.

I always think of this as "Erik's book," and it's at his insistence that I joined as an author. In writing this book together, we have complemented one another to present the complexities of "victims" and "offenders" as one and the same within our correctional system. His insider knowledge coexists alongside my outsider knowledge, and this book is the result of the voices of people who are impacted by the system conversing with the voices of people who study that system.[31] Participatory action research is research *with* the people most involved and impacted by that research rather than a traditional research approach *on* or even for those people.[32] This is a new form of life-history narrative for producing knowledge and solutions for our justice system. Credible messengers in the form of system-impacted people are pushed to the center—with scholars and science alongside them—and are given power to understand their own strengths in identifying solutions.[33]

How these stories are told and to whom matters. It gives people their lives, and their futures, back to them.

Functional fixedness is a cognitive bias where humans are limited to use an object only in the way that it is traditionally used.[34] This fixedness means no creativity and no innovation, business continues as usual and the status quo remains. Prisons as objects have been places of punishment used to turn criminals into noncriminals. We measure the success of this correctional system through how well it reduces recidivism.[35] A successful system produces not criminals, whereby an assumed criminal justice problem is met with a criminal justice solution. Any "innovative" approach, such as those rooted in Scandinavian principles, will be boxed in by this functional fixedness goal of reduced recidivism.

An about-face in how we view our prisons—a complete reversal in perspective on the function and purpose of our correctional system—could mean that a reimagined, human-centered system invests in *people* who are incarcerated.[36]

Instead of the reduced recidivism of criminals, our indicator of correctional success could be the increased well-being of people.[37] Prisons become places of opportunity designed to support people to be better than they arrived to the system.[38] The stories of the men in *Imprisoned Minds* support a reimagined corrections that repairs the harms of the past while empowering people in the present to become contributing citizens in the future.

People with an imprisoned mind have pasts that are dominated by those early and persistent memories of trauma, abuse, and neglect. These adverse childhood experiences are the foundation that enables destructive attitudes and behaviors into young adulthood and adulthood. The imprisoned mind and the cycle of incarceration means that nothing will change if these traumas go unaddressed. Programs that focus on changing criminal thinking errors, for example, may be treating the symptoms rather than treating the root causes.[39] Worse still, people who experience incarceration face an increased risk of adverse mental and physical health outcomes, from depression to premature death.[40] Here again there is a link between adverse childhood experiences and adverse adulthood health and mental health outcomes.[41] Prisons could be an opportunity to disrupt these links.

A trauma-informed correctional system could acknowledge and seek to minimize the long-term effects of childhood adversity.[42] Growing up with toxic stress (including in response to witnessing violence and living in extreme poverty) in the absence of any significant buffering support can derail normal functioning and development for children.[43] The experience of incarceration as an adult can make this worse, where past traumas can be exacerbated and new traumas can be introduced. Trauma-informed training for people who work in correctional settings can help avoid a worsening of the effects of adverse childhood experiences.[44] Trauma-specific treatments could explicitly acknowledge the impact of trauma, abuse, and neglect in an effort to help people understand how their past impacts their current thinking and behavior.[45]

Recognizing past childhood trauma is not excusing current adulthood behavior. The full motion picture of the stories in this book show how seemingly inexplicable harmful behavior can be associated with past harm. If we acknowledge this full complexity of the humanity of people on the inside, and if we change our measure of correctional success from reduced recidivism to increased well-being, then we can leverage new opportunities in innovation like a trauma-informed correctional system.

But what about the kids who experience significant trauma, neglect, and abuse whose minds and bodies remain unimprisoned? Aren't they evidence that "correlation does not equal causation"—that something else must be to blame for the link between these adverse childhood experiences and undesirable adulthood outcomes? These people hold immense value. They're not exceptions, they're exceptional. Rather than being held up as evidence that childhood trauma doesn't matter, they can serve as examples to identify the protective factors that break the cycle of abuse.[46] If we told their stories, we might learn of a supportive person or opportunity that interrupted their descent into the imprisoned mind. They're the evidence that pernicious outcomes of childhood abuse aren't inevitable.

The other group that falls outside of imprisoned mind expectations are men who are incarcerated with no history of childhood trauma. It's possible that these men have none of the characteristics of an imprisoned mind. They were wrong place–wrong time, hanging with the wrong crowd, beset by adverse adult experiences, or plagued by unhealthy addictions with origins beyond childhood. Or maybe they do have the characteristics of the imprisoned mind, and its source extends beyond childhood abuse and neglect. In either instance, a better than arrival approach to correctional success means that these men would still benefit from the reimagined system. They wouldn't be left to languish, nor would they be forced to go through treatment for a condition that they didn't possess.[47] Investing in people within our correctional system benefits all, imprisoned mind or not.

Reconceptualizing our measure of correctional success from reduced recidivism of criminals to increased well-being of people provides more possibilities of theories of human behavior to guide that system.[48] We no longer have to be limited to theories of deviant behavior and to theories of how to correct deviant behavior. We could look to theories of human motivation and to what gives people meaning in life.

People are intrinsically motivated when they have a sense of autonomy to direct their own lives.[49] It's often said that people are sent to prison because they've made bad choices, with the hope that experiencing incarceration will lead to better choices in the future. And yet nearly all opportunities to make choices in prison are removed. Opportunities that increase autonomy could increase well-being.

People are intrinsically motivated when they have the urge to get better and better at something that matters to them.[50] Providing opportunities for practice and learning of knowledge or a skill could increase well-being.

People are intrinsically motivated to do things in service of something larger than themselves.[51] It gives them purpose to contribute to others, especially when that means in support of the next generation. Providing opportunities for people in prison to support and mentor others or to give back to their communities can increase well-being.

When "evidence-based corrections" means "evidence for increased well-being," then a wealth of theoretical and applied knowledge becomes available to reimagine the correctional system.[52]

Empowering people in prison in the present in this manner can ensure that they are better than their arrival to the correctional system.[53] Erik's own transformation shows the potential for a reimagined system. He went from "just existing"—his words—to a star student in a college class, to a co-researcher on projects to enhance the correctional system, to published author in a journal, to researcher and author of a university press book.[54] And he now plans to extend the imprisoned mind idea into a class and workshop so that others in prison may free their mind. All of this provided him autonomy, mastery, and purpose. For Erik it was writing. For someone else it might be art. Someone else, computer coding. And still someone else, gardening. Possibly none of these have evidence to reduce recidivism.[55] But if that's no longer the metric of success, then that doesn't matter. Would anyone prefer their tax dollars pay for just-existing Erik who was getting tickets for fighting over the empowered Erik who is bettering the lives of the men around him? Just-existing Erik was dangerous to others. Empowered Erik is increasing the safety of people inside and out of prison.

Anyone who spends a significant amount of time in prison would be struck by how wasteful our current system is. The biggest waste is in stripping people of their humanity, of their identities, of their talents and abilities. When it becomes numbers over faces, we lose all of the levers that could be pulled to empower people to be better versions of themselves. Credible messengers make sense.[56] Peer mentors make sense.[57] Participatory action research makes sense.[58] Whenever I teach or do a workshop in prison—especially if I'm speaking about the value of incarcerated people to be a part of the solution—there's a moment where I often feel as if the audience finally engages with what I'm saying; more eyes look directly at me, and some heads nod affirmatively. It's the moment where I say, "I don't know what it's like to spend a night here, unable to leave." It's an acknowledgment that I'm an outsider and I'll never really "get it."

Imagine the power of a teacher, coach, or mentor who can say I know what it's like to spend that night and many more, unable to leave. Imagine the power of someone saying I used to have an imprisoned mind just like you do. Imagine the power of someone saying I found my mom after she shot herself and it messed me up, but I'm here today to tell you how I survived and now thrive. We're wasting opportunities to invest in people, both the mentors and the mentees, and we're limiting the success of our system in the process.

Last, if our correctional system is no longer solely a criminal justice problem requiring a criminal justice solution, then we open up more possibilities of who has expertise and resources that could be part of the solution.[59] A socially supportive, strengths-based correctional system could invest in people on the inside with resources from the outside to ensure they have sustaining and gainful futures.[60] State health, housing, and employment departments and agencies. Grassroots organizations and nonprofits. Faith-based organizations. Community health and mental health organizations. Employers. Veterans services. All reaching in.

And colleges and universities.

Mission-driven universities could share responsibility for the well-being of people who live and work in our correctional system. What other institution has the breadth and depth of knowledge and expertise to increase the well-being of people? Our charter here at ASU: *ASU is a comprehensive public research university, measured not by whom it excludes, but by whom it includes and how they succeed; advancing research and discovery of public value; and assuming fundamental responsibility for the economic, social, cultural, and overall health of the communities it serves.*

What would a prison unit look like that was infused with university resources?

We're figuring this out, through the design and implementation of the ASU POINT Model in both a men's and women's prison. POINT stands for Potential, Opportunity, Investment, Nurture, and Transformation. It's human-centered corrections designed to invest in people in prison to increase their well-being. Doctor of nursing practice students providing care during clinical rotations in prison. Interior design faculty and students transforming the physical space of a prison classroom so that it is trauma-informed. Social work faculty designing and implementing trauma and bereavement workshops. Counseling psychology faculty providing classes in how to manage stress in interpersonal relationships. Social work, justice studies, and social and family dynamics faculty sharing expertise to design a training for staff on gender and culturally informed practice. Journalism. Recreational therapy. Writing. Art. The faculty, the staff, the students, the interns—all investing in people on the inside so that they are better than their arrival to the system.

And, of course, we're doing all this while empowering incarcerated men and women as our collaborators in all of the work, providing them autonomy, mastery, and purpose. Erik is one member of our Arizona Transformation Project (ATP), a learning community of ASU faculty, students, and incarcerated men and women. The ATP is the organizing body of the ASU POINT Model, with a mission to enrich the lives of people inside and outside of the justice system through research and lived experience.

Inside and outside. Together, for a more holistic understanding of the challenges and potential solutions. Just like Erik and I in the writing of this book.

Why invest in people who are incarcerated? Why provide free opportunities and care for people who have broken the law while people who are free have to pay exorbitant sums for those opportunities? Why provide college classes and workshops to people who are supposed to be punished for their crimes? And what about the victims? What does it say to them when we invest in the people who harmed them?

Imprisonment of the body is the punishment.

I know the wonders and the fulfillment of on-campus higher education as both a student and a professor. And I also know how stifling and oppressive the experience of in-prison higher education can be. It's not the same thing.

If we want more from our correctional system, if we want it to produce people who contribute to our society rather than take from our society, then this is the cost of doing so.[61] We can't expect to produce men who are supporting partners, loving fathers, cooperating neighbors, and contributing citizens without building them up as individuals.[62] Most victims don't want themselves or anyone else to be victimized by that person again.[63] If we choose to not use incarceration as an opportunity to address the imprisoned mind and its causes, then we are tacitly okay with continued victimization.

Erik and I both lost our mothers to cancer in 2021. Our book is dedicated to them. My mother was diagnosed with stage IV pancreatic cancer at the end of 2019. The doctors guessed she had a year to live. That year to live was 2020, and COVID-19 travel restrictions and quarantines made a hard year even harder. I couldn't be with her at the end, and my Arizona family watched her New York funeral on YouTube. I can imagine some of what Erik felt as his mother lay dying, but I can't imagine all of it. Just like I can't imagine what any of the men in this book felt as they experienced loss as time passed while they were incarcerated.

Imprisonment of the body is the punishment. Ensuring the continued imprisonment of the mind is overpunishment.

What stands out most to me about the stories in this book is how close the men came to not ending up in prison. A loved one who died, a job that dried up, a mentor who moved, a school that closed—the men were an opportunity away from something else besides prison. A reimagined correctional system could redefine success as churning out productive members of society as measured through other indicators besides recidivism.[64] The opportunity of our correctional system is in treating the unaddressed neglect and trauma of the youth of yesterday. The opportunity of our correctional system is in achieving better mental health, better physical health, better financial health, better relationships, and better employability for people in the system; maybe most importantly, better parenting for their children facing imprisoned minds of their own. The opportunity of our correctional system is in creating meaning and purpose for the men and women who end up there. A reimagined system characterized by social support to promote human transformation is not "coddling criminals"—it is demanding a greater societal return on our investment for our response to crime while acknowledging the complexity of the lives of the people behind the walls.

This reimagined system will only succeed if it's dynamic and flexible enough to adapt to the humanity of people who engage in criminal behavior. No system will be perfectly designed; the best that we can do is to create an enabling environment with enough opportunities for the voices of the people who live and work there to make it even better.[65] The men in *Imprisoned Minds*—Erik among them—have given us knowledge for where to start.

The air is heavy and wet on a late July day at Canandaigua Lake in 2023. My four-year-old daughter springs off those same docks again and again into my arms. My one-year-old son looks on, held tight by Grampa. Maybe this moment will be my kids' earliest memory. Or maybe it will be my earliest memory for them.

I try hard to think back to being a toddler launching off the docks into my own father's arms. I think I remember the *clink* and the *clonk* of the aluminum docks banging together. I think I remember the beer bottle green of the lake water. I think I remember the giggle hiccups meaning this would be the last jump.

But what I know I remember is how fun it was to be a kid. I remember the many lake days and how fortunate my siblings and I were. I remember being loved. By my mom and my dad.

My earliest memory is a nice one. But it didn't change the people or the circumstances around me. It didn't change how others see or treat me. But maybe it changed and continues to change how I see the world.

Maybe it keeps my mind free, open to potential, opportunity, and possibility.

Conclusion

Liberation

It was emotionally challenging for me to write these stories. I found myself rooting for Oakland and his football career while knowing what the outcome would be, considering where he told me his story. I became frustrated by Unique's poor decision-making process just as his life seemed to finally be taking a favorable turn. I felt sorry for the trauma each kid was forced to endure, yet I was angered by many of their actions as adults. I had to remind myself that I shouldn't have been surprised or angered at all because each individual's behavior is indicative of the imprisoned mind. I had to recall my own flawed decision-making process growing up and remember that it's evidence of the immense adversity we experienced that affected our rationale. I realized it shouldn't be surprising that our lives went in the direction they did. If we had emerged from our trauma-filled childhood to become grounded successful adults, then our stories would be celebrated as exceptional.

A fellow prisoner once told me that our incarceration is a direct result of our best thinking. He wasn't claiming that prisoners had reached our intellectual peak. He wasn't implying that we're unable to be better people. He was simply clarifying that nobody commits a criminal act believing they'd be caught, meaning the planning and execution of our crimes, spontaneous or not, was done while using our best judgment at the time. Our rationale is flawed. The good news is, I believe this flaw doesn't have to be permanent. It can gradually be corrected in most who experience it.

I'd love to be able to tell you there's a pill one can take that would instantly correct the imprisoned mind. There isn't. The fact is, each person who experiences it only does so after enduring years of emotional stress as children.

People typically believe kids are resilient enough to overcome such traumatic experiences on our own, but very few truly can. The imprisoned mind can be avoided and even overcome, but to do that we must first be informed as to how it came to be in order to prevent the development, disrupt the progression, and reverse the permanence of it.

I was plagued by the lingering effects of the traumas I experienced as a kid. I didn't know what the constant anxiety or nervousness was, and I incorrectly assumed that what I felt was normal. I simply pushed the feelings aside and ignored them. Alone, I unknowingly tried to learn how to cope with the symptoms of childhood post-traumatic stress disorder (PTSD). I thought I was the only kid who struggled to cope with these feelings.

I was attacked by a twenty-five-year-old white supremacist and was forced to defend myself at the age of thirteen.[1] This traumatic event, compounded with my previous traumas, caused my decision-making process to become more rigid and reactive. I began to believe all white men were out to get me. I became aggressive whenever I felt challenged or confronted, and my aggression became habitual. I fought. I disrespected authority figures in school. And I learned to channel my fear and use it as fuel to attack rather than run from perceived threats. After a fight, my mother informed my school's principal about my past traumas, including the most recent, and the school provided a therapist for me to see once a week for a period of six weeks. He was a middle-aged white man who had no experience with traumatized young Black kids who distrusted white men. He was unable to connect with me because his middle-aged white cookie-cutter methods didn't fit my young Black angst. His inability to empathize with and adjust his methods to suit his patient, to gain my trust, left us with six uncomfortable one-hour sessions. And sadly, like the small minority of underprivileged kids who are provided therapy, the sessions ended with me being prescribed medication. Never again did I see a therapist.

Prescription medication merely masks the problem rather than addressing it. For me, my inability to overcome my mistrust of white men caused me to be reluctant to take what'd been prescribed by the therapist after only a short period of time. I suspected he'd purposely given me something that was detrimental for me. What I was given made me feel lethargic. It caused me to feel worse about myself than I already did. I later learned of other drugs that provided the relief I felt I needed. Like many kids, I sought out and found what worked best for me . . . marijuana. I started selling it to support my consumption. Others are led to more addictive substances—all to cope with what could've been immediately treated post-trauma. These series of events ultimately led to my imprisoned mind and plunged me down a path to criminality. Drugs didn't mask or relieve this problem. They made it worse.

My liberation from the imprisoned mind has been a long process. It took more than the shock of incarceration for me to overcome it. My imprisonment caused me to take a hard look at who I'd become and why I'd ended up in the situation I was in. I realized I had deficiencies in how I thought and saw the world, and I recognized the need for me to be better. I set out to discover how to do that. I focused on reading books to find answers. I studied psychology and sociology. I read biographies and nonfiction to expose myself to other people's lives and see how they thought and saw the world. I studied religion to find a spiritual perspective, and I talked with others in prison as a comparative approach to understand how we'd all ended up in the same place. I made a conscious effort to change how I thought and how I reacted to situations. Through years of trial and error I've focused on self-development, and I continue to do so. My liberation from the imprisoned mind has been and continues to be a long and arduous one, but it's been well worth it. I've evolved and overcome the mental suppression. Now my focus shifts to helping others.

Preventing the development of the imprisoned mind is essential for children exposed to trauma. It's imperative we focus on mental and emotional stability immediately after a traumatic event. Child Protective Services (CPS) could facilitate teaching each child how to properly process their experiences, how to use positive coping methods, and how to embrace conflict resolution skills to counteract their learned violent response. This can be done individually and through group therapy, all with trained specialists. Group therapy could be beneficial as it would allow the child to understand their experience is not unique to them alone by fostering social skills through team-building activities. CPS could be a key factor in protecting the child from developing an imprisoned mind.

Prevention can be done with the right therapeutic approach. It's my hope that the imprisoned mind will one day be classified as a personality disorder and recognized as a mental health condition. This would allow for further study and for the psychological community to train specialists in this area. Specialists could be taught to listen to the child better and to learn more about their experiences before committing to treatment options. Sergeant's and my therapists refused to listen to us or even consider alternative diagnoses and treatments. This caused us to check out on them, and they then probably checked out on us. Each child is different and may require a specialized approach to treating the imprisoned mind. Specialists could consider that the child's emotionally traumatizing experience likely damaged their ability to trust; therefore, the ability to gain trust is important. Some may take more time than others, but specialists could commit to convincing the child that they care and have their best interests at heart before attempting to treat them.

Children need a consistent and durable social support system. Simply having one person we believe cares can have a tremendous effect on the child. Take Kidd's and Oakland's stories. Each encountered individuals they believed cared about them, and this caused them both to make a conscious effort to stay out of trouble. They made tremendous progress in their personal, academic, and social development. Unfortunately, these positive influences were only temporary, and once gone, their negative behavior returned. This demonstrates the importance of a lasting social support system.

Organizations such as Big Brothers and Big Sisters and the YMCA are known to have permanent programs that have proven successful in providing the nurture needed to positively influence kids. Unfortunately, these organizations are not typically in the areas that need them the most. Imagine what could've been had each of these kids been given the opportunity to attend these places every day. It likely would've changed their lives. States could partner with these organizations and create funding to pay for their attendance and ensure these kids have daily transportation to access these programs. With knowledge of the imprisoned mind, these companies may be willing to develop group therapy sessions for those kids who've experienced trauma, with trained therapists. Not only would this provide a permanent safe place for these kids to process their experiences (with others who are similarly situated), but it'd also expose each child to a positive social support system and a world full of possibilities they never imagined.

How do we determine who needs such treatment? Our stories have demonstrated that these kids typically act out in school. Aside from Sergeant's story, each kid got into fights during school, and all had some interaction with the police or CPS—either called in response to domestic violence at home or because of some illegal behavior displayed by the child. Each chapter provides many examples of the child's circumstances having been witnessed by government employees and should've raised alarm bells indicating the child's need for help. Unfortunately, what we witnessed is what tends to happen all too often in underprivileged communities. The child is criminalized and thrown into a mental hospital like Kidd, placed in juvenile hall like Oso, Oakland, Dee, and Unique, or they're dropped off at a family member's house and forgotten like Sergeant. In each instance, the child was betrayed and failed not only by their parents, but also by government officials whose job it was to protect them. I believe that if there's a recognized need to remove a child from their home, then it's also essential for the child to receive some form of therapeutic treatment. Be it group therapy, inpatient or outpatient treatment, we can do better by each child.

Parents or guardians could be included in the child's treatment. Each story established that the child's dysfunctional home life contributed to their emotional stress. Therefore, it's important for the parent or guardian to be given the means to address their own mental and emotional stability in order to aid in the treatment of the child. This could include utilizing already existing programs such as anger management, Alcoholics Anonymous and Narcotics Anonymous, and parenting classes, as needed, along with individual and group therapy. Family counseling could be done as an initial assessment to determine the course of the parent's treatment in conjunction with the child's therapy.

The therapeutic treatment of indigent parents and children could be paid for by the state. Doing this would positively alter the child's and parent's life course and potentially prevent a future victim. I'm reminded of Dee's story. Imagine what could've been had the state mandated treatment for him and his family while he was in jail for assaulting Jay? Jay's life could've been saved, Dee could've avoided a lifetime of incarceration, and it could've healed the family divide by strengthening their bonds. All are positive outcomes. The associated costs of treatment could be seen as an investment in the children who'd otherwise become a perpetual drain on state resources. Doing this would actually save the state money on the cost of future investigations, court fees, and incarceration. There may be some instances where outpatient therapeutic treatment may not serve as a viable option to incarceration given the nature of the child's crime. In such cases, a sustained effort to disrupt the progression of the imprisoned mind will need to be the focus within juvenile and adult institutions.

Disrupting the progression of the imprisoned mind is more complex than its prevention. The child may be a teenager at this point and could've established negative habits and outlook on life. They may have experienced significant betrayals; therefore, gaining their trust may be more difficult than when they were children. I've found that sharing my own experiences allows youth to connect and be vulnerable in return. I believe it's vital to have those who've overcome the imprisoned mind themselves to be trained as specialists to assist with treatment. Only when trust is gained will the teenager expose what they're currently going through, and who better to connect with them than those who've been through it?

Being a teenager is difficult enough on its own. Teens who've experienced trauma need help with learning to differentiate between normal teenage feelings and symptoms of PTSD, and they need guidance with how to cope with these feelings. Teaching teens about trauma and its effects will bring about the realization of their altered mental state and life course. This can motivate them to change their behavior and adjust their life trajectory. Providing a guidance counselor could help them determine where they'd like to go in life, and having a mentor could then boost the self-confidence needed for them to pursue their new life.

Reversing the imprisoned mind could be the main focus during incarceration. While interviewing each subject for this book, I realized there was a therapeutic effect on each individual from simply talking about their traumatic experiences and learning about the effects of the imprisoned mind. I'm certainly not a trained therapist, but I discovered each individual became inspired to be and do better the more in-depth I went with them into their past traumas. For them, it was as if a weight had been removed from their shoulders, and a veil lifted from over their eyes. Each began to envision a better future for themselves and consider career options post-release. Some even considered going to college. They all seemed happier, and it showed in the way they carried themselves and in their social interactions. This didn't last. Once each interview was complete, most returned to their previous behaviors within three months. When I spoke with them, I found that the bleak reality of their current life course caused them to lose hope for a better future for themselves, so they reverted back to their old habits. Why work to be better people when the system seemed to be working against them? The absence of prospective job training, social skills development classes, and educational opportunities in prison left little hope of anything ever changing for them post-release, so why even try?

Reversing the imprisoned mind requires simple solutions to a complex problem. We could first teach the imprisoned mind to those who have it. They need to understand what it is, how it came to be, and the impact it has on how they came to be incarcerated. They need to identify the traumas they've experienced and come to terms with what happened to them. And they need to forgive those who traumatized them. More importantly, they must forgive themselves after taking accountability for their life choices. Only then will they be ready to move forward in life and commit to self-development.

People could provide assistance in helping prisoners determine career paths post-release. When one has shed the imprisoned mind, they need a direction to follow and goals to strive for. Exposing prisoners to different career paths is vital to avoiding regression to the imprisoned mind. It presents us with positive options to choose from. It allows us to finally experience autonomy after having never really felt in control of our lives. It gives us something to positively focus on and work toward while incarcerated. And it offers the most important ingredient to reversing the imprisoned mind: hope for a better future.

We can help the hopeless become hopeful by expanding access to therapy, helping to strengthen social support systems, and providing assistance in determining future career paths. We *can* have a positive impact on the lives of those who need it the most. By learning about the imprisoned mind through the stories of those who've experienced it, we can better understand crime and prevention rather than politicizing it.

I never imagined my voice could be important. After all, I'm just a prisoner. Who really cares what I have to say? It wasn't until meeting Dr. Kevin Wright that I began to understand my lived experience had value, and also that there's a demand for it. I never believed I possessed anything of value. In fact, I believed I'd be laughed at by Kevin when I told him about the imprisoned mind idea. He didn't laugh, and he validated my ideas by showing interest and asking questions. Some answers I had, and some answers I didn't, but that didn't matter to him. His belief in me motivated me to take on the monumental task of writing this book. I'd never written in this capacity before, so naturally I lacked the self-confidence and knowledge to complete this on my own. At times I doubted myself, and the thought of giving up crossed my mind a few times. But using his scholarly knowledge, Kevin was able to act as a mentor and guide me through the mentally demanding, and at times overwhelming, process of writing and completing this book. His support and the completion of this book is further evidence of the value of a social support system.

How we treat people matters. I may have never pursued writing had Dr. Wright laughed at me when I told him about the imprisoned mind. I never would've felt I had anything of value to contribute to the world, and I may have regressed from the liberation of my imprisoned mind. But he cared, and more importantly he believed in me. He offered his continued support, and with his help our book became a reality. I now have purpose in life, and with that I have hope. I became a better man and a better human being by having a mentor and a guide. Being imprisoned with those who have no purpose or hope, I'm reminded each day about the power of treating people humanely and what happens when we don't. Kevin was simply being who he is. He had no idea how he'd change my life or my perspectives. He had no way of knowing if I'd even accomplish what I have with his guidance. He simply took a chance and stuck with it. Imagine how many lives we can change if we all did the same with others like me.

It's common to hear people's stories and sometimes forget that they really happened. Some stories may be so tragic that we get caught up in the emotion of the tragedy and overlook empathy for the one who actually experienced it. We may even overlook the moral of the story. The stories I've shared are more common in prison than you might imagine. I believe three out of four prisoners are incarcerated because they made decisions that were influenced by the irrational thought process called the imprisoned mind. While crime will forever be a choice for anyone who commits it, it's the only choice for those with this mindset, because we're unable to perceive better options. Having an imprisoned mind isn't a choice. I do think there are bad people in prison, but that doesn't make all prisoners inherently bad. Were that true, the United States would have to consider ourselves, as a country, as having more "bad people" per capita than any other country in the world. While nobody will admit to that being the case, prisoners continue to be treated as if we're unable to be anything other than "criminals," deprived of practical rehabilitative opportunities throughout the vast majority of this nation's prisons. In a country that claims to be a nation of second chances, rehabilitation could be the primary goal throughout the justice system. We *can* be better. I believe the need for rehabilitation in our nation's prisons can be realized by telling the stories of people who experience an imprisoned mind. We just happen to be prisoners . . . but we can be much more.

Epilogue

Impermanence

Blam! Blam! Blam! The sound caught my attention while fixing a leaky sink. I worked in maintenance at East Unit, on Florence Prison Complex, and on this day I was tasked with changing out a p-trap in a shower hut. When I stopped what I was doing and looked, I was angered by what I saw. An older Mexican gentleman was beating on a clothes dryer. Without thinking I yelled, "Hey! Stop hitting that f-cking machine!" I stood up and walked toward the man. He looked frightened, so I composed myself before I reached him and asked, "Why are you hitting the machine like that?" I spoke in a way to convey my intention to help and not to be violent. Realizing I wasn't there to hurt him, the man confidently responded, "Oh! We hit the machine because it makes it dry quicker."

I was both surprised and puzzled. I'd never heard that one before, and I was speechless as I studied the individual who had caught me off guard. The man's gray hair and aged facial features showed he must've been in his mid- to late fifties. It's always stunning to witness such behavior from someone whose life experience should've taught them better, and with this man it was no different. It took a second before I hesitantly asked, "Does the machine not dry?" "Naw . . . it dries, but it takes longer than usual." He explained, "When you hit the machine it dries quicker."

It wouldn't occur to me to beat on a thing I thought was broken. That method can only make matters worse. As it was, I knew there was no way beating on the dryer made it dry quicker. It was irrational to think otherwise. The rational thing to do in prison, for one who knows how to fix things, is to first diagnose the problem, then determine which part is malfunctioning, and then figure out if it can be repaired or if it needs to be replaced. The final step is to grab the proper tools and get to work. If one has no working knowledge of how to fix that which is broken, then the only solution would be to find someone who does, and to allow them to show you or do it themselves. It's the practical way to ensure the proper outcome when something is broken or not duly functional.

I decided it'd be best to bring my dryer guy, Happy, and introduce him to the Mexican gentleman. After all, he can explain how the machines function better than me. Happy asked the Mexican gentleman what the problem with the machine was, and I listened while he was given the same answer as I was told. Happy paid close attention to every word and responded by giving his tutorial on the inner workings of the machine. He explained how beating on the machine couldn't possibly make it dry quicker by demonstrating how the heating element worked. To my surprise, the Mexican gentleman listened intently and started enthusiastically asking questions. The two men engaged in a conversation about dryers that was too dry for me, so I excused myself. They barely noticed as I walked away.

It was a month before the dryer broke again in that shower hut. This time, it was due to regular wear and tear. The Mexican gentleman showed up to maintenance one day and explained to Happy, in the proper technical language, that the dryer had broken and precisely what was wrong with it. After going and fixing the machine, Happy informed me that the man's diagnosis was spot-on. He was curious as to how the Mexican gentleman had known what was wrong with the machine and the technical language to explain it. He hadn't taught him that much about the dryers, so he asked him about it. The Mexican gentleman explained that he'd had his wife download technical manuals on the model of washers and dryers we had from the internet and send them to him. Apparently, he'd been vigorously studying the manuals and learning for weeks about the machines. "I was quite impressed by what he knew," Happy told me, "so I asked if I could take a look at those manuals."

The fact that the Mexican gentleman took initiative and went so far as to have technical manuals sent to him was quite impressive. *It made me want to help him further.* After talking with Happy, we went and spoke with our boss about the Mexican gentleman and were able to get him hired in maintenance as the washer and dryer apprentice. He came in and went right to work learning all he could, while putting what knowledge he'd gained from the manuals to good use. He worked diligently in maintenance for a couple of months and looked as if he'd been working on the machines for years. To our surprise, he was transferred to a minimum-custody unit after working with us for only a few months. However, in that time, he became very proficient with the machines. Our boss was so impressed that he had him hired as the washer and dryer guy at his new unit.

Carlos has since been released from prison. Whether or not he continued working with washers and dryers after his release, I couldn't say. I'd love to think our interaction in that shower hut led to him eventually starting a successful career or business. What really mattered to me was seeing him become impassioned by learning about something positive while in prison and witnessing such a dramatic shift in his focus. This is rare in prison.

I know from experience the frustration and disappointment that comes with not being able to develop knowledge about a thing that has piqued my interest in prison. To witness an older individual who was clearly making the transition away from the imprisoned mind when we met, seemingly flourish after finding a skill he could be passionate about was amazing. I wondered just how many others were transitioning away from the imprisoned mind and in need of finding their niche to complete the process of truly freeing themselves.

I've learned that most prisoners have an idea of what career path they'd like to pursue, but they typically have no clue as to what it takes to achieve it. For example, I found that many prisoners want to be truck drivers when they get out, but they can't tell you how to go about acquiring a commercial driver's license (CDL). I had information sent in about trucking schools, and each individual was shocked to learn the course length was two to three weeks. Many believed it'd take months, even years, to earn a CDL. I found that dispelling myths about career paths allowed prisoners to believe the particular career was more achievable, and, in response, they became more focused and determined to learn about what they had to do in order to realize their path post-release. It helps enable individuals to be released from prison focused, confident in themselves, and goal-oriented when we gain more knowledge of a preferred career. It's a far cry from the current status quo of being released feeling lost, with an imprisoned mind, and unsure of what it is they're going to do for a living. Imagine what ex-prisoners could accomplish if they're able to walk out of prison and immediately transition into their preferred career—I can assure you, the vast majority wouldn't recidivate.

I understand the public perception of "inmates" in this country is such that we're viewed as animals, or maybe machines, but this is far from reality. We are people. Many of us simply want to utilize our time in prison as positively and productive as possible to become better people. Instead, like a machine, we're thrown in a corner and forgotten until it's time to be called upon to perform its function. It only matters to those who own the machine if it's working properly. They don't beat on it or mistreat the machine when it doesn't work. They immediately scramble to have it fixed.

When prisoners are treated like machines we tend to shut down. Only, we're not machines. We're flawed human beings with emotions, so we act out of anger and frustration due to being treated as less than who we are. I can't imagine anyone who'd want prisoners to be released worse off than when we went to prison. Carlos is an example of our positive growth ability when given the opportunity to learn a skill. The general public could expect nothing less than prisoners returning to society better off than when we left it—which is the desire of many prisoners. The reality is, when treated humanely, people generally prove themselves to be worthy by holding themselves to that standard and exceeding expectations. While there are prisoners who may never change, there are many more who'd surprisingly flourish if given the opportunity.

Most people typically perceive prisons as being institutions that focus on rehabilitating prisoners. This isn't generally the case. Prisoner reform is currently not the primary focus. Whether this is by design or due to a failure to diagnose the problem, I can attest to the fact that simply warehousing prisoners and forcing idleness and punitive treatment on us in hopes of "correcting" criminality doesn't generally work. This is simply akin to beating a broken machine hoping it'll fix itself. We can do better. We can open the machine up and find the faulty or broken part. We can fix that broken part. With the proper tools, we can return the machine to its workable state rather than discarding it. Common sense doesn't have to be uncommon. Prisoners are not machines. Some of us have committed unspeakable acts, but this shouldn't disqualify us from being able to reinvent and redeem ourselves. We've already been broken, and our incarceration simply highlights our flaws due to our brokenness. Therefore, it's irrational to believe we can be mistreated and beaten to be fixed or improved upon. We've beaten on the beaten down long enough. What if we build them up? What if we invest in them? What if we provide the same care and attention as if it were a machine that belonged to you? Let's get the proper tools and get to work.

Appendix

Methodology

I've wanted to write this book for a while. I just didn't think that I could. I decided against it when I considered the obstacles I'd face as an incarcerated author. As I heard more and more stories from fellow prisoners, writing this book continued to occupy the forefront of my mind. I'd focus on the glaring similarities of each prisoner's story, and I immediately knew when I heard a story that it needed to be told. But I dismissed the thought each time because I told myself there were just too many things that stood in the way that would prevent the book from ever becoming a reality. It wasn't until after I was selected by Arizona State University's Dr. Kevin Wright to take part in Arizona's inaugural Inside-Out Prison Exchange Program that I came to understand the need for this book to be written. I discovered that there were actually people who wanted to hear what I had to say as a writer, but I also learned there were a lot more people who needed to learn about the imprisoned mind. I consulted Kevin about my idea for the book, and he immediately pledged his support. And with that, all the excuses I believed prevented me from writing this book began to dissipate.

My methodology and approach in interviewing subjects for the book was simple yet rigorous. My goal was to have the subjects in the book be representative of those with an imprisoned mind throughout the nation's prison population. Therefore, it was important for me that the book not only be racially diverse, but it also needed to have subjects from different socioeconomic classes and age groups. While I would've loved to include the female prisoner's perspectives, as one can imagine, my incarceration in a male prison prevented that from being a possibility. The chapters included here are the best representation of the male prison population given the limits placed upon me and the book's length.

Finding interview subjects wasn't the difficult part. Finding the *right* subjects proved to be extremely difficult. Stories are told all the time in prison. Only, a lot of what's told is clearly embellished. Each story made the one telling it appear bigger and tougher than I knew them to be, and they attempted to highlight how successful they were at selling drugs even though they were clearly drug users. The stories I wanted to tell had to perfectly highlight the imprisoned mind, but they had to be truthful accounts of the highs and lows of each life and representative of the flawed decision-making process. They had to be able to capture the reader with action and generate emotion. I knew when I heard a particular story that it'd be perfect for the book based upon these criteria, but I also knew when I heard one that wouldn't fit right as well.

Have you ever met someone and after having one conversation with them you walked away thinking, *there's something wrong with that dude*? I get that quite often in prison, and I've found it's likely the person has an imprisoned mind each time I walk away feeling this way. Every conversation is about them, and all they really know and care about is drugs, women, and the illegal things they've done. They're unable to think and talk about anything else. If they're forced to talk about something else, you'd quickly find how uninformed they are about things outside of what they've demonstrated as their priority. This is how I know when one has an imprisoned mind when I meet them.

I initially decided this book would have ten stories, with each individual narrative being a chapter. Long before writing this book, I determined Kidd, Dee, and Oakland's stories needed to be told as examples of the mindset. I'd observed each individual's character for some time, and I knew their stories were impactful. I'd observed Sergeant and Oso prior to meeting them. Sergeant was unlike everyone else I'd suspected as having an imprisoned mind. Prior to him, I thought the imprisoned mind's hyper-focus was only on drugs, women, and crimes committed. He made me realize that drugs were only one component that causes the imprisoned mind. He was the first to teach me that alcohol, seeking a family, and risk taking can equally take the place of drugs. His story seemed rare, and I felt it needed to be told.

I met Oso through mutual acquaintances preceding my first interview for the book. He was younger than me, but he was always more respectful with me than others his age. He was polite and courteous while appearing to be young and wild. It was a combination that made me curious about his story, so I began to question him one day. He quickly opened up to me, and I found his intravenous drug use to be an aspect that needed to be highlighted here.

Unique was the last subject interviewed. I met him the day he arrived on my unit. I could tell from the moment I saw him that, like me, he was from California. I introduced myself, and we instantly hit it off. He adamantly informed me he was not into prison gangs, prison politics, or drugs, and that he just wanted to do his time and learn a skill so he could go home and never return to prison again. This came from simply introducing myself. I instantly liked him. I suspected he was in the midst of naturally transitioning away from the imprisoned mind, and my further interactions with him confirmed that. When he did take the time to tell me his story, there was no doubt in my mind it needed to be told. But the determining factor was the need to tell the story of one who was in transition away from the mindset.

The interview process was quite frustrating at times. Given the sensitive nature of their stories, I wanted the interviewee to be as comfortable as possible and have as much privacy to share their stories with me. As one can imagine, prison has very few places away from ear hustling and prying eyes. We had to tune all of the noise out and maneuver through lockdowns and count times. We had to go to work and chow. We had to somehow find uninterrupted time around these obstacles.

I had each interviewee sign a contract prior to the interview giving me permission to write and potentially publish their stories. I promised each individual anonymity and allowed them to determine what name they'd go by. Once the contract was signed, I sat with each man for, at a minimum, a couple of hours each day and took notes by hand until their stories reached the present day. I began each interview by asking where they were born to get them talking, and I asked questions where need be to get a complete and accurate picture. I took notes by hand as recording devices are prohibited in prison. No story took longer than three days to be told.

I sat at the tiny desk in my dimly lit cell and used my notes to re-create what'd been told to me. There were many times when my notes weren't sufficient and I was forced to quit writing until I had the opportunity ask the interviewee clarifying questions in order to continue. As computers, word processors, and typewriters were prohibited, I had to write several rough drafts of each chapter in pencil. Once the first rough draft was completed, I asked each subject to read their story and sign a contract verifying accuracy—corrections were made where need be for the subject to sign the contract.

I wrote the chapter's second rough draft to make it more legible before turning it over to Kevin for editing. He made a photocopy of the rough draft, edited the copy, and returned both the original and edited draft to me at our monthly meeting. After receiving the suggested edits, I wrote the final rough draft in pen, while making the necessary revisions before turning it back over to Kevin to be typed up. Once the final rough draft was completed, I moved on to the next interview subject. The process from first interview to final draft took on average approximately six to eight weeks.

My incarceration prevents me from being able to corroborate each story. I knew the book couldn't work if the stories were not believable; therefore, it was important for me to express to each individual the significance of being truthful when relating their story. I used one tool in determining whether an interviewee was truthful: my experience in recognizing bullshit when I hear it. When I detected any inconsistency in an interviewee's story, I made it a point to ask probing questions so as to determine truthfulness, and I refused to allow embellishments. Any attempt by an interviewee to be less than forthright was not tolerated.

In total, I interviewed eleven men for the book. However, I only completed and wrote the stories of nine interviewees. I determined one subject was not being truthful due to the many contradictions between what he'd told me prior to the interview as opposed to during it. I terminated his interview halfway through after questioning him about the contradictions. Another subject's interview was terminated for his failure to give a full account of his life's story. And three interviews were unable to be added due to the book's overall word count limitations.

Writing this book has been difficult. It's also been the most meaningful thing I've accomplished to date. While there were times I doubted myself, the support of Kevin, Arizona State University grad students, family, and my fellow prisoners continued to give me the necessary confidence and support I needed to complete such a monumental project. Now that I'm done . . . it's on to the next one—whatever that may be.

Acknowledgments

There are many people, inside and outside of prison, who deserve to be acknowledged for their work, encouragement, and support of this book. We thank Madi Margolis, Genevieve McKenzie, Leya Reyes, and Madison Sutton for sharing their time to edit and comment on early versions of the book. We thank several additional people who agreed to read versions of the book at various stages: Shayla Evans, Greg Fizer, Marva Goodson-Miller, Gabe Groenig, Alexis Klemm, Travis Meyers, Stephanie Morse, Eric Stewart, and Cody Telep. Seven years is a long time to work on a project, and several people were responsible for pushing the book forward. Danielle Rudes, Jamie Fader, and Reuben Miller generously shared their time and their optimism when we felt lost. Shadd Maruna answered a cold email (over the winter holiday season), shared his time and wisdom, and wrote the perfect foreword to the book. Thank you. Peter Mickulas, Ray Michalowski, Luis Fernandez, and Rutgers University Press took a chance on the project when no one else would. We appreciate their enthusiasm and support from beginning to end. We thank Cheryl Jonson for stepping up for the project, but also for encouraging Kevin to teach Inside-Out many years ago—we wouldn't have met otherwise and this book wouldn't have happened. Joe Profiri and Ryan Thornell provided unexpected support to get the project to completion. We thank you both for your commitments to innovation and to impact.

Erik would like to thank all who are mentioned here for their contributions. I'm honored and humbled to know each person, and I'm incredibly thankful to those who gave their time and effort to ensure this book became a reality. Thank you all from the bottom of my heart for helping and believing in me. Thank you: Shadd Maruna, Greg Fizer, Genevieve McKenzie, Brian Cooper, Dean Gaines, Keith Avants, Tyrus Talbert, Robert Stanford,

Shaun Mills, Cedric Rue, Charles Gosmon, Gwendolyn Aiken, Mrs. DeVilliers, and Malik and Khadijah Hernandez. Thank you to my sister, Susan Eversoll, my nephew Michael Wilson, and my niece Sharday Ware. I appreciate your love and support. And a special thanks goes to all who contributed your stories. Thank you for trusting me enough to be vulnerable with me in such an environment and believing that I'd honor my word with your stories. Though your names may be anonymous, your stories will help change hearts and minds.

Last but not least . . . the most special of thanks goes to the one person who, if not for him, this book would've never been written, let alone published. This man is the most incredible person I've ever met. From editing each chapter to finding a publisher, there's not one part of this book he didn't have a hand in. He encouraged me whenever I doubted myself and gave me the confidence needed to finish this book. I'm extremely honored and grateful for his friendship, and I'm even more humbled to be considered his colleague. Thank you for everything you've done for me, Dr. Kevin Wright.

Kevin would like to thank the organizations and people who made this project possible. The faculty, staff, and students of Arizona State University are champions of work that makes an impact in the community. I'm especially appreciative of leadership from the Watts College and the School of Criminology and Criminal Justice—Scott Decker, Cassia Spohn, Beth Huebner, Cody Telep, and Cynthia Lietz. Students and alumni of the Center for Correctional Solutions have enhanced the lives of other people, including mine: Danielle Haverkate, Alexis Klemm, Caitlin Matekel, Gen McKenzie, Travis Meyers, Stephanie Morse, and Raven Simonds. Students of our Inside-Out community, both inside and out of prison, and past and present members of the Arizona Transformation Project have provided inspiration and motivation to get this thing done.

Natasha and I met when this project started. The book, and our relationship and eventual marriage, all made it. Thank you for the love and support and for believing "the book" would come to be. Annika and Grady were both born during those seven years. They may never know it, but their contributions to this project were invaluable. Brian, Lisa, Aunt Patty, and Uncle John have been a consistent support of all my endeavors. And thank you always to Mom and Dad—I love you both.

The men who courageously shared their stories for this book will impact people they've never met, near and far. Their stories may be the source of support needed for someone else to overcome the challenges that they've experienced. Thank you.

As a lifelong student, there have been a few teachers who changed how I see the world. Erik Maloney is one of them. Like any good collaborator, he pushed my thinking on our work, and he has enriched my understanding of what could be done in our prisons. But his lessons extend beyond work. On many occasions I've observed Erik meet and inspire students who come into the prison. It's like watching an art form—he mixes laughter and smiles with moments of profound seriousness. When I talk to those students later about their time in prison, they all talk about Erik. They talk about him as if they've known him their entire life, and they share how he provided them needed perspective. The lesson he's taught me is this: Whenever things aren't going your way. When all seems lost. When everything is taken from you. You give.

Notes

Foreword

1   Stanley Cohen, *Against Criminology* (New Brunswick, NJ: Transaction, 1988), 299.

Introduction

1   Danielle L. Haverkate et al., "On PAR with the Yard: Participatory Action Research to Advance Knowledge in Corrections," *Corrections: Policy, Practice and Research* 5, no. 1 (2020): 28–43; Justin Thrasher et al., "Reimagining Prison Research from the Inside-Out," *Journal of Prisoners on Prisons* 28, no. 1 (2019): 12–28.

About-Faces

1   E. A. Carson and Rich Kluckow, *Correctional Populations in the United States, 2021* (Washington, DC: U.S. Department of Justice, 2023).
2   Sara Wakefield and Christopher Wildeman, *Children of the Prison Boom: Mass Incarceration and the Future of American Inequality* (New York: Oxford University Press, 2014).
3   Vincent J. Felitti et al., "Relationship of Childhood Abuse and Household Dysfunction to Many of the Leading Causes of Death in Adults: The Adverse Childhood Experience (ACE) Study," *American Journal of Preventative Medicine* 14, no. 4 (1998): 245–258.
4   Christian L. Bolden, *Out of the Red: My Life of Gangs, Prison, and Redemption* (New Brunswick, NJ: Rutgers University Press, 2020).
5   Stephanie J. Morse, Kevin A. Wright, and Max Klapow, "Correctional Rehabilitation and Positive Psychology: Opportunities and Challenges," *Sociological Compass* 16, no. 3 (2022): e12960.
6   A number of excellent books detail the lives of boys growing up surrounded by adverse experiences. Among them are Jamie J. Fader, *Falling Back: Incarceration and Transitions to Adulthood among Urban Youth* (New Brunswick, NJ: Rutgers

University Press, 2013); Victor M. Rios, *Punished: Policing the Lives of Black and Latino Boys* (New York: New York University Press, 2011); and Michaela Soyer, *Lost Childhoods: Poverty, Trauma, and Violent Crime in the Post-Welfare Era* (Oakland: University of California Press, 2018).

7 Nadine Burke Harris, *The Deepest Well: Healing the Long-Term Effects of Childhood Trauma and Adversity* (Boston: Mariner Books, 2018).

8 Shadd Maruna, *Making Good: How Ex-Convicts Reform and Rebuild Their Lives* (Washington, DC: American Psychological Association, 2001).

9 Shadd Maruna, "Qualitative Research, Theory Development, and Evidence-Based Corrections: Can Success Stories Be 'Evidence'?," in *Qualitative Research in Criminology: Advances in Criminological Theory*, ed. Jody Miller and Wilson R. Palacios (New York: Routledge, 2017), 311–337.

10 To learn more about the international Inside-Out Prison Exchange program, go to http://www.insideoutcenter.org. To learn about its origins, see Lori Pompa, "One Brick at a Time: The Power and Possibility of Dialogue across the Prison Wall," *Prison Journal* 93 (2013): 127–134. To learn about our class impact in Arizona, see Cassandra Philippon et al., "Learning with the Others: Perspective-Taking and the Future of Criminal Justice in the Inside-Out Prison Exchange Program," *Journal of Criminal Justice Education* 35, no. 1 (2024): 136–155.

11 Shadd Maruna and Marieke Liem, "Where Is This Story Going? A Critical Analysis of the Emerging Field of Narrative Criminology," *Annual Review of Criminology* 4 (2021): 125–146.

12 Robert K. Merton, "Social Structure and Anomie," *American Sociological Review* 3, no. 5 (1938): 672–682.

13 Robert Agnew, "Foundation for a General Strain Theory of Crime and Delinquency," *Criminology* 30, no. 1 (1992): 47–88.

14 Michael R. Gottfredson and Travis Hirschi, *A General Theory of Crime* (Stanford, CA: Stanford University Press, 1990).

15 See, for example, Diane K. Fast, Julianne Conry, and Christine A. Loock, "Identifying Fetal Alcohol Syndrome among Youth in the Criminal Justice System," *Journal of Developmental & Behavioral Pediatrics* 20, no. 5 (1999): 370–372; Hannah Uebel et al., "Reasons for Rehospitalization in Children Who Had Neonatal Abstinence Syndrome," *Pediatrics* 136, no. 4 (2015): e811–e920; Karen M. Abram et al., "Posttraumatic Stress Disorder and Trauma in Youth in Juvenile Detention," *Archives of General Psychiatry* 61, no. 4 (2004): 403–410; Eric Durand et al., "History of Traumatic Brain Injury in Prison Populations: A Systematic Review," *Annals of Physical and Rehabilitation Medicine* 60 (2017): 95–101; Karen Hughes et al., "The Effect of Multiple Adverse Childhood Experiences on Health: A Systematic Review and Meta-Analysis," *The Lancet: Public Health* 2, no. 8 (2017): e356–e366.

16 Ronald Akers, *Social Learning and Social Structure: A General Theory of Crime and Deviance* (New York: Routledge, 2009).

17 Travis Hirschi, *Causes of Delinquency* (Berkeley: University of California Press, 1969); Francis T. Cullen, "Social Support as an Organizing Concept for Criminology: Presidential Address to the Academy of Criminal Justice Sciences," *Justice Quarterly* 11, no. 4 (1994): 527–559.

18 Robert J. Sampson, *Great American City: Chicago and the Enduring Neighborhood Effect* (Chicago: University of Chicago Press, 2012).

19 See, for example, Michelle Alexander, *The New Jim Crow: Mass Incarceration in the Age of Colorblindness* (New York: New Press, 2010); Elijah Anderson, *Black in White Space: The Enduring Impact of Color in Everyday Life* (Chicago: University of Chicago Press, 2022); Marc Mauer, *Race to Incarcerate* (New York: New Press, 2006).

20 Alfred Blumstein et al., *Criminal Careers and "Career Criminals"* (Washington, DC: National Academies Press, 1986).

21 Terrie E. Moffitt, "Adolescence-Limited and Life-Course-Persistent Antisocial Behavior: A Developmental Taxonomy," *Psychological Review* 100, no. 4 (1993): 674–701.

22 Robert J. Sampson and John H. Laub, *Crime in the Making: Pathways and Turning Points through Life* (Cambridge, MA: Harvard University Press, 1993); Peggy Giordano, Stephen A. Cernkovich, and Jennifer L. Rudolph, "Gender, Crime, and Desistance: Toward a Theory of Cognitive Transformation," *American Journal of Sociology* 107, no. 4 (2002): 990–1064.

23 Christoffer Carlsson, "Masculinities, Persistence, and Desistance," *Criminology* 51, no. 3 (2013): 661–693.

24 Ray Paternoster and Shawn Bushway, "Desistance and the Feared Self: Toward an Identity Theory of Criminal Desistance," *Journal of Criminal Law and Criminology* 99, no. 4 (2009): 1103–1156; Maruna, *Making Good*.

25 Shadd Maruna and Heith Copes, "What Have We Learned from Five Decades of Neutralization Research?," *Crime and Justice* 32 (2005): 221–320.

26 Kevin A. Wright and Leana A. Bouffard, "Capturing Crime: The Qualitative Analysis of Individual Cases for Advancing Criminological Knowledge," *International Journal of Offender Therapy and Comparative Criminology* 60, no. 2 (2016): 123–145.

27 James Bennett, *Oral History and Delinquency: The Rhetoric of Criminology* (Chicago: Chicago University Press, 1981).

28 Loïc Wacquant, "The Curious Eclipse of Prison Ethnography in the Age of Mass Incarceration," *Ethnography* 3, no. 4 (2002): 371–397.

29 Danielle L. Haverkate et al., "On PAR with the Yard: Participatory Action Research to Advance Knowledge in Corrections," *Corrections: Policy, Practice and Research* 5, no. 1 (2020): 28–43.

30 Gillian Buck, Philippa Tomczak, and Kaitlyn Quinn, "This Is How It Feels: Activating Lived Experience in the Penal Voluntary Sector," *British Journal of Criminology* 62, no. 4 (2022): 822–839.

31 Haverkate et al., "On PAR with the Yard"; Justin Thrasher et al., "Reimagining Prison Research from the Inside-Out," *Journal of Prisoners on Prisons* 28, no. 1 (2019): 12–28.

32 Michelle Fine, *Just Research in Contentious Times: Widening the Methodological Imagination* (New York: Teacher's College Press, 2017).

33 Lauren Farrell, Bethany Young, and Janeen Buck Willison, *Participatory Research in Prisons* (Washington, DC: Urban Institute, 2021).

34 Karl Duncker, "On Problem-Solving," *Psychological Monographs* 58, no. 5 (1945): i–113.

35 Kevin A. Wright, Stephanie J. Morse, and Madison M. Sutton, "The Limits of Recidivism Reduction: Advancing a More Comprehensive Understanding of Correctional Success," in *Transforming Criminal Justice: An Evidence-Based Agenda for Reform*, ed. Jon B. Gould and Pamela R. Metzger (New York: New York University Press, 2022), 149–172.

36 Kevin A. Wright, "Time Well Spent: Misery, Meaning, and the Opportunity of Incarceration," *Howard Journal of Criminal Justice* 59, no. 1 (2020): 44–64.

37 Wright, Morse, and Sutton, "The Limits of Recidivism Reduction."

38 Kevin A. Wright, "A High Potential for Something Good: Reflections on When Lived Experience Meets What Works," in *Handbook on Prisons and Jails*, ed. Danielle Rudes, Gaylene Armstrong, Kimberly Kras, and TaLisa Carter (New York: Routledge, 2024), 433–445.

39 Savanah Mueller, Mark Hart, and Cary Carr, "Resilience Building Programs in U.S. Corrections Facilities: An Evaluation of Trauma-Informed Practices in Place," *Journal of Aggression, Maltreatment & Trauma* 32, nos. 1–2 (2023): 242–261.

40 Jason Schnittker, Michael Massoglia, and Christopher Uggen, *Prisons and Health in the Age of Mass Incarceration* (New York: Oxford University Press, 2022).

41 Burke Harris, *The Deepest Well*.

42 Sheryl P. Kubiak, Stephanie S. Covington, and Carmen Hillier, "Trauma-Informed Corrections," in *Social Work in Juvenile and Criminal Justice Systems*, ed. David W. Springer and Albert R. Roberts (Springfield, IL: Charles C. Thomas, 2017), 92–104.

43 Charles A. Nelson et al., "Adversity in Childhood is Linked to Mental and Physical Health throughout Life," *BMJ* 371 (2020).

44 Kubiak, Covington, and Hillier, "Trauma-Informed Corrections"

45 Mueller, Hart, and Carr, "Resilience Building Programs."

46 Kevin A. Wright et al., "The Cycle of Violence Revisited: Childhood Victimization, Resilience, and Future Violence," *Journal of Interpersonal Violence* 34, no. 6 (2019): 1261–1286.

47 Wright, "Time Well Spent."

48 Wright, Morse, and Sutton, "The Limits of Recidivism Reduction."

49 Richard M. Ryan and Edward L. Deci, *Self-Determination Theory: Basic Psychological Needs in Motivation, Development, and Wellness* (New York: Guilford Press, 2017).

50 Ryan and Deci, *Self-Determination Theory*.

51 Ryan and Deci, *Self-Determination Theory*.

52 Wright, Morse, and Sutton, "The Limits of Recidivism Reduction."

53 Wright, "A High Potential for Something Good."

54 Erik Maloney, "Violence: The Invisible Bars," *Journal of Contemporary Criminal Justice* 38, no. 2 (2022): 207–210.

55 Lynette C. Lee and Mary K. Stohr, "A Critique and Qualified Defense of 'Correctional Quackery,'" *Journal of Contemporary Criminal Justice* 28, no. 1 (2012): 96–112.

56 Thomas P. LeBel, Matt Richie, and Shadd Maruna, "Helping Others as a Response to Reconcile a Criminal Past: The Role of the Wounded Healer in Prisoner Reentry Programs," *Criminal Justice and Behavior* 41, no. 1 (2015): 108–120.

57 Esther Matthews, "Peer-Focused Prison Reentry Programs: Which Peer Characteristics Matter Most?," *Incarceration: An International Journal of Imprisonment, Detention and Coercive Confinement* 2, no. 2 (2021): 1–19.

58 Cody W. Telep et al., "The Value of Participatory Action Research in Corrections: Introduction to the Special Issue," *Corrections: Policy, Practice and Research* 5, no. 1 (2020): 1–5.

59 Wright, Morse, and Sutton, "The Limits of Recidivism Reduction."
60 Francis T. Cullen, "The End of American Exceptionalism: An Enlightened Corrections," *Criminology & Public Policy* 21, no. 4 (2022): 769–786.
61 Wright, "Time Well Spent."
62 Reuben J. Miller, *Halfway Home: Race, Punishment, and the Afterlife of Mass Incarceration* (New York: Little, Brown and Company, 2020).
63 Danielle Sered, *Until We Reckon: Violence, Mass Incarceration, and a Road to Repair* (New York: New Press, 2019).
64 Wright, Morse, and Sutton, "The Limits of Recidivism Reduction."
65 Ben Crewe and Alice Ievins, "The Prison as a Reinventive Institution," *Theoretical Criminology* 24, no. 4 (2020): 568–589.

Conclusion

1 Erik Maloney, "Violence: The Invisible Bars," *Journal of Contemporary Criminal Justice* 38, no. 2 (2022): 207–210.

Bibliography

Abram, Karen M., Linda A. Teplin, Devon R. Charles, Sandra L. Longworth, Gary M. McClelland, and Mina K. Dulcan. "Posttraumatic Stress Disorder and Trauma in Youth in Juvenile Detention." *Archives of General Psychiatry* 61, no. 4 (2004): 403–410.

Agnew, Robert. "Foundation for a General Strain Theory of Crime and Delinquency." *Criminology* 30, no. 1 (1992): 47–88.

Akers, Ronald. *Social Learning and Social Structure: A General Theory of Crime and Deviance.* New York: Routledge, 2009.

Alexander, Michelle. *The New Jim Crow: Mass Incarceration in the Age of Colorblindness.* New York: New Press, 2010.

Anderson, Elijah. *Black in White Space: The Enduring Impact of Color in Everyday Life.* Chicago: University of Chicago Press, 2022.

Bennett, James. *Oral History and Delinquency: The Rhetoric of Criminology.* Chicago: Chicago University Press, 1981.

Blumstein, Alfred, Jacqueline Cohen, Jeffrey A. Roth, and Christy A. Visher. *Criminal Careers and "Career Criminals."* Washington, DC: National Academies Press, 1986.

Bolden, Christian L. *Out of the Red: My Life of Gangs, Prison, and Redemption.* New Brunswick, NJ: Rutgers University Press, 2020.

Buck, Gillian, Philippa Tomczak, and Kaitlyn Quinn. "This Is How It Feels: Activating Lived Experience in the Penal Voluntary Sector." *British Journal of Criminology* 62, no. 4 (2022): 822–839.

Burke Harris, Nadine. *The Deepest Well: Healing the Long-Term Effects of Childhood Trauma and Adversity.* Boston: Mariner Books, 2018.

Carlsson, Christoffer. "Masculinities, Persistence, and Desistance." *Criminology* 51, no. 3 (2013): 661–693.

Carson, E. A., and Rich Kluckow. *Correctional Populations in the United States, 2021.* Washington, DC: U.S. Department of Justice, 2023.

Cohen, Stanley. *Against Criminology.* New Brunswick, NJ: Transaction, 1988.

Crewe, Ben, and Alice Ievins. "The Prison as a Reinventive Institution." *Theoretical Criminology* 24, no. 4 (2020): 568–589.

Cullen, Francis T. "The End of American Exceptionalism: An Enlightened Corrections." *Criminology & Public Policy* 21, no. 4 (2022): 769–786.

———. "Social Support as an Organizing Concept for Criminology: Presidential Address to the Academy of Criminal Justice Sciences." *Justice Quarterly* 11, no. 4 (1994): 527–559.

Duncker, Karl. "On Problem-Solving." *Psychological Monographs* 58, no. 5 (1945): i–113.

Durand, Eric, Mathilde Chevignard, Alexis Ruet, A. Dereix, Claire Jourdan, and Pascale Pradat-Diehl. "History of Traumatic Brain Injury in Prison Populations: A Systematic Review." *Annals of Physical and Rehabilitation Medicine* 60 (2017): 95–101.

Fader, Jamie J. *Falling Back: Incarceration and Transitions to Adulthood among Urban Youth*. New Brunswick, NJ: Rutgers University Press, 2013.

Farrell, Lauren, Bethany Young, and Janeen Buck Willison. *Participatory Research in Prisons*. Washington, DC: Urban Institute, 2021.

Fast, Diane K., Julianne Conry, and Christine A. Loock. "Identifying Fetal Alcohol Syndrome among Youth in the Criminal Justice System." *Journal of Developmental & Behavioral Pediatrics* 20, no. 5 (1999): 370–372.

Felitti, Vincent J., Robert F. Anda, Dale Nordenberg, David F. Williamson, Alison M. Spitz, Valerie Edwards, Mary P. Koss, and James S. Marks. "Relationship of Childhood Abuse and Household Dysfunction to Many of the Leading Causes of Death in Adults: The Adverse Childhood Experience (ACE) Study." *American Journal of Preventative Medicine* 14, no. 4 (1998): 245–258.

Fine, Michelle. *Just Research in Contentious Times: Widening the Methodological Imagination*. New York: Teacher's College Press, 2017.

Giordano, Peggy, Stephen A. Cernkovich, and Jennifer L. Rudolph. "Gender, Crime, and Desistance: Toward a Theory of Cognitive Transformation." *American Journal of Sociology* 107, no. 4 (2002): 990–1064.

Gottfredson, Michael R., and Travis Hirschi. *A General Theory of Crime*. Stanford, CA: Stanford University Press, 1990.

Haverkate, Danielle L., Travis J. Meyers, Cody W. Telep, and Kevin A. Wright. "On PAR with the Yard: Participatory Action Research to Advance Knowledge in Corrections." *Corrections: Policy, Practice and Research* 5, no. 1 (2020): 28–43.

Hirschi, Travis. *Causes of Delinquency*. Berkeley: University of California Press, 1969.

Hughes, Karen, Mark A. Bellis, Katherine A. Hardcastle, Dinesh Sethi, Alexander Butchart, Christopher Mikton, Lisa Jones, and Michael P. Dunne. "The Effect of Multiple Adverse Childhood Experiences on Health: A Systematic Review and Meta-Analysis." *The Lancet: Public Health* 2, no. 8 (2017): e356–e366.

Kubiak, Sheryl P., Stephanie S. Covington, and Carmen Hillier. "Trauma-Informed Corrections." In *Social Work in Juvenile and Criminal Justice Systems*, edited by David W. Springer and Albert R. Roberts, 92–104. Springfield, IL: Charles C. Thomas, 2017.

LeBel, Thomas P., Matt Richie, and Shadd Maruna. "Helping Others as a Response to Reconcile a Criminal Past: The Role of the Wounded Healer in Prisoner Reentry Programs." *Criminal Justice and Behavior* 41, no. 1 (2015): 108–120.

Lee, Lynette C., and Mary K. Stohr. "A Critique and Qualified Defense of 'Correctional Quackery.'" *Journal of Contemporary Criminal Justice* 28, no. 1 (2012): 96–112.

Maloney, Erik. "Violence: The Invisible Bars." *Journal of Contemporary Criminal Justice* 38, no. 2 (2022): 207–210.

Maruna, Shadd. *Making Good: How Ex-Convicts Reform and Rebuild Their Lives.* Washington, DC: American Psychological Association, 2001.

———. "Qualitative Research, Theory Development, and Evidence-Based Corrections: Can Success Stories Be 'Evidence'?" In *Qualitative Research in Criminology: Advances in Criminological Theory,* edited by Jody Miller and Wilson R. Palacios, 311–337. New York: Routledge, 2017.

Maruna, Shadd, and Heith Copes. "What Have We Learned from Five Decades of Neutralization Research?" *Crime and Justice* 32 (2005): 221–320.

Maruna, Shadd, and Marieke Liem. "Where Is This Story Going? A Critical Analysis of the Emerging Field of Narrative Criminology." *Annual Review of Criminology* 4 (2021): 125–146.

Matthews, Esther. "Peer-Focused Prison Reentry Programs: Which Peer Characteristics Matter Most?" *Incarceration: An International Journal of Imprisonment, Detention and Coercive Confinement* 2, no. 2 (2021): 1–19.

Mauer, Marc. *Race to Incarcerate.* New York: New Press, 2006.

Merton, Robert K. "Social Structure and Anomie." *American Sociological Review* 3, no. 5 (1938): 672–682.

Miller, Reuben J. *Halfway Home: Race, Punishment, and the Afterlife of Mass Incarceration.* New York: Little, Brown and Company, 2020.

Moffitt, Terrie E. "Adolescence-Limited and Life-Course-Persistent Antisocial Behavior: A Developmental Taxonomy." *Psychological Review* 100, no. 4 (1993): 674–701.

Morse, Stephanie J., Kevin A. Wright, and Max Klapow. "Correctional Rehabilitation and Positive Psychology: Opportunities and Challenges." *Sociological Compass* 16, no. 3 (2022): e12960.

Mueller, Savanah, Mark Hart, and Cary Carr. "Resilience Building Programs in U.S. Corrections Facilities: An Evaluation of Trauma-Informed Practices in Place." *Journal of Aggression, Maltreatment & Trauma* 32, nos. 1–2 (2023): 242–261.

Nelson, Charles A., Zulfiqar A. Bhutta, Nadine Burke Harris, Andrea Danese, and Muthanna Samara. "Adversity in Childhood Is Linked to Mental and Physical Health throughout Life." *BMJ* 371 (2020).

Paternoster, Ray, and Shawn Bushway. "Desistance and the Feared Self: Toward an Identity Theory of Criminal Desistance." *Journal of Criminal Law and Criminology* 99, no. 4 (2009): 1103–1156.

Philippon, Cassandra, Kevin A. Wright, Cody W. Telep, and Olivia P. Shaw. "Learning with the Others: Perspective-Taking and the Future of Criminal Justice in the Inside-Out Prison Exchange Program." *Journal of Criminal Justice Education* 35, no. 1 (2024): 136–155.

Pompa, Lori. "One Brick at a Time: The Power and Possibility of Dialogue across the Prison Wall." *Prison Journal* 93 (2013): 127–134.

Rios, Victor M. *Punished: Policing the Lives of Black and Latino Boys.* New York: New York University Press, 2011.

Ryan, Richard M., and Edward L. Deci. *Self-Determination Theory: Basic Psychological Needs in Motivation, Development, and Wellness.* New York: Guilford Press, 2017.

Sampson, Robert J. *Great American City: Chicago and the Enduring Neighborhood Effect.* Chicago: University of Chicago Press, 2012.

Sampson, Robert J., and John H. Laub. *Crime in the Making: Pathways and Turning Points through Life.* Cambridge, MA: Harvard University Press, 1993.

Schnittker, Jason, Michael Massoglia, and Christopher Uggen. *Prisons and Health in the Age of Mass Incarceration*. New York: Oxford University Press, 2022.

Sered, Danielle. *Until We Reckon: Violence, Mass Incarceration, and a Road to Repair*. New York: New Press, 2019.

Soyer, Michaela. *Lost Childhoods: Poverty, Trauma, and Violent Crime in the Post-Welfare Era*. Oakland: University of California Press, 2018.

Telep, Cody W., Kevin A. Wright, Danielle L. Haverkate, and Travis J. Meyers. "The Value of Participatory Action Research in Corrections: Introduction to the Special Issue." *Corrections: Policy, Practice and Research* 5, no. 1 (2020): 1–5.

Thrasher, Justin, Erik Maloney, Shaun Mills, Johnny House, Timm Wroe, and Varrone White. "Reimagining Prison Research from the Inside-Out." *Journal of Prisoners on Prisons* 28, no. 1 (2019): 12–28.

Uebel, Hannah, Ian M. Wright, Lucy Burns, Lisa Hilder, Barbara Bajuk, Courtney Breen, Mohamed E. Abdel-Latif, et al. "Reasons for Rehospitalization in Children Who Had Neonatal Abstinence Syndrome." *Pediatrics* 136, no. 4 (2015): e811–e820.

Wacquant, Loïc. "The Curious Eclipse of Prison Ethnography in the Age of Mass Incarceration." *Ethnography* 3, no. 4 (2002): 371–397.

Wakefield, Sara, and Christopher Wildeman. *Children of the Prison Boom: Mass Incarceration and the Future of American Inequality*. New York: Oxford University Press, 2014.

Wright, Kevin A. "A High Potential for Something Good: Reflections on When Lived Experience Meets What Works." In *Handbook on Prisons and Jails*, edited by Danielle Rudes, Gaylene Armstrong, Kimberly Kras, and TaLisa Carter, 433–445. New York: Routledge, 2024.

———. "Time Well Spent: Misery, Meaning, and the Opportunity of Incarceration." *Howard Journal of Criminal Justice* 59, no. 1 (2020): 44–64.

Wright, Kevin A., and Leana A. Bouffard. "Capturing Crime: The Qualitative Analysis of Individual Cases for Advancing Criminological Knowledge." *International Journal of Offender Therapy and Comparative Criminology* 60, no. 2 (2016): 123–145.

Wright, Kevin A., Stephanie J. Morse, and Madison M. Sutton. "The Limits of Recidivism Reduction: Advancing a More Comprehensive Understanding of Correctional Success." In *Transforming Criminal Justice: An Evidence-Based Agenda for Reform*, edited by Jon B. Gould and Pamela R. Metzger, 149–172. New York: New York University Press, 2022.

Wright, Kevin A., Jillian J. Turanovic, Eryn N. O'Neal, Stephanie J. Morse, and Evan T. Booth. "The Cycle of Violence Revisited: Childhood Victimization, Resilience, and Future Violence." *Journal of Interpersonal Violence* 34, no. 6 (2019): 1261–1286.

Index

About the Authors

ERIK S. MALONEY is a co-founding member of the Arizona Transformation Project. He works every day to change the world and leave it better than he found it. Outside of his lifelong pursuit of knowledge and self-development, his focus is on redeeming his past through mentoring and positively influencing all he encounters. He currently develops and teaches classes to inspire and empower other prisoners.

KEVIN A. WRIGHT is an associate professor in the School of Criminology and Criminal Justice and director of the Center for Correctional Solutions at Arizona State University. He earned his PhD in criminal justice from Washington State University in 2010. His work focuses on enhancing the lives of people living and working in the correctional system through research, education, and community engagement.

Available titles in the Critical Issues in Crime and Society series

Laura S. Abrams and Ben Anderson-Nathe, *Compassionate Confinement: A Year in the Life of Unit C*

Laura S. Abrams and Diane J. Terry, *Everyday Desistance: The Transition to Adulthood among Formerly Incarcerated Youth*

Tammy L. Anderson, ed., *Neither Villain nor Victim: Empowerment and Agency among Women Substance Abusers*

Miriam Boeri, *Women on Ice: Methamphetamine Use among Suburban Women*

Christian L. Bolden, *Out of the Red: My Life of Gangs, Prison, and Redemption*

Scott A. Bonn, *Mass Deception: Moral Panic and the U.S. War on Iraq*

Mary Bosworth and Jeanne Flavin, eds., *Race, Gender, and Punishment: From Colonialism to the War on Terror*

Henry H. Brownstein, Timothy M. Mulcahy, and Johannes Huessy, *The Methamphetamine Industry in America: Transnational Cartels and Local Entrepreneurs*

Ben Brucato, *Race and Police: The Origin of Our Peculiar Institutions*

Loretta Capeheart and Dragan Milovanovic, *Social Justice: Theories, Issues, and Movements*, Revised and expanded edition

Kim Cook, *Shattered Justice: Crime Victims' Experiences with Wrongful Convictions and Exonerations*

Alexandra Cox, *Trapped in a Vice: The Consequences of Confinement for Young People*

Anna Curtis, *Dangerous Masculinity: Fatherhood, Race, and Security inside America's Prisons*

Hilary Cuthrell, Luke Muentner, and Julie Poehlmann, *When Are You Coming Home? How Young Children Cope When Parents Go to Jail*

Walter S. DeKeseredy and Martin D. Schwartz, *Dangerous Exits: Escaping Abusive Relationships in Rural America*

Patricia E. Erickson and Steven K. Erickson, *Crime, Punishment, and Mental Illness: Law and the Behavioral Sciences in Conflict*

Jamie J. Fader, *Falling Back: Incarceration and Transitions to Adulthood among Urban Youth*

Luis A. Fernandez, *Policing Dissent: Social Control and the Anti-Globalization Movement*

Angela J. Hattery and Earl Smith, *Way Down in the Hole: Race, Intimacy, and the Reproduction of Racial Ideologies in Solitary Confinement*

Mike King, *When Riot Cops Are Not Enough: The Policing and Repression of Occupy Oakland*

Ronald C. Kramer, *Carbon Criminals, Climate Crimes*

Timothy R. Lauger, *Real Gangstas: Legitimacy, Reputation, and Violence in the Intergang Environment*

Margaret Leigey, *The Forgotten Men: Serving a Life without Parole Sentence*

Andrea Leverentz, *The Ex-Prisoner's Dilemma: How Women Negotiate Competing Narratives of Reentry and Desistance*

Ethan Czuy Levine, *Rape by the Numbers: Producing and Contesting Scientific Knowledge about Sexual Violence*

Clara S. Lewis, *Tough on Hate? The Cultural Politics of Hate Crimes*

Michael J. Lynch, *Big Prisons, Big Dreams: Crime and the Failure of America's Penal System*

Erik S. Maloney and Kevin A. Wright, *Imprisoned Minds: Lost Boys, Trapped Men, and Solutions from Within the Prison*

Liam Martin, *The Social Logic of Recidivism: Cultural Capital from Prisons to the Streets*

Allison McKim, *Addicted to Rehab: Race, Gender, and Drugs in the Era of Mass Incarceration*

Raymond J. Michalowski and Ronald C. Kramer, eds., *State-Corporate Crime: Wrongdoing at the Intersection of Business and Government*

Susan L. Miller, *Victims as Offenders: The Paradox of Women's Violence in Relationships*

Torin Monahan, *Surveillance in the Time of Insecurity*

Torin Monahan and Rodolfo D. Torres, eds., *Schools under Surveillance: Cultures of Control in Public Education*

Ana Muñiz, *Police, Power, and the Production of Racial Boundaries*

Marianne O. Nielsen and Linda M. Robyn, *Colonialism Is Crime*

Leslie Paik, *Discretionary Justice: Looking Inside a Juvenile Drug Court*

Yasser Arafat Payne, Brooklynn Hitchens, and Darryl L. Chambers, *Murder Town, USA: Homicide, Structural Violence, and Activism*

Anthony M. Platt, *The Child Savers: The Invention of Delinquency*, 40th anniversary edition with an introduction and critical commentaries compiled by Miroslava Chávez-García

Lois Presser, *Why We Harm*

Joshua M. Price, *Prison and Social Death*

Heidi Reynolds-Stenson, *Cultures of Resistance: Collective Action and Rationality in the Anti-Terror Age*

Diana Rickard, *Sex Offenders, Stigma, and Social Control*

Jeffrey Ian Ross, ed., *The Globalization of Supermax Prisons*

Dawn L. Rothe and Christopher W. Mullins, eds., *State Crime, Current Perspectives*

Jodi Schorb, *Reading Prisoners: Literature, Literacy, and the Transformation of American Punishment, 1700–1845*